T0134835

Model and Design of Improved Current Mode Logic Gates

Kirti Gupta · Neeta Pandey · Maneesha Gupta

Model and Design of Improved Current Mode Logic Gates

Differential and Single-ended

Kirti Gupta
Department of Electronics
and Communication
Bharati Vidyapeeth's College
of Engineering
New Delhi, Delhi, India

Neeta Pandey
Department of Electronics
and Communication
Delhi Technological University
New Delhi, Delhi, India

Maneesha Gupta
Department of Electronics
and Communication
Netaji Subhas University of Technology
Dwarka, Delhi, India

ISBN 978-981-15-0984-1   ISBN 978-981-15-0982-7   (eBook)
https://doi.org/10.1007/978-981-15-0982-7

This Springer imprint is published by the registered company Springer Nature Singapore Pte Ltd.
The registered company address is: 152 Beach Road, #21-01/04 Gateway East, Singapore 189721, Singapore

Preface

Technological evolution has facilitated the coexistence of digital and analog circuits on a single chip. A single-chip realization has a profound impact on performance, cost, and size. Such chip eases signal acquisition which falls primarily in analog domain and signal processing that is predominately done in the digital domain. The digital circuit design revolves around CMOS due to negligible static power, but it consumes dynamic power which becomes severe at high frequencies and also results in large current spikes during switching event (switching noise). As a consequence, the resolution of analog circuits may decrease; therefore, this issue needs special attention. Alternate logic styles are explored to reduce switching noise which work on keeping power supply current nearly constant during the switching event and/or working with smaller voltage swings. Current mode logic (CML) style is one among these which addresses both the issues and is the main focus of the book.

The book presents the background and a brief review of available literature on CML gates in Chap. 1. The remaining chapters of the book describe newer topologies obtained by modifying the basic parts of CML, namely pull-down network, current source, and load. Chapter 2 is devoted to detailed analysis and design procedure of differential CML and single-ended (PFSCL) gates. The realization of the basic logic gates in differential CML and the single-ended (PFSCL) style is also included. Chapter 3 details the inclusion of triple-tail cell concept in pull-down network of the differential CML gate. This modification leads to lower power supply requirement. It, however, increases the implementation area. The multiple threshold transistor-based triple-tail cell is described next that reduces the overall area requirement. Mathematical formulations for the design-oriented model are elucidated with an intention to develop an understanding of the impact of design and process parameters. The performance of the proposed topologies is illustrated for low-power, high-speed, and power-efficient design cases.

Chapter 4 presents improved dynamic CML (D-CML) gates and self-timed buffer for design of multi-stage applications. Chapter 5 deals with the speed improvement in the CML gates by modifying their load. The load uses the capacitive coupling phenomenon. A complete mathematical model for static parameters and the delay is developed for differential CML and PFSCL gates.

A systematic design procedure to size the bias current and the transistor's aspect ratio to meet design goals is also presented.

Efficient realization of a logic function in PFSCL style is the aim of Chap. 6. A method to reduce the gate count in comparison with the conventional NOR-based logic function realization is described. A new fundamental cell developed by applying triple-tail cell concept in PFSCL style is presented and analyzed. The use of fundamental cell in realizing various logic functions is discussed, and the overall improvement in terms of gate count, propagation delay, and power is compared with the conventional ones.

Tri-state circuits are the essential elements in bus-organized and programmable logic devices and are explored in Chap. 7. Tri-state circuits in CML style are worked upon in this chapter.

This book details the improved designs of CML gates that are suited to mixed-signal environments. An in-depth analysis and step-by-step design procedure will help the researcher to design a gate for given constraints.

New Delhi, India   Kirti Gupta
New Delhi, India   Neeta Pandey
New Delhi, India   Maneesha Gupta

Acknowledgements

The authors would like to take this opportunity to thank Bharati Vidyapeeth's College of Engineering, New Delhi, Delhi Technological University, New Delhi, and Netaji Subhas University of Technology, New Delhi, for their support in carrying out the work on current mode logic (CML) style. We are thankful to our students Ms. Ranjana Sivaram, Ms. Garima Bhatia, Mr. Ankit Mittal, and Dr. Bharat Choudhuary for fruitful discussions in formalizing multiple threshold voltage transistor triple-tail cell-based differential CML gates and developing new tri-state buffers.

We are grateful to our friends, colleagues, and family members who have always encouraged us to push our limits and have supported us endlessly in all our endeavors.

There was sincere support from the editorial staff of Springer from Ms. Suvira Srivastav since initial proposal submission. A similar gesture was extended by Mr. Antony Raj Joseph during book submission. We are thankful to both of you and in fact the entire editorial team.

Contents

1 **Introduction** 1
   1.1 Background 1
   1.2 Current Mode Logic 2
   References 4

2 **Current Mode Logic (CML): Basic Concepts** 13
   2.1 Introduction 13
   2.2 Basic Concepts 13
   2.3 Differential CML Gates 17
      2.3.1 Analysis of Differential CML Gates 18
      2.3.2 Design of a Differential CML Inverter 24
      2.3.3 Analysis of Two-Level CML Gates 27
   2.4 Single-Ended CML Gates 28
      2.4.1 PFSCL Gates 28
      2.4.2 Analysis of a PFSCL Inverter 30
      2.4.3 Design of a PFSCL Inverter 32
   2.5 Summary 35
   References 35

3 **Differential CML Gates with Modified PDN** 37
   3.1 Introduction 37
   3.2 Triple-Tail Cell-Based Approach 37
   3.3 Triple-Tail Cell (TT-1)-Based Differential CML Gates ... 41
      3.3.1 Analysis of TT-1-Based CML Gates 42
      3.3.2 Design of TT-1-Based CML Gates 45
      3.3.3 Performance Comparison 50
      3.3.4 Extension to D Latch Design 56
   3.4 Triple-Tail Cell (TT-2)-Based Differential CML Gates ... 58
      3.4.1 Analysis of TT-2 Based CML Gates 59

3.4.2   Design of TT-2-Based CML Gates   61
3.4.3   Performance Comparison   67
3.5   Summary   69
References   70

4   CML Gates with Modified Current Source   71
4.1   Introduction   71
4.2   Dynamic CML Gates   72
4.3   Dynamic Differential CML Gates   74
4.3.1   Dy-DCML-NN Gates   74
4.3.2   Dy-DCML-NP Gates   79
4.3.3   General Discussion on Dynamic Differential
CML Gate   82
4.4   Dynamic PFSCL Gates   83
4.4.1   Dy-PFSCL-NN Gates   84
4.4.2   Dy-PFSCL-NP Gates   88
4.4.3   General Discussion on Dy-PFSCL Gates   93
4.5   Multi-stage Applications   94
4.5.1   Multi-stage D-CML Design Using STB-1   95
4.5.2   Multi-stage D-CML Design Using STB-2   96
4.6   Performance Comparison with Static Gates   97
4.6.1   Performance Comparison of Differential CML Gates   97
4.6.2   Performance Comparison of PFSCL Gates   99
4.7   Summary 100
References 101

5   CML Gates with Modified Load 103
5.1   Introduction 103
5.2   Available Loads 103
5.3   NP-Load 105
5.3.1   Analysis of NP-Load 105
5.3.2   Resistance of NP-Load 106
5.4   Differential CML Gates with NP-Load (CML-CC) 107
5.4.1   Operation of Differential CML-CC Inverter 108
5.4.2   Analysis of Differential CML-CC Inverter 108
5.4.3   Design of Differential CML-CC Inverter 111
5.4.4   Performance Comparison 114
5.5   PFSCL Gates with Modified NP-Load (PFSCL-CC) 116
5.5.1   Operation of PFSCL-CC Inverter 116
5.5.2   Analysis of PFSCL-CC Inverter 117
5.5.3   Design of PFSCL-CC Inverter 120
5.5.4   Performance Comparison 122
5.6   Summary 125
References 125

6   PFSCL Circuits with Reduced Gate Count 127
   6.1   Introduction 127
   6.2   Realization of PFSCL Circuits (Method-1) 127
   6.3   Realization of PFSCL Circuits (Method-2) 129
         6.3.1   Analysis of Fundamental Cell 130
         6.3.2   Design of Fundamental Cell 134
         6.3.3   Basic Gate Realization 137
   6.4   Performance Comparison 140
   6.5   Design Examples 141
         6.5.1   LFSR Design 142
         6.5.2   Adder Design 144
   6.6   Summary 148
   References 148

7   Tri-state CML Circuits 151
   7.1   Introduction 151
   7.2   Differential Tri-state CML Circuits 151
         7.2.1   Switch-Based Differential Tri-state CML Circuit 152
         7.2.2   Voltage Follower-Based Differential Tri-state CML
                 Circuit 152
         7.2.3   Low-Power Differential Tri-state CML Circuit 153
         7.2.4   Performance Comparison 154
         7.2.5   Application Examples 155
   7.3   Tri-state PFSCL Circuits 158
         7.3.1   Switch-Based Tri-state PFSCL Circuits 158
         7.3.2   Sleep Transistor-Based PFSCL Tri-state Circuits 163
   7.4   Summary 170
   References 171

About the Authors

Dr. Kirti Gupta received B.Tech. in Electronics and Communication Engineering from Indira Gandhi Institute of Technology, Delhi in 2002, M. Tech. in Information Technology from School of Information Technology in 2006. She received her Ph.D. in Electronics and Communication Engineering from Delhi Technological University, in 2016. Since 2002, she is with Bharati Vidyapeeth's College of Engineering, New Delhi and is presently serving as Professor in the same institute. A life member of ISTE, and senior member of IEEE, she has published more than 100 research papers in international, national journals and conferences. Her teaching and research interest is in digital VLSI design.

Dr. Neeta Pandey received her M.E. in Microelectronics from Birla Institute of Technology and Sciences, Pilani in 1991 and Ph.D. from Guru Gobind Singh Indraprastha University, Delhi in 2009. She has served in Central Electronics Engineering Research Institute, Pilani, Indian Institute of Technology, Delhi, Priyadarshini College of Computer Science, Noida and Bharati Vidyapeeth's College of Engineering, Delhi in various capacities. At present, she is a professor in the ECE department, Delhi Technological University. Her teaching and research interests include analog and digital VLSI design.

A life member of ISTE, and senior member of IEEE, USA, she has coauthored over 100 papers in international, national journals of repute and conferences.

Dr. Maneesha Gupta is currently a Professor at the Electronics & Communication Engineering Department of the Netaji Subhas University of Technology, India. She received her B.E. in Electronics & Communication Engineering from the Government Engineering College, Jabalpur in 1981, M.E. in Electronics & Communication Engineering from the same university in 1983, and her PhD. in Electronics Engineering (Analysis, Synthesis & Applications of Switched Capacitor Circuits) from the Indian Institute of Technology, Delhi in 1990.

Her teaching and research interests include switched capacitor circuits and analog signal processing. Dr. Gupta has co-authored over 150 research papers in the above areas in various international/national journals and conferences.

Chapter 1
Introduction

1.1 Background

Digital integrated circuits have witnessed a phenomenal growth in the past few decades due to technological advancements and availability of electronic design automation tools. The development of single-chip mixed mode systems requires integration of digital circuits and analog circuits on the same chip [1–3]. Conventional CMOS logic is predominant in digital circuit design owing to negligible static power consumption; high packing density; and well tested and documented design methodologies [4–6]. At the time of switching, the CMOS-based digital circuits generate noise which is coupled to analog circuits through substrate and limits analog circuit resolution [6, 7]. Many methods are suggested in the literature to address this issue that works at different levels of abstraction [7–11]. At a technology level, substrate coupling is reduced by Silicon on Insulator (SOI) or highly doped epitaxial layer. It leads to fabrication complexity and also increases the cost. Careful floor planning and skilled layout techniques are used at physical level. The former is achieved through separate placement of digital and analog blocks, while diffused guard bands are suggested for the later one. At circuit level, fully differential and substrate referenced analog architectures are preferred due to their intrinsic noise immunity features. Separate power grids, multiple supply pins, and bonding wires are suggested at the system level.

Apart from the methods discussed above, alternate high-speed digital circuits styles have also been explored and investigated that may coexist with analog circuits [12–26]. These styles either use smaller voltage swing or employ a mechanism to cancel transient currents occurring in switching events, thereby maintaining a nearly constant current. The MOS current mode logic (CML) gates need a single current source and work on smaller voltage swing; therefore, it is a preferred choice for mixed-signal IC applications [23–26].

© Springer Nature Singapore Pte Ltd. 2020
K. Gupta et al., *Model and Design of Improved Current Mode
Logic Gates*, https://doi.org/10.1007/978-981-15-0982-7_1

1.2 Current Mode Logic

The current mode logic (CML) is built around differential amplifier and therefore consists of a source-coupled pair operating as logic evaluation block (pull-down network (PDN)); a current source whose current is steered through one of the transistor of source-coupled pair; and a load that converts current to voltage [23–26]. The logic is further viewed as differential or single ended depending upon nature of input(s) being processed and availability of output.

Researchers have investigated CML style, and the work is broadly directed toward analysis and design of these gates; developing topologies for better performance and system applications. The CML gate is analyzed in terms of static parameters—voltage swing, noise margin and gain, and delay. MOS models such as Sah [27], BSIM [28, 29, 30, 31, 32, 33] and alpha power law [34, 35] are used for analysis purpose. The design is aimed at finding an aspect ratio of transistors as per design specifications and choosing bias current according to design constraints. The design is elucidated using three approaches which are based on simulation, analytical, and algorithmic.

In simulation-based design approach, the transistors are sized as per performance specification—high speed or low power [26]. In high-speed design, delay needs to be minimized and this criterion is fulfilled by applying higher bias current. It results in larger transistor sizes and higher power supply. The low-power gate necessitates the selection of smaller bias current, and therefore, the static parameter specifications may be met with smaller sized transistors and power supply values. This approach, though seems simple, requires tedious simulation iterations and is time-consuming too. The analytical approach [27–42] is suitable in early design phases and is based on linearization of the transistor parameters. The aspect ratios of the transistors are expressed as a function of the bias current and are computed to meet the design criterion—power-efficient, high-speed, and low-power design criteria. In algorithmic approach [43–50], the design is treated as an optimization problem with nonlinear design constraints and linear goal function.

The topological modifications in different sections of a CML gate [51–63] are also suggested in the literature in order to improve performance. The issue of threshold voltage fluctuation during fabrication is addressed by introducing feedback transistors [51, 52] in PDN. The concept is supported by mathematical formulations and is tested through optical-fiber-link multiplexer and demultiplexer IC. This modification also benefits speed.

In yet another modification in PDN, either different threshold transistors are employed at each level of source-coupled transistor pairs in [53, 54] or an extra invalid level in addition to the high and low logic levels [55, 56]. Former gates are named as multi-threshold CMOS (MTCMOS) MOS current mode logic gates. This modification culminates into the reduction in the minimum power supply requirement and lowers power consumption. The gate-based on later modification is called triple-rail MOS current mode logic (Tr-MCML). The Tr-MCML style proves to be beneficial in pipeline operations and supports power-on-demand operations in pipeline architectures.

In an effort to improve the performance of single-ended CML style, positive feedback is applied to replace the voltage reference source, and resulting topology is termed as positive-feedback source-coupled logic (PFSCL) [57]. This change provides significant improvement in switching speed, power, and area. The analysis, modeling, and design of the PFSCL gate are presented in [58–62].

The discussion till this point focuses on modification in PDN. Here, the modification in load section of CML gate is discussed. The load primarily does current to voltage conversion and determines the voltage swing and speed of the gate. Typically, a passive resistor or a PMOS transistor operating in the linear region [36] is used as a load. In adaptable MOS current mode logic (AMCML), the load is adjusted according to the real-time need. Here, adaptable bias and swing controllers are employed in [63, 64] for resistance variations. The controllers set the bias voltages of all the PMOS load transistors according to the desired current and voltage swing, thereby making circuits ready for real-time adaptation. Shunt peaking [65–74] is also introduced, to improve the speed of the CML gate, wherein an inductor (passive or active) is connected in series with conventional resistive load. The use of passive inductor is not recommended due to the large component size and lengthier design process [69]. In active inductor, an NMOS transistor with its gate connected to separate supply via a resistor is used as an alternative [73, 74]. A bulk–drain connected PMOS load [75] provides a high resistance and is used widely in subthreshold source-coupled logic (STSCL) gates [75–82], a variant of CML that operates in subthreshold region.

The CML gates consume static power due to the presence of current source. In an attempt to reduce static power consumption, the current source is allowed to operate whenever there is a change in input values. This scheme is named as self-timed MOS current mode logic (ST-MCML) style [83]. A pulse generator and a sense amplifier are essential for proper operation. The sense amplifier measures the small changes at the inputs and amplifies it to the desired output levels.

Dynamic current mode logic gates [84, 85] are another variation of CML wherein both load and current section of a CML gate are simultaneously modified. An additional clock signal is used to control the operation, namely precharging of the output node and its subsequent evaluation. Both load and current source sections are modified to support the operation. These gates do not consume static power but show small dynamic power due to the small instantaneous current during switching transitions.

The sleep method is well known for lowering the power consumption in CMOS logic style, and it is applied to differential MOS current mode logic circuits [86–89] also. Here, sleep transistor is placed in series with the power supply. Depending on the state of sleep transistor, the circuit operates in sleep or active mode. The power consumption is reduced in sleep mode as the connection to supply ceases to exist in sleep mode. The sleep transistor connects the power supply to the circuit, and operation is resumed in active mode.

CML gates are extensively used in a wide variety of applications due to its high-speed and reduced switching noise characteristics. Typical application areas include communication systems, optical fiber links, microprocessors, and signal processors. In communication systems, a phase-locked loop (PLL) is the key element used for frequency synthesis, clock generation, data recovery, and synchronization. A typical PLL consists of a mixer/phase detector, low pass filter, voltage controlled oscillator, and a frequency divider. The phase detector primarily uses an XOR gate or D latch. Frequency divider realized as a cascade of divide-by-two stages can be classified as regenerative and static type. Various implementations for phase detector and frequency divider are available in the literature [63–65, 90–100]. The oscillators also play an important role in the modulation and demodulation of the signals. The implementations of the ring oscillators and their design are presented in [101, 102]. An LFSR comprises of a shift register and a feedback network consisting of XOR/XNOR gates. It is implemented with both differential and PFSCL style [103, 104].

Another important application field for CML circuits is the optical-fiber-link system wherein multiplexing and demultiplexing of signals is commonly used for the efficient utilization of the optical fiber channel bandwidth. A multiplexer transfers the data serially across the optical fiber which is then transferred in parallel through a demultiplexer. The realizations of multiplexer and demultiplexer involving D latch are shown in [51, 52, 105–107].

The CML gates are employed in the design of a number of circuits often used in the datapaths of microprocessors and signal processors [108–135]. The datapath is the core of the processor and consists of an interconnection of basic combinational functions such as arithmetic (addition, multiplication, shift, and comparison) and logic operators. A variety of complex building blocks such as adders, compressors, and multipliers are available. The use of CML circuits to implement pipeline datapath systems is also demonstrated in the literature.

References

1. S. Kiaei, D. Allstot, Low-noise Logic for Mixed-mode VLSI Circuits. Microelectron. J. **23** (2), 103–114 (1992)
2. B. Razavi, *Design of Analog CMOS Integrated Circuits* (Tata McGraw Hill Edition, 2007)
3. P.E. Allen, D.R. Holberg, *CMOS Analog Circuit Design*, 2nd edn. (Oxford University Press, 2007)
4. S.M. Kang, Y. Leblebici, *CMOS Digital Integrated Circuits: Analysis and Design* (Tata McGraw Hills, Third Edition, 2006
5. J.M. Rabaey, A. Chandrakasan, B. Nikolic, *Digital Integrated Circuits*, 2nd edn. (Pearson Education, 2003)
6. S. Kiaei, S. Chee, D. Allstot, CMOS source-coupled logic for mixed-mode VLSI, in *Proceedings of IEEE International Symposium on Circuits and Systems* (New Orleans, 1990), pp. 1608–1611
7. B. Stanistic, N. Verghese, R. Rutenbar, L. Carley, D. Allstot, Addressing substrate coupling in mixed-mode ICs: simulation and power distribution synthesis. IEEE J. Solid-State Circ. **29**(3), 226–238 (1994)
8. D. Su, M. Loinaz, S. Masui, B. Wooley, Experimental results and modeling techniques for substrate noise in mixed-signal integrated circuits. IEEE J. Solid-State Circ. **28**(4), 420–430 (1993)

9. S. Masui, Simulation of substrate coupling in mixed-signal MOS circuits, in *Proceedings of IEEE Symposium on VLSI Circuits* (Seattle, 1992), pp. 42–43
10. R. Sàez, M. Kayal, M. Declercq, M. Schneider, Digital circuit techniques for mixed analog/digital circuits applications, in *Proceedings of IEEE International Conference on Electronics, Circuits and System* (Rodos, 1996), pp. 956–959
11. D. Allstot, S. Chee, S. Kiaei, M. Shristawa, Folded source-coupled logic versus CMOS static logic for low-noise mixed-signal ICs. IEEE Trans. Circ. Sys. I **40**(9), 553–563 (1993)
12. S. Badel, in *MOS Current-Mode Logic Standard Cells for High-Speed Low-Noise Applications* (thesis no. 4098, 2008)
13. E. Albuquerque, J. Fernandes, M. Silva, NMOS current-balanced logic. Electron. Lett. **32** (11), 997–998 (1996)
14. L. Yang, J.S. Yuan, Enhanced techniques for current balanced logic in mixed-signal ICs, in *Proceedings of IEEE Computer Society Annual Symposium on VLSI* (2003), pp. 1–2
15. E.F.M. Albuquerque, M.M. Silva, An experimental comparison of substrate noise generated by CMOS and by low-noise digital circuit, in *Proceedings of IEEE International Symposium on Circuits and Systems*, (2004), pp. II-481–II-482
16. P. Saxena, K.M. Sudheer, V.B. Chandratre, Design of novel current balanced voltage controlled delay element. Int. J. VLSI Des. Commun. Syst. **5**(3), 37–45 (2014)
17. H. Ng, D. Allstot, CMOS current steering logic for low-voltage mixed-signal integrated circuits. IEEE Trans. VLSI Syst. **5**(3), 301–308 (1997)
18. S. Radiom, B. Sheikholeslami, H. Aminzadeh, R. Lotfi, Folded-current-steering DAC: an approach to low-voltage high-speed high-resolution D/A converters, in *Proceedings of IEEE International Symposium on Circuits and Systems* (2006), pp. 4783–4786
19. D.Y. Jeong, S.H. Chai, W.C. Song, G.H. Cho, CMOS current-controlled oscillators using multiple-feedback-loop ring architectures, in *Proceedings of IEEE International Solid-state Circuits Conference* (1997), pp. 386–491
20. S. Maskai, S. Kiaei, D. Allstot, Synthesis techniques for CMOS folded source-coupled logic circuits. IEEE J. Solid-State Circ. **27**(8), 1157–1167 (1992)
21. J. Kundan, S. Hasan, Enhanced folded source-coupled logic technique for low-voltage mixed-signal integrated circuits. IEEE Trans. Circ. Syst. II **47**(8), 810–817 (2000)
22. M. Maleki, S. Kiaei, Enhancement source-coupled logic for mixed-mode VLSI circuits. IEEE Trans. Circ. Syst. II **39**(7), 399–402 (1992)
23. M. Yamashina, H. Yamada, An MOS current mode logic (MCML) circuit for low-power sub-GHz processors. IEICE Trans. Electr. **E75-C**(10), 1181–1187 (1992)
24. M. Yamashina, M. Mizuno, K. Furuta, H. Igura, M. Nomura, H. Abiko, K. Okabe, A. Ono, H. Yamad, A low-supply voltage GHz MOS integrated circuit for mobile computing systems, in *Proceedings of IEEE Symposium on Low Power Electronics* (San Diego, 1994), pp. 80–81
25. M. Mizuno, M. Yamashina, K. Furuta, H. Igura, H. Abiko, K. Okabe, A. Ono, H. Yamada, A GHz MOS adaptive pipeline technique using MOS current-mode logic. IEEE J. Solid-State Circ. **31**(6), 784–791 (1996)
26. J.M. Musicer, J. Rabaey, MOS current mode logic for low power, low noise, CORDIC computation in mixed-signal environments, in *Proceedings of International Symposium of Low Power Electronics and Design* (2000), pp. 102–107
27. S. Bruma, Impact of on-chip process variations on MCML performance, in *Proceedings of IEEE Conference on Systems-on-Chip* (2003), pp. 135–140
28. M. Alioto, G. Palumbo, Design strategies for source coupled logic gates. IEEE Trans. Circ. Syst. I **50**(5), 640–654 (2003)
29. M. Alioto, G. Palumbo, S. Pennisi, Modelling of source-coupled logic gates. Int. J. Circ. Theory Appl. **30**(4), 459–477 (2002)
30. M. Hassan, M. Anis, M. Elmasry, MOS current mode circuits: analysis, design, and variability. IEEE Trans. Very Large Scale Integr. VLSI Syst. **13**(8), 885–898 (2005)

31. M. Alioto, G. Palumbo, Power-delay optimization of D-latch/MUX source coupled logic gates. Int. J. Circ. Theory Appl. **33**(1), 65–85 (2005)
32. M. Alioto, L. Pancioni, S. Rocchi, V. Vignoli, Analysis and design of MCML gates with hysteresis, in *Proceedings of International Symposium on Circuits and Systems* (Island of KOS, 2006), pp. 1263–1267
33. M. Alioto, G. Palumbo, Modelling and design considerations on CML gates under high-current effects. Int. J. Circ. Theory Appl. **33**, 503–518 (2005)
34. M. Alioto, G. Palumbo, Nanometer MCML gates: models and design considerations, in *Proceedings of IEEE International Symposium on Circuits and Systems* (Marrakech, 2006)
35. M. Alioto, Design of nanometer MOS current mode logic: from very high-speed down to ultra-low power, in *Proceedings of International Conference on Microelectronics* (2009), pp. 12–13
36. M. Alioto, G. Palumbo, Model and design of bipolar and MOS current-mode logic (CML, ECL and SCL Digital Circuits) (Kluwer Academic Publications, 2005)
37. N. Pandey, K. Gupta, G. Bhatia, B. Choudhary, MOS current mode logic exclusive-OR gate using multi-threshold triple-tail cells. Microelectr. J. **57**, 13–20 (2016)
38. N. Pandey, M. Gupta, K. Gupta, A PFSCL based configurable logic block, in *Proceedings of Annual IEEE India International Conference INDICON* (2015), pp. 1–4
39. N. Pandey, K. Gupta, M. Gupta, An efficient triple-tail cell based PFSCL D-latch. Microelectr. J. **45**(8), 1001–1007 (2014)
40. K. Gupta, N. Pandey, M. Gupta, Analysis and design of MOS current mode logic exclusive-OR gate using triple-tail cells. Microelectr. J. **44**(6), 561–567 (2013)
41. K. Gupta, N. Pandey, M. Gupta, Low-voltage MOS current mode logic multiplexer. Radio Eng. **22**(1), 259–268 (2013)
42. K. Gupta, N. Pandey, M. Gupta, MCML D-latch using triple-tail cells: analysis and design. Active Passive Electr. Comp. **2013**, 9 (2013). (Article ID: 217674)
43. A.H. Ismail, M.I. Elmasry, A low power design approach for MOS current mode logic, in *Proceedings of IEEE Conference on Systems on-Chip* (2003), pp. 143–146
44. G. Caruso, Design of MOS current mode logic gates-computing the limits of voltage swing and bias current, in *Proceedings of IEEE International Symposium on Circuits and Systems* (2005), pp. 5637–5640
45. G. Caruso, A. Macchiarella, Optimum design of two-level MCML gates, in *Proceedings of IEEE International Conference on Electronics, Circuits and Systems* (St. Julien's, 2008), pp. 141–144
46. O. Musa, M. Shams, An efficient delay model for MOS current-mode logic automated design and optimization. IEEE Trans. Circ. Syst. I **57**(8), 2041–2052 (2010)
47. U. Seckin, C.K. Yang, A comprehensive delay model for CMOS CML circuits. IEEE Trans. Circ. Syst. I Regul. Papers **55**(9), 2608–2618 (2010)
48. H. Hassan, M. Anis, M. Elmasry, Design and optimization of MOS current mode logic for parameter variations. Integr. VLSI J. Special Issue: ACM Great Lakes Symp. VLSI **38**(3), 417–437 (2005)
49. R.P. Arroyo, P.A. Moya, H. Wolfgang, Design of a MCML gate library applying multiobjective optimization, in *Proceedings of the IEEE Computer Society Annual Symposium on VLSI* (Porto. Alegre, 2007), pp. 310–314
50. R. Pereira, P. Alvarado, H. Krautschneider, Multi-objective optimization of MCML circuits using a genetic algorithm, in *Workshop on Iberchip In Memorias* (2006), pp. 1–4
51. A. Tanabe, M. Umetani, I. Fujiwara, T. Ogura, K. Kataoka, M. Okihara, H. Sakuraba, T. Endoh, F. Masuoka, 0.18-μm CMOS 10-Gb/s multiplexer/demultiplexer ICs using current mode logic with tolerance to threshold voltage fluctuation. IEEE J. Solid-State Circ. **36**(6), 988–996 (2001)
52. A. Tanabe, M. Umetani, I. Fujiwara, T. Ogura, K. Kataoka, M. Okihara, H. Sakuraba, T. Endoh, F. Masuoka, A 10-Gb/s multiplexer/demultiplexer IC in 0.18 μm CMOS using current mode logic with tolerance to threshold voltage fluctuation, in *Proceedings of IEEE International Conference on Solid-State Circuits* (San Francisco, 2000), pp. 62–63

53. H. Hassan, M. Anis, M. Elmasry, Low power multi-threshold MCML: analysis, design and variability. Microelectron. J. **37**(10), 1097–1104 (2006)
54. H. Hassan, M. Anis, M. Elmasry, Analysis and design of low-power multi-threshold MCML, in *Proceedings of the IEEE International Conference on System-on-Chip* (2004), pp. 25–29
55. K. Zhou, S. Chen, A. Rucinski, J.F. McDonald, T. Zhang, Self-timed triple-rail MOS current mode logic pipeline for power-on-demand design, in *Proceedings of IEEE International Symposium on Circuits and Systems* (2005), pp. 1394–1397
56. K. Zhou, Y. Luo, S. Chen, A. Drake, J.F. McDonald, T. Zhang, Triple-rail MOS current mode logic for high-speed self-timed pipeline applications, in *Proceedings of IEEE International Symposium on Circuits and Systems* (Island of KOS, 2006), pp. 3654–3657
57. M. Alioto, L. Pancioni, S. Rocchi, V. Vignoli, Modeling and evaluation of positive-feedback source-coupled logic. IEEE Trans. Circ. Syst. I Regul. Papers **51**(4), 2345–2355 (2004)
58. M. Alioto, A. Fort, L. Pancioni, S. Rocchi, V. Vignoli, Positive-feedback source-coupled logic: a delay model, in *Proceedings of IEEE Symposium on Circuits and Systems* (2004), pp. II/641–644
59. M. Alioto, A. Fort, L. Pancioni, S. Rocchi, V. Vignoli, An approach to the design of PFSCL gates, in *Proceedings of IEEE Symposium on Circuits and Systems* (2005), pp. 2437–2440
60. M. Alioto, L. Pancioni, S. Rocchi, V. Vignoli, Power-delay-area-noise margin trade-offs in positive-feedback source-coupled logic gates. IEEE Trans. Circ. Syst. I Regul. Papers **54**(9), 1916–1928 (2007)
61. M. Alioto, L. Pancioni, S. Rocchi, V. Vignoli, Exploiting hysteresys in MCML circuits. IEEE Trans. Circ. Syst. II **53**(11), 1170–1174 (2006)
62. R. Cao, J. Hu, Near-threshold computing of single-rail MOS current mode logic circuits. Res. J. Appl. Sci. Eng. Technol. **5**, 2991–2996 (2013). (Article ID: 836019)
63. M.P. Houlgate, D.J. Olszewski, K. Abdelhalim, L.M. Eachern, Adaptable performance MOS current mode logic for use in a 3 GHz programmable frequency divider, in *Proceedings of IEEE Conference on Circuits and Systems* (2003), pp. 1303–1306
64. M.P. Houlgate, D.J. Olszewski, K. Abdelhalim, L.M. Eachern, Adaptable MOS current mode logic for use in a multi-band RF prescaler, in *Proceedings of IEEE Conference on Circuits and Systems* (2004), pp. 329–332
65. A. Worapishet, M. Thamsirianunt, An NMOS inductive loading technique for extended operating frequency CMOS ring oscillators, in *Proceedings of IEEE Midwest Symposium on Circuits and Systems* (2002), pp. 116–119
66. H.T. Bui, Y. Savaria, 10 GHz PLL using active shunt-peaked MCML gates and improved frequency acquisition XOR phase detector in 0.18 μm CMOS, in *Proceedings of the IEEE International Workshop SOC for Real-Time Applications* (2004), pp. 115–118
67. S.S. Mohan, M.del Mar Hershenson, S.P. Boyd, T.H. Lee, Bandwidth extension in CMOS with optimized on-chip inductors. IEEE J. Solid-State Circ. **35**(3), 346–354 (2000)
68. H.T. Bui, Y. Savaria, Shunt-peaking of MCML gates using active inductors, in *Proceedings of IEEE Northeast Workshop on Circuits and Systems* (2004), pp. 361–364
69. F. Yuan, in *CMOS active inductors and transformers: principle, implementation and applications* (Springer, 2008)
70. S. Mohan, S. Hershenson, M. Boyd, T. Lee, Simple accurate expressions for planar spiral inductances. IEEE J. Solid-State Circ. **34**(10), 1419–1424 (1999)
71. B. Sun, F. Yuan, A New inductor series-peaking technique for bandwidth enhancement of CMOS current-mode circuits. Analog Integr. Circ. Sig. Process **37**, 259–264 (2003)
72. F. Yuan, in *CMOS Current-Mode Circuits for Data Communications* (Springer, 2007)
73. H.T. Bui, Dual-path and diode-tracking active inductors for MCML gates, in *Canadian Conference on Electrical and Computer Engineering* (2006), pp. 1060–1063
74. S.M. Masood, in *Active Loads in Current-Mode Logic (CML) Topology* (Technical University of Denmark, 2006)

75. A. Tajalli, E. Vittoz, Y. Leblebici, Ultra low power subthreshold MOS current mode logic circuits using a novel load device concept, in *Proceedings of International Conference on Solid State Circuits* (Munich, 2007), pp. 304–307

76. A. Tajalli, E. VIttoz, Y. Leblebici, E.J. Brauer, Ultra-low power subthreshold current-mode logic utilizing PMOS load device. Electr. Lett. **43**(17), 911–912 (2007)

77. M. Alioto, Y. Leblebici, Analysis and design of ultra-low power subthreshold MCML gates, in *Proceedings of IEEE International Symposium on Circuits and System* (Taipei, 2009), pp. 2557–2560

78. E.A. Shapiro, E.G. Friedman, Performance characteristics of 14 nm near threshold MCML circuits, in *Proceedings of IEEE Unified Conference on SOI-3D-Subthreshold Microelectronics Technology* (Monterey, 2013), pp. 1–2

79. A. Tajalli, Y. Leblebici, Subthreshold source-coupled logic, in *Advanced Circuits for Emerging Technologies*, ed. by K. Iniewski (Wiley, Hoboken, NJ, USA, 2012)

80. A. Tajalli, E.J. Brauer, Y. Leblebici, E. Vittoz, Subthreshold source-coupled logic circuits for ultra-low-power applications. IEEE J. Solid-State Circ. **43**(7), 1699–1710 (2008)

81. R. Cao, J. Hu, Near-threshold computing and minimum supply voltage of single-rail MCML circuits. J. Electr. Comput. Eng. **2014**, 10 (2014). (Article ID 836019)

82. F. Cannillo, C. Toumazou, T.S. Lande, Nanopower subthreshold MCML in submicrometer CMOS technology. IEEE Trans. Circ. Syst. I Regul. Papers **56**(8), 1598–1611 (2009)

83. M.H. Anis, M.I. Elmasry, Self-timed MOS current mode logic for digital applications, in *Proceedings of IEEE International Symposium on Circuits and Systems* (2002), pp. 113–116

84. M.W. Allam, M.I. Elmasry, Dynamic current mode logic (DyMCML): a new low-power high performance logic style. IEEE J. Solid-State Circ. **36**(3), 550–558 (2001)

85. G. Caruso, D. Sclafani, Analysis of compressor architectures in MOS current-mode logic, in *Proceedings of IEEE International Conference on Electronics, Circuits, and Systems* (Athens, 2010), pp. 13–16

86. J.B. Kim, Low-power MCML circuit with sleep-transistor, in *Proceedings of IEEE International Conference on Application-Specific Integrated Circuits* (2009), pp. 25–28

87. K. Zou, J. Hu, A power-gating scheme for MOS current mode logic circuits. Telkomnika **11** (10), 6111–6119 (2013)

88. Y. Wu, X. Fan, H. Ni, J. Hu, Low-power near-threshold MOS current mode logic with power-gating techniques, in *Proceedings of the 2nd International Conference on Computer Science and Electronics Engineering, Changsha* (2013), pp. 1694–1697

89. A. Cevrero, F. Regazzoni, M. Schwander, S. Badel, P. Ienne, Y. Leblebici, Power-gated MOS current mode logic (PG-MCML): a power aware DPA-resistant standard cell library, in *Proceedings of in IEEE International Conference on Design Automation* (New York, 2011), pp. 1014–1019

90. J.K. Shin, T.W. Yoo, M.S. Lee, Design of half-rate linear phase detector using MOS current mode logic gates for 10-Gb/s clock and data recovery circuits, in *Proceedings of International Conference on Advanced Communication Technology* (Phoenix Park, 2005), pp. 205–210

91. P. Heydari, R. Mohavavelu, Design of ultra high-speed CMOS CML buffers and latches, in *Proceedings of IEEE Conference on Circuits and Systems* (2003), pp. 208–211

92. M. Sumanthi, Y.C. Kartheek, Performance and analysis of CML logic gates and latches, in *Proceedings of IEEE International Symposium on Microwave, Antenna, Propagation and EMC Technologies for Wireless Communications*, Hangzhou (2007), pp. 1428–1432

93. P. Heydari, R. Mohavavelu, Design of ultra high-speed CMOS CML buffers and latches, in *Proceedings of the International Symposium on Circuits and Systems* (2003), pp. II-208–II-211

94. M. Usama, Tad A. Kwasniewski, Design and comparison of CMOS current mode logic latches, in *Proceedings of IEEE International Symposium on Circuits and Systems* (2004), pp. 353–356

95. M. Alioto, R. Mita, G. Palumbo, Design of high-speed power efficient MOS current mode logic frequency dividers. IEEE Trans. Circ. Syst. II: Expr. Briefs **53**(11), 1165–1169 (2006)
96. R. Nonis, E. Palumbo, P. Palestri, L. Selmi, A design methodology for MOS current-mode logic frequency dividers. IEEE Trans. Circ. Syst. I Regul. Papers **54**(2), 245–254 (2007)
97. B. Razavi, A model to understand current consumption, maximum operating frequency and scaling trends of MCML frequency dividers. RF Microelectronics (Prentice Hall, 1998)
98. U. Singh, M.M. Green, High-frequency CML clock dividers in 0.13-m CMOS operating up to 38 GHz. IEEE J. Solid-State Circ. **40**(8), 1658–1661 (2005)
99. R.K. Agrawal, N. Pandey, K. Gupta, Implementation of PFSCL razor flip flop, in *Proceedings of IEEE 2017 International Conference on Computing Methodologies and Communication*, ICCMC, pp. 6–11
100. Radhika, N. Pandey, K. Gupta, M. Gupta, Low power D-latch design using MCML tri-state buffers, in *Proceedings of IEEE International Conference on Signal Processing and Integrated Networks* (SPIN) (2014), pp. 531–534
101. M. Nocente, D. Fontanelli, P. Palestri, R. Nonis, D. Esseni, L. Selmi, A numerical model for the oscillation frequency, the amplitude and the phase-noise of MOS-current-mode-logic ring oscillators. Int. J. Circ. Theory Appl. **38**(6), 591–623 (2009)
102. A.H. Ismail, M. Sharifkhani, M I. Elmasry, On the design of low power MCML based ring oscillators, in *Proceedings of IEEE Canadian Conference on Electrical and Computer Engineering* (2004), pp. 2383–2386
103. A. Tyagi, N. Pandey, K. Gupta, PFSCL based linear feedback shift register, in *Proceedings of IEEE International Conference on Computational Techniques in Information and Communication Technologies, ICCTICT* (2016), pp. 580–585
104. S. Agarwal, N. Pandey, K. Gupta, Bharat Choudhary, Design of MCML based LFSR for low power and mixed signal applications, in *Proceedings of Annual IEEE India International Conference INDICON* (2015), pp. 1–6
105. K. Gupta, N. Pandey, M. Gupta, A new active shunt-peaked MCML based high performance 1:8 demultiplexer for serial communication. Int. J. Eng. Technol. **2**(10), 4632–4639 (2010)
106. K. Gupta, U. Mittal, R. Baghla, P. Shukla, N. Pandey, On the implementation of PFSCL serializer, in *Proceedings of IEEE International Conference on Signal Processing and Integrated Networks (SPIN)* (2016), pp. 436–440
107. K. Gupta, U. Mittal, R. Baghla, N. Pandey, Implementation of PFSCL based demultiplexer, in *Proceedings of IEEE International Conference on Computational Techniques in Information and Communication Technologies, ICCTICT* (2016), pp. 490–494
108. L. Li, S. Raghavendran, D.T. Comer, CMOS current mode logic gates for high speed applications, in *Proceedings of NASA Symposium on VLSI Design* (Coeurd' Alene, Idaho, 2005), pp. 1–3
109. S. Kabiri, M. Shams, Implementation of MCML universal logic for 10 GHz range in a 0.13 μm CMOS technology, in *Proceedings of the International Symposium on Circuits and Systems* (2004), pp. 653–656
110. P. Heydari, Design and analysis of low-voltage current-mode logic buffers, in *Proceedings of IEEE International Symposium on Quality Electronic Design* (2003), pp. 293–298
111. M. Alioto, G. Palumbo, Power aware design of nanometer MCML tapered buffers. IEEE Trans. Circ. Syst. II: Expr. Briefs **55**(1), 16–20 (2008)
112. Y.M. El-Hariry, A.H. Madian, MOS current mode logic realization of digital arithmetic circuits, in *Proceedings of International Conference on Microelectronics* (Cairo, 2010), pp. 128–131
113. S. Badel, Y. Leblebici, Tri-state buffer/bus driver circuits in MOS current-mode logic, in *Proceedings of Research in Microelectronics and Electronics Conference* (Bordeaux, 2007), pp. 237–240
114. N. Haiyan, H. Jianping, The layout implementations of high-speed low-power MCML cells, in *Proceedings of IEEE International Conference on Electronics, Communication and Control* (Zhejiang, 2011), pp. 2936–2939

115. M. Haghi, J. Draper, A single-event upset hardening technique for high speed MOS current mode logic, in *Proceedings of IEEE International Symposium on Circuits and Systems* (Paris, 2010), pp. 4137–4140

116. S. Khabiri, M. Shams, An MCML four-bit ripple-carry adder design in 1 GHz range, in *Proceedings of IEEE International Symposium on Circuits and Systems* (2005), pp. 1634–1637

117. B. Liang, K. Ma, Z. Ding, X. Fu, The structure design of MOS current mode logic adder, in *Proceedings of International Conference on Millimeter Wave Technology*, vol. 4 (Shenzen, 2012), pp. 1–4

118. Y. Delican, T. Yildirim, High performance 8-bit MUX based multiplier design using MOS current mode logic, in *Proceedings of International Conference on Electrical and Electronics Engineering* (Bursa, 2011), pp. II-89–II-93

119. A. Saha, D. Pal, M. Chandra, M.K. Goswami, Novel high speed MCML 8-bit by 8-bit multiplier, in *Proceedings of International Conference on Devices and Communications* (Mesra, 2011), pp. 1–5

120. V. Srinivasan, S.H. Dong, J.B. Sulistyo, Gigahertz-range MCML multiplier architectures, in *Proceedings of the International Symposium on Circuits and Systems* (2004), pp. 785–788

121. Y. Delcan, A. Morgul, High performance 16-bit MCML multiplier, in *Proceedings of IEEE European Conference on Circuit Theory and Design, Antalya* (2009), pp. 157–160

122. M. Mizuno, M. Yamashina, K. Furuta, H. Igura, H. Abiko, K. Okabe, A. Ono, H. Yamada, A GHz MOS adaptive pipeline technique using variable delay circuits, in *IEEE International Symposium on VLSI circuits* (1994), pp. 27–28

123. T.W. Kwan, M. Shams, Multi-GHz energy-efficient asynchronous pipelined circuits in MOS current mode logic, in *Proceedings of IEEE International Symposium on Circuits and Systems* (2004), pp. II-645–II-648

124. T.W. Kwan, M. Shams, Design of multi-GHz asynchronous pipelined circuits in MOS current mode logic, in *Proceedings of International Conference on VLSI Design* (2005), pp. 301–305

125. T.W. Kwan, M. Shams, Design of asynchronous circuit primitives using MOS current mode logic, in *Proceedings of International Conference on VLSI Design* (2004), pp. 170–173

126. T.W. Kwan, M. Shams, Design of high-performance power-aware asynchronous pipelined circuits in MOS current mode logic, in *Proceedings of IEEE International Symposium on Asynchronous Circuits and Systems* (2005), pp. 1–10

127. K. Gupta, N. Pandey, M. Gupta, Multi-threshold MOS current mode logic based asynchronous pipeline circuits. ISRN Electr **2012**, 7 (2012). (Article ID 529194)

128. K. Gupta, N. Pandey, M. Gupta, A novel active shunt-peaked MCML array multiplier. J. Multi Discipl. Eng. Technol. **6**(2), 8 (2012)

129. K. Gupta, N. Pandey, N. Saxena, S. Dutta, Implementation and performance comparison of a four-bit ripple-carry adder using different MOS current mode logic topologies, in *Proceedings of International Conference on Computational Science and Its Applications —ICCSA* (2017), pp. 299–313

130. N. Pandey, K. Gupta, S. Gupta, S. Kumari, MCML based priority encoders, in *4th International Conference on Recent Advances in Engineering Science and Management (ICRAESM-17)*, pp. 246–254

131. K. Gupta, P. Shukla, N. Pandey, On the implementation of PFSCL adders, in *Second International Innovative Applications of Computational Intelligence on Power, Energy and Controls with their Impact on Humanity* (2016), pp. 287–291

132. K. Gupta, R. Tanwar, N. Pandey, M. Gupta, A novel high speed MCML square root carry select adder for mixed-signal applications, in *Proceedings of IEEE International Conference on Multimedia, Signal Processing and Communication Technologies* (2013), pp. 194–197

133. K. Gupta, N. Pandey, M. Gupta, Low power multi-threshold MOS current mode logic asynchronous pipeline circuits, in *Proceedings of IEEE 5th India International Conference on Power Electronics (IICPE)* (2012), pp. 1–4

134. K. Gupta, N. Pandey, M. Gupta, A novel active shunt-peaked MOS current mode logic C-element for asynchronous pipelines, in *Proceedings of IEEE International Conference on Multimedia, Signal Processing and Communication Technologies* (2011), pp. 122–125
135. K. Gupta, N. Pandey, M. Gupta, Shunt-peaking in MCML memory element design in 0.18 μm CMOS technology, in *Proceedings of Annual IEEE India Conference (INDICON)* (2010), pp. 1–4

Chapter 2
Current Mode Logic (CML): Basic Concepts

2.1 Introduction

In the last few decades, the electronic industry has witnessed a phenomenal growth due to the advancements in the integration technologies. The current trend is toward the high-resolution mixed-signal integrated circuits. The current mode logic style is preferred in digital circuit design over CMOS logic style due to its low noise characteristics. The current mode logic gates were originally implemented by using bipolar transistor [1] and currently due to the advantages offered by MOS transistors; current mode logic gates employing them are favored. This chapter presents the basic concepts of the MOS-based current mode logic (CML) gate. The operation of a CML gate is described first, followed by the analysis and design of differential and the single-ended CML gates. The realization of basic digital gates in CML style is also discussed.

2.2 Basic Concepts

The basic structure of a CML gate consists of a pull-down network (PDN), a current source, and a load. The PDN uses source-coupled transistors pairs to implement the logic function, the current source maintains a constant bias current, and the load performs the current-to-voltage conversion [2–4]. These gates can be differential or single-ended depending on the type of operation. Let us consider differential and single-ended inverters of Fig. 2.1 to further elucidate the operation of these gates. The current source in both the inverters is realized by biasing a NMOS transistor $M1$ in saturation region. Also, they use source-coupled transistor pair ($M2$–$M3$) in the PDN. The differential CML inverter (Fig. 2.1a) operates with differential inputs $(v_{in\_1} - v_{in\_2})$ and uses equal-valued load resistors (R_{L1} and R_{L2}) for converting the

© Springer Nature Singapore Pte Ltd. 2020
K. Gupta et al., *Model and Design of Improved Current Mode Logic Gates*, https://doi.org/10.1007/978-981-15-0982-7_2

current through the source-coupled transistor pair (*M2–M3*) to differential outputs ($v_{out\_1} - v_{out\_2}$). In contrast, a single-ended CML inverter (Fig. 2.1b) operates on single input (v_{in}) that drives transistor *M2* and a reference voltage source (V_{REF}) is connected to the gate terminal of *M3*. The output v_{out} is obtained from resistor R_{L1} as shown. The CML gates work on the principle of current steering. This can be explained by analyzing the operation for a differential CML inverter. In Fig. 2.1a, by assuming, *M2* and *M3* as matched and operating in the saturation region, following relations can be written:

$$v_{in\_d} = v_{in\_1} - v_{in\_2} = \left(\frac{2i_{D\_M2}}{\mu_n C_{ox} \frac{W_N}{L_N}} \right)^{1/2} - \left(\frac{2i_{D\_M3}}{\mu_n C_{ox} \frac{W_N}{L_N}} \right)^{1/2} \tag{2.1a}$$

$$I_{CS} = i_{D\_M2} + i_{D\_M3} \tag{2.1b}$$

where v_{in_d} is the differential input voltage; i_{D_M2}, i_{D_M3} are the drain currents of *M2* and *M3*, respectively. The parameters μ_n, C_{ox}, W_N, and L_N corresponds to electron mobility, the oxide capacitance per unit area, the effective channel width, and length of the transistor.

By substituting Eq. (2.1b) into Eq. (2.1a), i_{D_M2} and i_{D_M3} can be expressed as a function of the differential input voltage as:

$$i_{D\_M2} = \frac{I_{CS}}{2} + \frac{I_{CS}}{2} \left(\frac{\mu_n C_{ox} \frac{W_N}{L_N} v_{in\_d}^2}{I_{CS}} - \frac{\left(\mu_n C_{ox} \frac{W_N}{L_N} \right)^2 v_{in\_d}^4}{4 I_{CS}^2} \right)^{1/2} \tag{2.2}$$

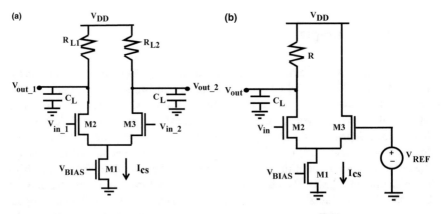

Fig. 2.1 CML inverter: a differential and b single-ended

and

$$i_{D\_M3} = \frac{I_{CS}}{2} - \frac{I_{CS}}{2}\left(\frac{\mu_n C_{ox}\frac{W_N}{L_N}v_{in\_d}^2}{I_{CS}} - \frac{\left(\mu_n C_{ox}\frac{W_N}{L_N}\right)^2 v_{in\_d}^4}{4I_{CS}^2}\right)^{1/2} \quad (2.3)$$

The differential drain current can be calculated as:

$$i_{D\_M2} - i_{D\_M3} = \frac{1}{2}\mu_n C_{ox}\frac{W_N}{L_N}v_{in\_d}\sqrt{\frac{4I_{CS}}{\mu_n C_{ox}\frac{W_N}{L_N}} - v_{in\_d}^2} \quad (2.4)$$

Equation (2.4) predicts an equal current flow in transistors M2 and M3 at two instances of v_{in_d}. But this behavior is not observed in the practice. The reason being that the above results are derived by assuming both the transistors ON and operating in saturation region. However, in reality as the differential input exceeds a limit $\left(= \sqrt{2I_{CS}/\mu_n C_{ox}\frac{W_N}{L_N}}\right)$, either of the transistor carries the entire current I_{CS}, and turns OFF the other. This explains the current steering operation in CML gates and is illustrated by plotting the currents in two transistors for various values of v_{in_d} in Fig. 2.2. The same can be summarized as [1]:

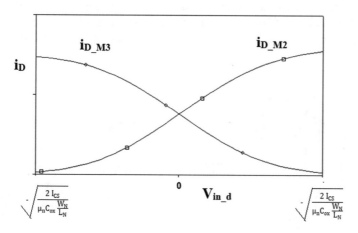

Fig. 2.2 Current steering in CML gate

$$i_{D\_M2} = \begin{cases} 0 & v_{\text{in}\_d} < -\sqrt{\dfrac{2I_{CS}}{\mu_n C_{ox}\frac{W_N}{L_N}}} \\[3mm] \dfrac{I_{CS}}{2} + \dfrac{v_{\text{in}\_d}}{2}\sqrt{\mu_n C_{ox}\dfrac{W_N}{L_N}I_{CS} - \left(\mu_n C_{ox}\dfrac{W_N}{L_N}\dfrac{v_{\text{in}\_d}}{2}\right)^2} & |v_{\text{in}\_d}| \le \sqrt{\dfrac{2I_{CS}}{\mu_n C_{ox}\frac{W_N}{L_N}}} \\[3mm] I_{CS} & v_{\text{in}\_d} > \sqrt{\dfrac{2I_{CS}}{\mu_n C_{ox}\frac{W_N}{L_N}}} \end{cases}$$

$$\text{(2.5a)}$$

$$i_{D\_M3} = I_{CS} - i_{D\_M2} \tag{2.5b}$$

The differential output voltage as the function of differential input voltage may be written as [1]:

$$v_{\text{out}\_d} = \begin{cases} \delta V & v_{\text{in}\_d} < -\sqrt{\dfrac{2I_{CS}}{\mu_n C_{ox}\frac{W_N}{L_N}}} \\[3mm] -v_{\text{in}\_d}\,\delta V\sqrt{\dfrac{\mu_n C_{ox}}{I_{CS}}\dfrac{W_N}{L_N} - \left(\dfrac{\mu_n C_{ox}}{2}\dfrac{W_N}{L_N}v_{\text{in}\_d}\right)^2} & |v_{\text{in}\_d}| \le \sqrt{\dfrac{2I_{CS}}{\mu_n C_{ox}\frac{W_N}{L_N}}} \\[3mm] -\delta V & v_{\text{in}\_d} > \sqrt{\dfrac{2I_{CS}}{\mu_n C_{ox}\frac{W_N}{L_N}}} \end{cases} \tag{2.6}$$

where δV is the voltage drop across R_{L1} (R_{L2}) when complete bias current I_{CS} is steered through it. The resistors R_{L1}, R_{L2} can be replaced by MOSFET as load device since the area occupied by a transistor is usually smaller than that occupied by the comparable resistive load. A PMOS transistor operating in the linear region is generally used as load. The circuit of differential and single-ended CML inverters

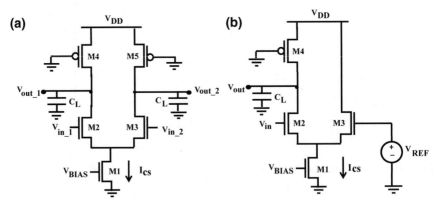

Fig. 2.3 CML inverters with PMOS load: **a** differential [1] and **b** single ended

with PMOS load is shown in Fig. 2.3. Using the standard BSIM3v3 MOSFET model [5], the resistance offered by the load transistors $M4$ and $M5$ is given as [1]:

$$R_{LP} = \frac{R_{int\_p}}{1 - \frac{(R_{DSW}10^{-6})/W_P}{R_{int\_p}}} \qquad (2.7)$$

where R_{DSW} is the empirical model parameter, W_P is the effective channel width of PMOS transistors $M4$, $M5$. The parameter R_{int_p} corresponds to the intrinsic resistance of the transistors in the linear region and is given as [1]:

$$R_{int\_p} = \left[\mu_{eff,p} C_{ox} \frac{W_P}{L_P} \left(V_{DD} - |V_{T,P}|\right)\right]^{-1} \qquad (2.8)$$

Here, the parameters $\mu_{eff,p}$, $V_{T,P}$, and L_P are the effective hole mobility, the threshold voltage, and the effective channel length of the PMOS transistors $M4$, $M5$, respectively. With the foundation of CML-related basic concepts, an in-depth analysis on differential and single-ended CML gates is discussed further.

2.3 Differential CML Gates

The differential CML gates use differential signaling. The PDN realizes the functionality by using series-gating design approach [1]. It is a systematic general approach wherein a N-input logic function $F(Y1, \ldots, Y_N)$ is implemented as a network of source-coupled transistor pairs having all transistor paths associated with the 2^N possible input combinations and then properly connecting each of the upper drain nodes to the output nodes.

The following rules are generally followed while realizing a logic function.

(i) The source-coupled transistor pairs are not allowed to share their source terminal with other transistor pair.

(ii) The current source must be connected to the source of only one transistor pair.

(iii) Each of the two drain nodes of a transistor pair is connected to the source of another stacked transistor pair.

By iterating this reasoning, a tree with N-levels of source-coupled transistor pairs is obtained. A generalized differential CML gate for two inputs $Y1$ and $Y2$ is shown in Fig. 2.4. The drain terminals of the transistor pairs at the highest level are connected to the appropriate output nodes according to the logic function. Based on the outlined concept, the circuits of basic combinational gates such as exclusive-OR

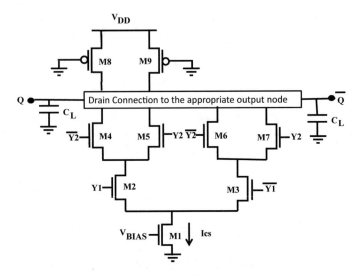

Fig. 2.4 A generalized two-level differential CML gate

(XOR) gate, 2:1 multiplexer (MUX), and a sequential circuit such as D latch are drawn in Fig. 2.5.

2.3.1   Analysis of Differential CML Gates

The behavior of a CML gate can be analyzed in terms of static and delay parameters [1]. The static parameters include voltage swing (V_{SWING}), small-signal gain (A_{v_d}), noise margin (NM), and power (P) of the CML gate. A CML inverter is considered first, and then, the established theoretical concepts are extended to the complex CML circuits. For an inverter (Fig. 2.3a), the differential input (v_{in_d}) and output (v_{out_d}) voltages [1] are defined as:

$$v_{in\_d} = v_{in\_1} - v_{in\_2} \tag{2.9a}$$

$$v_{out\_d} = v_{out\_1} - v_{out\_2} = -R_{LP}(i_{D\_M2} - i_{D\_M3}). \tag{2.9b}$$

For the analysis, two simple cases are being considered. For the case, with high differential input voltage v_{in_d}, i.e., when $v_{in\_1} > v_{in\_2}$, the bias current I_{CS} flows through transistor $M2$. Therefore, by substituting $i_{D\_M2} = I_{CS}$ and $i_{D\_M3} = 0$ in Eq. (2.9b), low differential output voltage ($V_{OL} = v_{out\_d}$) [1] is derived as:

Fig. 2.5 Differential CML gates: **a** XOR gate, **b** 2:1 MUX, and **c** D latch

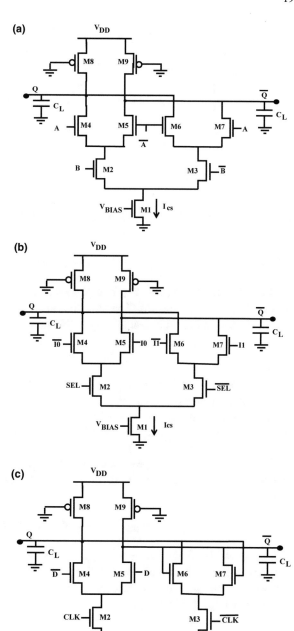

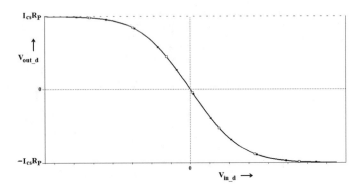

Fig. 2.6 Voltage transfer characteristic of a differential CML inverter

$$V_{OL} = -I_{CS} R_{LP} \tag{2.10}$$

Similarly, for low value of differential input $v_{\text{in}\_1} < v_{\text{in}\_2}$, the bias current I_{CS} gets steered to transistor $M3$. The substitution of $i_{D\_M2} = 0$ and $i_{D\_M3} = I_{CS}$ in Eq. (2.9b) yields high differential output voltage ($V_{OH} = v_{\text{out}\_d}$) [1] as:

$$V_{OH} = I_{CS} R_{LP} \tag{2.11}$$

The same is illustrated through voltage transfer characteristic (VTC) of differential CML inverter plotted in Fig. 2.6. It is to be noted that the characteristic is symmetrical around a logic threshold voltage $V_{LT} = 0$. From this, it can be inferred that at this point on VTC, differential output voltage is equal to the differential input voltage which occurs only when both the inputs are equal ($v_{\text{in}\_1} = v_{\text{in}\_2}$).

From the above two expressions given in Eqs. (2.10) and (2.11), the voltage swing (V_{SWING}) defined as the difference in the high and low output voltages [1] is found as:

$$V_{SWING} = V_{OH} - V_{OL} = 2 I_{CS} R_{LP} \tag{2.12}$$

The small-signal voltage gain (A_{v_d}) is the gain evaluated around the logic threshold voltage. As the differential CML gate is symmetric and has fully differential inputs therefore in accordance with half circuit concept, A_{v_d} around the logic threshold voltage [1] is computed as:

$$A_{v\_d} = g_{m,n}R_{LP} = R_{LP}\sqrt{2\,\mu_{\text{eff},n}C_{ox}\frac{W_N}{L_N}\frac{I_{CS}}{2}} \tag{2.13}$$

where $g_{m,n}$ is defined as the transconductance and is substituted as $\sqrt{\mu_{\text{eff},n}C_{ox}\frac{W_N}{L_N}I_{CS}}$.

Using Eq. (2.12), to replace R_{LP}, we get the resulting expression of A_{v_d} as:

$$A_{v\_d} = \frac{v_{\text{SWING}}}{2} \sqrt{\mu_{\text{eff},n} C_{ox} \frac{W_N}{L_N} \frac{1}{I_{CS}}} \tag{2.14}$$

The noise margin of the CML gate defines its noise tolerance. Typically, noise margins for low signal levels (NM_L) and high signal value (NM_H), respectively, are considered and are expressed as:

$$NM_H = V_{OH} - V_{IH} \tag{2.15a}$$

$$NM_L = V_{IL} - V_{OL} \tag{2.15b}$$

where V_{IH} (V_{IL}) is the minimum (maximum) differential input voltage which can be interpreted as logic '1' (logic '0') and corresponds to the points on VTC at which $\frac{\partial v_{\text{out}\_d}}{\partial v_{\text{in}\_d}} = -1$. However, as the VTC of CML gate is symmetric, the values of NM_L and NM_H are equal ($NM = NM_L = NM_H$) [6]. To evaluate NM, V_{IH} is first derived by differentiating Eq. (2.6) and then equating to -1. The simplified expression for V_{IH} [1] is derived as:

$$V_{IH} = \sqrt{\frac{2 I_{CS}}{\mu_{\text{eff},n} C_{ox} \frac{W_N}{L_N}} \left(1 - \frac{1}{\sqrt{2} A_{v\_d}}\right)} \tag{2.16}$$

where $\delta V = I_{CS} R_{LP}$ is substituted. Now, putting the values form Eqs. (2.11) and (2.16) in Eq. (2.15), NM [1] is calculated as:

$$NM = \frac{V_{\text{SWING}}}{2} \left(1 - \frac{\sqrt{2}}{A_{v\_d}}\right) \tag{2.17}$$

It is to be noted in Eq. (2.17) that the noise margin is proportional to half the voltage swing and approximately assumes this value for large values of A_{v_d}. To complete the static analysis, it is worth mentioning that due to the presence of constant current source, CML gates consume static power. The static power of CML gates is computed as the product of bias current I_{CS} and the power supply value V_{DD}, which can be written as:

$$P = V_{DD} I_{CS} \tag{2.18}$$

The propagation delay of a differential CML inverter is evaluated as the time it takes to charge or discharge the load capacitor C_L from 50% of the differential input value to 50% of the differential output value. The delay is derived by linearizing the circuit around logic threshold. The corresponding equivalent linear half circuit is shown in Fig. 2.7. The parasitic capacitances associated with the NMOS transistor

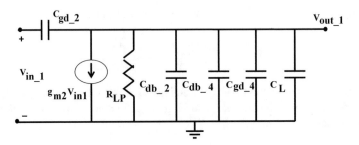

Fig. 2.7 Half circuit of a differential CML inverter

$M2$ and PMOS transistors $M4$ are considered, wherein C_{db_i}, C_{gd_i} represents drain–bulk junction capacitance and the gate-to-drain capacitance of ith transistor ($i = 2, 4$).

The resulting circuit models a first-order circuit therefore by using the open-circuit time constant method; the propagation delay t_{PD_d} for a unit-step input waveform is expressed as:

$$t_{PD\_d} = 0.69\, R_{LP}\left(C_{gd\_2} + C_{db\_2} + C_{db\_4} + C_{gd\_4} + C_L\right) \qquad (2.19)$$

The value of NMOS parasitic capacitance is calculated by assuming it to operate in saturation region most of the time. Thus, gate-to-drain capacitance C_{gd_i} of ith NMOS transistor is calculated as:

$$C_{gd\_i} = C_{gdo} W_n \qquad (2.20)$$

where C_{gdo} is a model parameter representing the overlap gate-to-drain capacitance per unit channel width. The junction capacitance C_{db_i} [7] is expressed as:

$$C_{db\_i} = W_n\left(K_{jn} C_{jn} L_{dn} + 2K_{jswn} C_{jswn}\right) + 2K_{jswn} C_{jswn} L_{dn} \qquad (2.21)$$

where C_{jn} and C_{jswn} are the zero-bias junction capacitance per unit area and zero-bias sidewall capacitance per unit parameter, respectively. The parameter L_{dn} is extrapolated form layout design rules. The coefficients K_{jn}, and K_{jswn} are the voltage equivalence factor for the junction and the sidewall capacitances [7]. The value of coefficient K_j is calculated as:

$$K_j = \frac{-\varnothing_0^m}{V_1 - V_2(1 - m)}\left[(\varnothing_0 - V_1)^{1-m} - (\varnothing_0 - V_2)^{1-m}\right] \qquad (2.22)$$

where $\varnothing_0$ is the built-in potential difference across the junction, m is the grading coefficient of the junction, and V_1 and V_2 are the minimum and maximum voltages across the junction. The sidewall coefficients K_{jsw} are determined in a similar fashion. Since PMOS operates in linear region, the calculation of gate drain capacitance differs from that of NMOS transistor considered above [1]. The gate-to-drain capacitance is evaluated as the sum of the overlap capacitance and capacitance due to the channel charge of PMOS working in linear region. Thus, it can be written as:

$$C_{\text{gd\_p}} = C_{\text{gd\_0}} W_P + C_{\text{gd\_int}} \tag{2.23}$$

where $C_{\text{gd\_int}}$ is the intrinsic capacitance, represents the channel charge, and is evaluated as the differential of total charge associated with the MOSFET with respect to the drain terminal voltage. From BSIM3v3 capacitance model [5], the channel charge Q_d for 40/60 charge portioning is given [1] as:

$$Q_d = -W_P L_P C_{ox} \left[\frac{V_{\text{SG}} - |V_T|}{2} - \frac{3 A_{\text{bulk}} V_{\text{SD}}}{4} + \frac{(A_{\text{bulk}} V_{\text{SD}})^2}{8 \left(V_{\text{SG}} - |V_T| - \frac{A_{\text{bulk}}}{2} V_{\text{SD}} \right)} \right] \tag{2.24}$$

$$\approx -W_P L_P C_{ox} \left[\frac{V_{\text{SG}} - |V_T|}{2} - \frac{3 A_{\text{bulk}} V_{\text{SD}}}{4} \right] \tag{2.25}$$

where $V_{\text{SD}} \ll \frac{V_{\text{SG}} - |V_T|}{A_{\text{bulk}}}$ was assumed. The A_{bulk} parameter [1] in terms other BSIM3v3 model parameters is defined as:

$$A_{\text{bulk}} = \frac{1}{1 + K_{\text{ETA}}} \left\{ 1 + \frac{K_{10X}}{2\sqrt{\emptyset_s - |V_{\text{SB}}|}} \left[\frac{A_0 L_P}{L_P + 2\sqrt{X_J X_{\text{dep}}}} \right. \right.$$
$$\left. \left. \left(1 - A_{\text{GS}}(|V_{\text{GS}}| - |V_T|) \left(\frac{L_P}{L_P + 2\sqrt{X_J X_{\text{dep}}}} \right)^2 \right) + \frac{b_0}{W_P + B_1} \right] \right\} \tag{2.26}$$

The parameter A_{bulk} is maximized by setting W_P to its minimum value and maximizing the A_{bulk} for L_P. As an example, for the PMOS in 0.18 μm CMOS technology, with $V_{\text{DD}} = 1.8$ V, the maximum value of $A_{\text{bulk,max}}$ is 1.29. Thus, $C_{\text{gd\_int}}$ [1] is written as:

$$C_{\text{gd\_int}} = \frac{\partial Q_d}{\partial V_d} = \frac{3}{4} A_{\text{bulk,max}} W_P L_P C_{ox} \tag{2.27}$$

The above capacitance values can be substituted in delay equation [Eq. (2.19)] to determine the delay of a differential CML inverter.

2.3.2   Design of a Differential CML Inverter

The design of a differential CML inverter refers to the determination of the aspect ratios of the transistors such that they satisfy given specifications on noise margin and bias current [1]. The steps involved in the design of CML inverter is explained below:

For a given *NM* value, and by assuming A_{v_d} (>1.4 for differential CML gates [8]), the voltage swing [1] by using Eq. (2.12) is calculated as:

$$V_{\text{SWING}} = \frac{2NM}{1 - \frac{\sqrt{2}}{A_{v\_d}}} \qquad (2.28)$$

The value of equivalent load resistance required to achieve the above V_{SWING} can thus be found out as:

$$R_{\text{LP}} = \frac{V_{\text{SWING}}}{2I_{\text{CS}}} \qquad (2.29)$$

Further, it is worth mentioning here that to get the desired value of resistance, it necessary to decide which parameter out of length and width is to be calculated or kept at its minimum value. To determine this, the equivalent resistance, $R_{\text{LP\_MIN}}$, for the minimum-sized PMOS transistor is first computed. The high current value I_{HIGH} [1] for the required voltage swing is determined as:

$$I_{\text{HIGH}} = \frac{V_{\text{SWING}}}{2R_{\text{LP\_MIN}}}. \qquad (2.30)$$

If the bias current is higher than I_{HIGH}, then R_{LP} should be less than $R_{\text{LP\_MIN}}$. For this, L_P is set to its minimum value; i.e., L_{MIN} and W_P [1] are calculated by solving Eqs. (2.7) and (2.8) as:

$$W_P = \frac{2I_{\text{CS}}}{V_{\text{SWING}}\,\mu_{\text{eff},p}C_{ox}\left(V_{\text{DD}} - |V_{T,P}|\right)} \frac{L_{\text{MIN}}}{\left\{1 - \frac{R_{\text{DSW}}10^{-6}}{L_{\text{MIN}}}\left[\mu_{\text{eff},p}C_{ox}\left(V_{\text{DD}} - |V_{T,P}|\right)\right]\right\}} \qquad (2.31)$$

Similarly, if the bias current is lower than I_{HIGH}, then R_{LP} should be greater than $R_{\text{LP\_MIN}}$ which is achieved by setting W_P to its minimum value, i.e., W_{MIN} and calculating L_P [1] by solving Eqs. (2.7) and (2.8) as:

$$L_P = W_{\text{MIN}}\,\mu_{\text{eff},p}C_{ox}\left(V_{\text{DD}} - |V_{T,P}|\right)\left(\frac{V_{\text{SWING}}}{2I_{\text{CS}}} - \frac{R_{\text{DSW}}10^{-6}}{W_{\text{MIN}}}\right) \qquad (2.32)$$

Now, to size PDN transistors ($M2$, $M3$), the small-signal gain (A_{v_d}) is used. Assuming minimum channel length for the said transistors, the width (W_N) [1] is computed as:

$$W_N = \frac{4}{\mu_{\mathrm{eff},n} C_{ox}} \left(\frac{A_{v\_d}}{V_{\mathrm{SWING}}} \right)^2 I_{CS} L_{\mathrm{MIN}} \tag{2.33}$$

Sometimes, Eq. (2.33) results in a value of W_N smaller than the minimum channel width; therefore, in such cases, W_N is also set to W_{MIN}. This happens when the bias current is lower than the current of the minimum-sized NMOS transistor, I_{LOW}. Using Eq. (2.13), I_{LOW} [1] is given as:

$$I_{\mathrm{LOW}} = \frac{1}{4} \frac{W_{\mathrm{MIN}}}{L_{\mathrm{MIN}}} \mu_{\mathrm{eff},n} C_{ox} \left(\frac{V_{\mathrm{SWING}}}{A_{v\_d}} \right)^2 \tag{2.34}$$

As an example, for the adopted 0.18 μm CMOS technology (refer Table 2.1), for $V_{\mathrm{DD}} = 1.8$ V, the value of I_{HIGH}, I_{LOW} is evaluated as 23 μA, 1 μA, respectively. The size of transistors for a $NM = 130$ mV and $I_{CS} = 20$ μA is $W_N = 5.38$ μm, $L_N = 0.18$ μm, $W_P = 0.27$ μm, $L_P = 0.2$ μm, respectively.

The above design expressions [Eqs. (2.28–2.34)] relate the dimensions of the transistor to the bias current and the voltage swing. Hence, these can further be utilized to express the capacitances used in the delay equation (Eq. 2.19) which can later be used to design CML gates satisfying delay requirements [1]. For the bias current I_{CS} ranging from I_{LOW} to I_{HIGH} and using Eqs. (2.20–2.27), various capacitances in Eq. (2.19) may be expressed as:

$$C_{\mathrm{gd}\_2} = C_{\mathrm{gd}0} W_2 = 4A_{v\_d}^2 C_{\mathrm{gd}0} \frac{L_{\mathrm{MIN}}}{\mu_{\mathrm{eff},n} C_{ox}} \frac{I_{CS}}{(V_{\mathrm{SWING}})^2} \tag{2.35}$$

$$C_{\mathrm{db}\_2} = W_2 \left(K_{\mathrm{jn}} C_{\mathrm{jn}} L_{\mathrm{dn}} + 2K_{\mathrm{jswn}} C_{\mathrm{jswn}} \right) + 2K_{\mathrm{jswn}} C_{\mathrm{jswn}} L_{\mathrm{dn}} \tag{2.36}$$

$$= 4A_{v\_d}^2 \frac{L_{\mathrm{MIN}}}{\mu_{\mathrm{eff},n} C_{ox}} \left(K_{\mathrm{jn}} C_{\mathrm{jn}} L_{\mathrm{dn}} + 2K_{\mathrm{jswn}} C_{\mathrm{jswn}} \right) \frac{I_{CS}}{(V_{\mathrm{swing}})^2} + 2K_{\mathrm{jswn}} C_{\mathrm{jswn}} \tag{2.37}$$

$$C_{\mathrm{gd}\_4} = C_{\mathrm{gd}0} W_{\mathrm{MIN}} + \frac{3}{4} A_{\mathrm{bulk,max}} W_{\mathrm{MIN}} L_P C_{ox} \tag{2.38}$$

Table 2.1 Process parameters for the used 0.18 μm CMOS technology

Parameter	Values
C_{ox}	8.54 fF/mm^2
$\mu_{\mathrm{eff},n} C_{ox}$	264 μ A/V^2
$\mu_{\mathrm{eff},p} C_{ox}$	64 μ A/V
$\dfrac{W_{\mathrm{MIN}}}{L_{\mathrm{MIN}}}$	0.27 μm 0.18 μm
V_{TN}	0.5 V
V_{TP}	−0.5 V

$$= C_{gd0}W_{MIN} + \frac{3}{4}A_{bulk,max}W_{MIN}C_{ox}\{\mu_{eff,p}C_{ox}W_{MIN}(V_{DD} - |V_{T,P}|)$$
$$\left(\frac{V_{SWING}}{2I_{CS}} - \frac{R_{DSW} * 10^{-6}}{W_{MIN}}\right)\}$$

(2.39)

$$C_{db\_4} = W_{MIN}\left(K_{jp}C_{jp}L_{dp} + 2K_{jswp}C_{jswp}\right) + 2K_{jswp}C_{jswp}L_{dp}$$ (2.40)

On careful examination, a generalized expression for all the above capacitance can be written. The capacitance between two terminals x and y in general form can be expressed as:

$$C_{xy} = \frac{a_{xy}}{(V_{SWING})^2}I_{CS} + \frac{b_{xy}V_{SWING}}{I_{CS}^2} + c_{xy}$$ (2.41)

The expressions of the coefficients a_{xy}, b_{xy}, and c_{xy} in all the capacitances in Eq. (2.23) are summarized in Table 2.2.

Using Eqs. (2.35–2.40), Eq. (2.19) can be written as:

$$t_{PD} = 0.69V_{SWING}\left(\frac{a}{V_{SWING}^2} + b\frac{V_{SWING}}{I_{CS}^2} + \frac{c + C_L}{I_{CS}}\right)$$ (2.42)

where

$$a = a_{db2} + a_{gd2}$$ (2.42a)

$$b = b_{gd4}$$ (2.42b)

$$c = c_{db2} + c_{gd4} + c_{db4}$$ (2.42c)

Table 2.2 Coefficients of the capacitances for differential CML inverter [1]

NMOS coefficients	
a_{db2}	$\frac{4A_{v\_d}^2 L_{MIN}}{\mu_{eff,n}C_{ox}}\left(K_{jn}C_{jn}L_{dn} + 2K_{jswn}C_{jswn}\right)$
a_{gd2}	$4A_{v\_d}^2 C_{gdo}\frac{L_{MIN}}{\mu_{eff,n}C_{ox}}$
c_{db2}	$2K_{jswn}C_{jswn}L_{dn}$
b_{db2}, b_{gd2},c_{gd2}	0
PMOS coefficients	
b_{gd4}	$\frac{3}{8}A_{bulk,max}\mu_{eff,p}C_{ox}^2 W_{MIN}^2(V_{DD} - |V_{T,P}|)$
c_{gd4}	$C_{gdo}W_{MIN} - \frac{3}{4}A_{bulk,max}\mu_{eff,p}C_{ox}^2 W_{MIN}(V_{DD} - |V_{T,P}|)R_{DSW}10^{-6}$
c_{db4}	$K_{jp}C_{jp}L_{dp}W_{MIN} + 2K_{jswp}C_{jswp}(L_{dp} + W_{MIN})$
a_{gd4}, a_{db4}, b_{db4}	0

Where the symbols have their usual meaning

For the completeness of the delay model, it is necessary to discuss its validity for I_{CS} values lying outside the range I_{LOW} to I_{HIGH}. For $I_{CS} > I_{HIGH}$, it can be observed that the capacitance coefficients of PMOS transistor in Eq. (2.42) differ as explained in design procedure. But it may be noted that for such values of I_{CS} the capacitive contribution of PMOS transistor is negligible; therefore, Eq. (2.19) can predict the delay. Similarly, for $I_{CS} < I_{HIGH}$, the delay majorly depends on the capacitances of PMOS transistor; therefore, the capacitance coefficients of NMOS transistor do not affect the delay. So, the delay expression represented in (Eq. 2.42) can estimate the delay.

2.3.3 Analysis of Two-Level CML Gates

The above discussion is related to differential CML inverter which has a single level of source-coupled transistor pair. To develop a complete understanding of concept, the analysis of two-level CML circuits is also discussed. The static model for CML circuit holds same as explained for CML inverter, but the delay differs due to its dependence on the parasitic capacitances of the transistor in the PDN. Therefore, the delay model for a two-level CML gate is also included. A 2:1 multiplexer drawn in Fig. 2.5b is considered. The corresponding equivalent linear half circuit is drawn

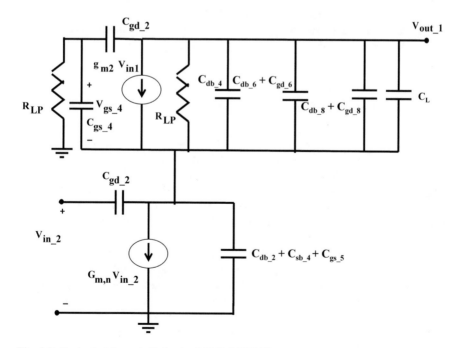

Fig. 2.8 Equivalent linear half circuit of CML MUX [1]

in Fig. 2.8 [1]. By assuming a switching transition in the input connected at the lower level, the propagation delay [1] by using the open-circuit time constant method can be expressed as:

$$t_{PD\_d} = 0.69 \Big[R_{LP} \big(2C_{gd_4} + C_{db_4} + C_{gd_6} + C_{db_6} + C_{gd_8} + C_{db_8} + C_L \big)$$
$$+ \frac{1}{G_{m,n}} \big(C_{gd_2} + C_{db_2} + C_{gs_4} + C_{sb_4} + C_{gs_5} + C_{sb_5} \big) \Big] \qquad (2.43)$$

where $G_{m,n} \left(= \sqrt{\frac{\mu_{eff,n} C_{ox}}{2} \frac{W_N}{L_N} I_{CS}} = \frac{g_{m,n}}{2} \right)$ is the equivalent transconductance of M4. Substituting the value, the simplified delay expression [1] is:

$$t_{PD\_d} = 0.69\, R_{LP} \Big[3C_{gd\_2} + 2C_{db\_4} + C_{gd\_8} + C_{db\_8} + C_L + \frac{2}{A_{v\_d}} \big(2C_{gd\_2} + 3C_{db\_2} + C_{gs\_4} \big) \Big]$$
$$(2.44)$$

2.4 Single-Ended CML Gates

The single-ended CML gates use single-ended signaling. The schematic of a single-ended CML inverter [10] is already shown in Fig. 2.3b. The transistors M1, M2–M3, M4–M5 form the current source, PDN, and load of the gate. The input (v_{in}) is applied to M2 while the gate of M3 is connected to a voltage reference source V_{REF}. The circuit provides a single-ended output (v_{out}).

2.4.1 PFSCL Gates

An improved form of single-ended CML gate named as positive-feedback source-coupled logic (PFSCL) gate is suggested in the literature [9–11]. In this type of gate, a positive feedback replaces the reference voltage source used in single-ended CML gate. Due to their improved performance, PFSCL gates are chosen as a representative of single-ended CML gate in this chapter. A generic N-input PFSCL gate (Fig. 2.9a) realizes a N-input NOR function by connecting NMOS transistors in parallel to each other and finally inverting the input [10]. The PFSCL realizations of an inverter [12] and a buffer are shown in Fig. 2.9b, c. The inverter circuit has input transistor M2 which is source-coupled with a feedback transistor M3 whose gate is connected to the output node. The constant current source M1 provides the bias current I_{CS} while the PMOS load transistor M4 performs the current-to-voltage conversion. In case of PFSCL buffer, the circuit remains the same as inverter, but the output is obtained from the alternate branch as shown in Fig. 2.9c.

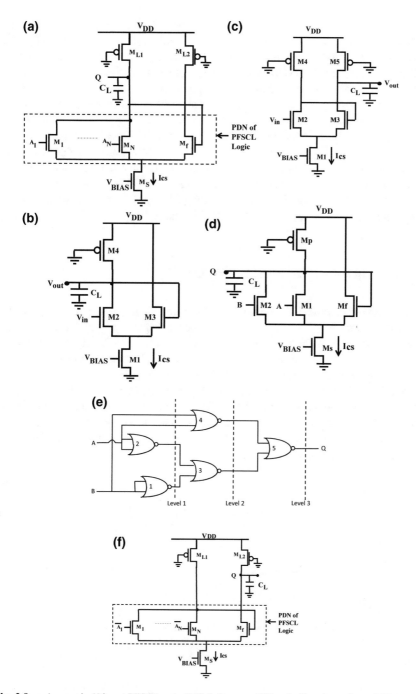

Fig. 2.9   a A generic *N*-input PFSCL gate [10], **b** inverter [12], **c** buffer, **d** two-input NOR gate, **e** two-input XOR realization [13], **f** *N*-input PFSCL NAND gate [12]

The two-input NOR gate has two transistor $M2$, $M3$ connected in parallel as depicted in Fig. 2.9d. The basic structure of PFSCL style recommends NOR-based realization of a logic function [9]. Based on this, the gate-level schematic for a PFSCL XOR gate using NOR-based approach is shown in Fig. 2.9e [13]. It consists of five identical two-input PFSCL NOR gates arranged in three levels. The first level is responsible for generating the complement of the applied inputs, whereas the subsequent two levels implement the XOR functionality. Other combinational gates can also be realized in the similar manner. It is suggested that the same topology of Fig. 2.9a can be used for N-input NAND gate with the help of De Morgan's law [9]. The inputs need to be applied in the inverted form, and the output is taken from the other branch as drawn in Fig. 2.9f [12]. Therefore, PFSCL gates using NAND-based realization use cascading of stages instead of the stacking of transistor pairs employed in differential CML gates.

2.4.2 Analysis of a PFSCL Inverter

The behavior is modeled in terms of static and delay parameters [9–11]. The parameters namely voltage swing, small-signal voltage gain, and the noise margin are derived for a PFSCL inverter. The circuit of a PFSCL inverter shown in Fig. 2.9b is analyzed. For a high value of input v_{in}, the bias current I_{CS} is steered through $M2$ and a low voltage ($V_{OL} = V_{DD} - R_{LP}I_{CS}$) is obtained at the output. Similarly, $M2$ is turned OFF for low value of input v_{in}, and a high voltage ($V_{OH} = V_{DD}$) is obtained at the output. The voltage transfer characteristics of the PFSCL inverter is plotted in Fig. 2.10 and is found to be symmetrical around the logic threshold voltage $V_{LT} = V_{DD} - R_{LP}I_{CS}/2$. As discussed above, the high (V_{OH}) and low (V_{OL}) output voltages are

$$V_{OH} = V_{DD} \tag{2.45a}$$

$$V_{OL} = V_{DD} - I_{CS} R_{LP} \tag{2.45b}$$

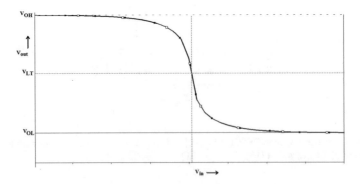

Fig. 2.10 Voltage transfer characteristic of a PFSCL inverter

The voltage swing (V_{SWING}) is computed [10] as:

$$V_{\text{SWING}} = V_{\text{OH}} - V_{\text{OL}} = I_{\text{CS}} R_{\text{LP}} \tag{2.46}$$

The small-signal voltage gain (A_{v_p}) [9, 10] is evaluated around the logic threshold voltage. By applying the superposition of the input voltages at the gate of $M2$ and $M3$, the value of A_{v_p} around the logic threshold voltage [10] is computed as:

$$A_{v\_p} = \frac{g_{m,n} R_{\text{LP}}/2}{1 - g_{m,n} R_{\text{LP}}/2} \tag{2.47}$$

where $g_{m,n}$ is the transconductance of the NMOS transistor computed around the logic threshold as $\sqrt{\mu_{\text{eff},n} C_{ox} \frac{W_N}{L_N} I_{\text{CS}}}$.

The noise margin (*NM*) of a PFSCL inverter [10] is evaluated as:

$$NM = \frac{V_{\text{SWING}}}{2} f\left(g_{m,n} R_P/2\right) \tag{2.48a}$$

where function f is expressed [10] as:

$$f(x) = 2 \sqrt{\frac{1}{2}(1 - 1/16x^2)\left(1 - \sqrt{1 - \frac{1 - 1/4x^2}{(1 - 1/16x^2)^2}}\right)} \cdot \left[2 \sqrt{1 - \frac{1}{2}(1 - 1/16x^2)\left(1 - \sqrt{1 - \frac{1 - 1/4x^2}{(1 - 1/16x^2)^2}}\right)} - \frac{1}{x}\right] \cdot \tag{2.48b}$$

The function f(x) represented in Eq. (2.48b) can be approximated by the expression [10]

$$f(x) = 1.4x - 0.65 \tag{2.48c}$$

The above relation is valid for $x = g_{m,n} R_P/2 < 1$, whereas it exhibits hysteresis for values greater than 1. Alternatively, by using the piecewise-linear approximation of the VTC [9], the *NM* can also be computed as:

$$NM = \frac{V_{\text{SWING}}}{2}\left(1 - \frac{1}{A_{v\_p}}\right) \tag{2.48d}$$

The delay of a PFSCL inverter can be analytically evaluated by linearizing the circuit around the logic threshold. The presence of a feedback, however, makes the analysis complex, so an alternate approach [10] is followed. According to the approach, when the input voltage switches abruptly from low logic level to the high logic level, the propagation delay t_{PD} is evaluated as [10]:

$$t_{PD} = R_{LP} C_{out} = R_{LP} \left(C_{db\_2} + C_{gd\_2} + C_{db\_4} + C_{gd\_4} + C_{gd\_3} + \frac{1}{2} C_{gs\_3} + C_L \right)$$

(2.49)

where all the capacitances have their usual meaning and are computed as discussed in detail for differential CML gates. It may be noted that the capacitance C_{gs_3} is multiplied with ½ due to the miller effect associated with the gain from the gate to source of transistor $M3$ [11]. The delay derived for the inverter can be extended for a n-input generalized PFSCL gate (Fig. 2.9a) as:

$$t_{PD} = R_{LP} C_{out}$$
$$= R_{LP} \left(n(C_{db\_n} + C_{gd\_n}) + C_{db\_p} + C_{gd\_p} + C_{gd\_f} + \frac{1}{2} C_{gs\_f} + C_L \right) \quad (2.50)$$

where C_{out} is the total capacitance at the output node which includes the load capacitance C_L and the parasitic capacitances associated with the transistors. C_{db_n}, C_{gd_n} are the respective drain–bulk and gate-to-drain capacitances of the input transistors; C_{gs_f}, C_{gd_f} represents the gate-to-source and gate-to-drain capacitances of feedback transistor Mf, respectively. The capacitances C_{db_p}, C_{gd_p} represent the drain–bulk and gate–drain capacitance associated with the load transistor.

2.4.3 Design of a PFSCL Inverter

In this section, the design approach of a PFSCL inverter for a given value of the bias current I_{CS} and the noise margin is presented [10].

For a specified value of NM, and by assuming $g_{m,n} R_{LP}/2 = 1$, the value of voltage swing for which the NMOS transistors in the PDN remain in saturation is calculated using Eq. (2.48d) as:

$$V_{SWING} = 2NM \tag{2.51}$$

The voltage swing obtained requires sizing of the load transistor with equivalent resistance $R_{LP} \left(= \frac{V_{SWING}}{I_{CS}} \right)$. To this end, the equivalent resistance, R_{LP_MIN}, for the minimum-sized PMOS transistor is first determined and then the bias current I_{HIGH} [10] for the required voltage swing is determined as:

$$I_{HIGH} = \frac{V_{SWING}}{R_{P\_MIN}} \tag{2.52}$$

If the bias current is higher than I_{HIGH}, then R_{LP} should be less than R_{LP_MIN} and this is achieved by setting L_P to its minimum value, i.e., L_{MIN} and W_P which is calculated by solving Eqs. (2.7) and (2.8) as:

$$W_P = \frac{I_{CS}}{V_{SWING} \, \mu_{\text{eff},p} C_{ox} \left(V_{DD} - |V_{T,P}|\right) \left\{ 1 - \frac{R_{DSW} 10^{-6}}{L_{MIN}} \left[\mu_{\text{eff},p} C_{ox} \left(V_{DD} - |V_{T,P}|\right) \right] \right\}} \cdot \frac{L_{MIN}}{}$$

(2.53)

Similarly, if the bias current is lower than I_{HIGH}, then R_{LP} should be greater than R_{LP_MIN} and this is achieved by setting W_P to its minimum value, i.e., W_{MIN} and L_P [10] which is calculated by solving Eqs. (2.7) and (2.8) as:

$$L_P = W_{MIN} \, \mu_{\text{eff},p} C_{ox} \left(V_{DD} - |V_{T,P}|\right) \left(\frac{V_{SWING}}{I_{CS}} - \frac{R_{DSW} 10^{-6}}{W_{MIN}} \right)$$

(2.54)

The size of the transistors $M2$ and $M3$ can be computed by expressing $g_{m,n} R_{LP}/2$ in terms of the bias current and voltage swing. The term $g_{m,n} R_{LP}/2$ can be expressed as:

$$\frac{g_{m,n} R_{LP}}{2} = \frac{V_{SWING}}{2} \sqrt{\mu_{\text{eff},n} C_{ox} \frac{W_N}{L_N} \frac{1}{I_{CS}}}$$

(2.55)

Solving the above equation, with the minimum channel length, the width W_N [10] of $M2$ and $M3$ transistors can be computed as:

$$W_N = \frac{4}{\mu_{\text{eff},n} C_{ox}} \frac{I_{CS} L_{MIN}}{V_{SWING}^2}$$

(2.56)

Sometimes, Eq. (2.56) results in a value of W_N smaller than the minimum channel width; therefore, in such cases, W_N is also set to W_{MIN}. This happens when the bias current is lower than the current of the minimum-sized NMOS transistor, I_{LOW}. Using Eq. (2.56), I_{LOW} [10] is given as:

$$I_{LOW} = \frac{1}{4} \frac{W_{MIN}}{L_{MIN}} \mu_{\text{eff},n} C_{ox} V_{SWING}^2$$

(2.57)

According to the above design procedure, the dimensions of the transistors are being expressed in terms of bias current and the voltage swing. The parasitic capacitances associated with the delay expressions can now also be expressed in terms of these parameters. As already discussed for differential CML gate, rewriting the generalized expression for capacitance C_{xy} connected between terminals x and y

$$C_{xy} = \frac{a_{xy}}{\left(V_{SWING}\right)^2} I_{CS} + b_{xy} \frac{V_{SWING}}{I_{CS}} + c_{xy}$$

Using design Eqs. (2.54) and (2.56), various capacitances in Eq. (2.50) for I_{CS} ranging from I_{LOW} to I_{HIGH} may be expressed as:

$$C_{\text{gd}\_2} = C_{\text{gdo}} W_2 = 4 C_{\text{gdo}} \frac{L_{\text{MIN}}}{\mu_{\text{eff},n} C_{ox}} \frac{I_{\text{CS}}}{\left(V_{\text{SWING}}\right)^2} \tag{2.58}$$

$$C_{\text{db}\_2} = W_2 \left(K_{\text{jn}} C_{\text{jn}} L_{\text{dn}} + 2 K_{\text{jswn}} C_{\text{jswn}} \right) + 2 K_{\text{jswn}} C_{\text{jswn}} L_{\text{dn}} \tag{2.59}$$

$$= 4 \frac{L_{\text{MIN}}}{\mu_{\text{eff},n} C_{ox}} \left(K_{\text{jn}} C_{\text{jn}} L_{\text{dn}} + 2 K_{\text{jswn}} C_{\text{jswn}} \right) \frac{I_{\text{CS}}}{\left(V_{\text{SWING}}\right)^2} + 2 K_{\text{jswn}} C_{\text{jswn}} L_{\text{dn}} \tag{2.60}$$

$$C_{\text{gs}\_3} = \frac{2}{3} W_3 C_{ox} L_{\text{MIN}} \tag{2.61}$$

$$= \frac{8}{3} \frac{L_{\text{MIN}}^2}{\mu_{\text{eff},n}} \frac{I_{\text{CS}}}{\left(V_{\text{SWING}}\right)^2} \tag{2.62}$$

$$C_{\text{gd}\_4} = C_{\text{gdo}} W_{\text{MIN}} + \frac{3}{4} A_{\text{bulk,max}} W_{\text{MIN}} L_P C_{ox} \tag{2.63}$$

$$= C_{\text{gdo}} W_{\text{MIN}} + \frac{3}{4} A_{\text{bulk,max}} W_{\text{MIN}} C_{ox} \left\{ \mu_{\text{eff},p} C_{ox} W_{\text{MIN}} \left(V_{\text{DD}} - |V_{T,P}| \right) \left[\frac{V_{\text{SWING}}}{I_{\text{CS}}} - \frac{R_{\text{DSW}} 10^{-6}}{W_{\text{MIN}}} \right] \right\} \tag{2.64}$$

$$C_{\text{db}\_4} = W_{\text{MIN}} \left(K_{\text{jp}} C_{\text{jp}} L_{\text{dp}} + 2 K_{\text{jswp}} C_{\text{jswp}} \right) + 2 K_{\text{jswp}} C_{\text{jswp}} L_{\text{dp}} \tag{2.65}$$

where the symbols have their usual meaning.

The coefficients $a_{xy}, b_{xy},$ and c_{xy} of all the capacitances [10] in Eq. (2.49) are summarized in Table 2.3.

The various capacitances in the delay expression can now be substituted by their respective coefficients. The delay expression for the PFSCL inverter using Eqs. (2.58–2.65) can be written as:

Table 2.3 Coefficients of the capacitances for PFSCL inverter [10]

NMOS coefficients	
a_{db2}	$\frac{4 L_{\text{MIN}}}{\mu_{\text{eff},n} C_{ox}} \left(K_{\text{jn}} C_{\text{jn}} L_{\text{dn}} + 2 K_{\text{jswn}} C_{\text{jswn}} \right)$
a_{gd2}	$4 C_{\text{gdo}} \frac{L_{\text{MIN}}}{\mu_{\text{eff},n} C_{ox}}$
a_{gs3}	$\frac{8}{3} \frac{L_{\text{MIN}}^2}{\mu_{\text{eff},n}}$
c_{db2}	$2 K_{\text{jswn}} C_{\text{jswn}} L_{\text{dn}}$
$b_{\text{db2}}, \ b_{\text{gd2}}, c_{\text{gd2}}$	0
PMOS coefficients	
b_{gd4}	$\frac{3}{4} A_{\text{bulk,max}} \mu_{\text{eff},p} C_{ox}^2 W_{\text{MIN}}^2 \left(V_{\text{DD}} - |V_{T,P}| \right)$
c_{gd4}	$C_{\text{gdo}} W_{\text{MIN}} - \frac{3}{4} A_{\text{bulk,max}} \mu_{\text{eff},p} C_{ox}^2 W_{\text{MIN}} \left(V_{\text{DD}} - |V_{T,P}| \right) R_{\text{DSW}} 10^{-6}$
c_{db4}	$K_{\text{jp}} C_{\text{jp}} L_{\text{dp}} W_{\text{MIN}} + 2 K_{\text{jswp}} C_{\text{jswp}} \left(L_{\text{dp}} + W_{\text{MIN}} \right)$
$a_{\text{gd4}}, \ a_{\text{db4}}, \ b_{\text{db4}}$	0

The symbols have their usual meaning

$$t_{PD} = V_{SWING}\left(\frac{a}{V_{SWING}^2} + b\frac{V_{SWING}}{I_{CS}^2} + \frac{c+C_L}{I_{CS}}\right) \tag{2.66}$$

where

$$a = a_{db2} + a_{gd2} + \frac{1}{2}a_{gs3} \tag{2.67a}$$

$$b = b_{gd4} \tag{2.67b}$$

$$c = c_{db2} + c_{gd4} + c_{db4} \tag{2.67c}$$

The above procedure can be illustrated by designing a PFSCL inverter with $V_{DD} = 1.8$ V, $V_{SWING} = 350$ mV, and $I_{CS} = 30$ μA for the taken 0.18 μm CMOS technology parameters. The values I_{HIGH}, I_{LOW}, L_P, and W_N are calculated as 19 μA, 12 μA, 1.5 μm, 0.66 μm, respectively. As per the procedure, W_P and L_N are set to their minimum values. Using the coefficients in Eq. (2.66), the propagation delay with the capacitance 10 fF is evaluated as 0.8 ns while a delay of 1 ns is obtained through simulations. As explained for differential CML gates, the derived delay equation can also be used to evaluate the delay for I_{CS} values lying outside the range I_{LOW} to I_{HIGH}.

2.5 Summary

In this chapter, the basic concepts related to the CML gates are presented. The operating principles of the differential and single-ended CML gates are discussed. An improved version of the single-ended CML gate named as positive-feedback source-coupled logic (PFSCL) gate is presented and is worked upon. The behavior modeling of differential CML and PFSCL gates is described first which is followed by systematic design procedure. The approach to realize logic function in differential CML as well as in PFSCL styles is discussed, and the realization of few common digital logic gates is drawn.

References

1. M. Alioto, G. Palumbo, in *Modeling of MOS Current-Mode Gates (CML, ECL and SCL Digital Circuits)* (Springer, US, 2005) (Reprinted by permission from Springer Nature Customer Service Centre GmbH [COPYRIGHT])
2. M. Yamashina, H. Yamada, An MOS current mode logic (MCML) circuit for low-power sub-GHz processors. IEICE Trans. Electr. **75**(10), 1181–1187 (1992)

3. M. Yamashina, M. Mizuno, K. Furuta, H. Igura, M. Nomura, H. Abiko, K. Okabe, A. Ono, H. Yamad, A low-supply voltage GHz MOS integrated circuit for mobile computing systems, in *Proceedings of IEEE Symposium on Low Power Electronics* (San Diego, 1994), pp. 80–81
4. M. Mizuno, M. Yamashina, K. Furuta, H. Igura, H. Abiko, K. Okabe, A. Ono, H. Yamada, A GHz MOS adaptive pipeline technique using MOS current-mode logic. IEEE J. Solid-State Circ. **31**(6), 784–791 (1996)
5. Y. Cheng, Hu C, MOSFET Modeling and BSIM3 user's guide (Kluwer Academic Publishers, Boston, 1999)
6. S.M. Kang, Y. Leblebici, CMOS digital integrated circuits: analysis and design, 3rd edn. (Tata McGraw Hills, 2006)
7. J.M. Rabaey, A. Chandrakasan, B. Nikolic, Digital integrated circuits, 2nd edn. (Pearson Education, 2003)
8. H. Hassan, M. Anis, M. Elmasry, MOS current mode circuits: analysis, design, and variability. IEEE Trans. Very Large Scale Integr. (VLSI) Syst. **13**(8), 885–898 (2005)
9. M. Alioto, L. Pancioni, S. Rocchi, V. Vignoli, Modeling and evaluation of positive-feedback source-coupled logic. IEEE Trans. Circ. Syst. I, Regul. Papers **51**(4), 2345–2355 (2004)
10. M. Alioto, L. Pancioni, S. Rocchi, V. Vignoli, Power-delay-area-noise margin trade-offs in positive-feedback source-coupled logic gates. IEEE Trans. Circ. Syst. I Regul. Papers **54**(9), 1916–1928 (2007)
11. M. Alioto, A. Fort, L. Pancioni, S. Rocchi, V. Vignoli, An Approach to the Design of PFSCL gates. in *Proceedings of IEEE Symposium on Circuits and Systems* (2005), pp. 2437–2440
12. N. Pandey, K. Gupta, M. Gupta, An efficient triple-tail cell based PFSCL D-latch. Microelectr. J. **45**(8), 1001–1007 (2014). (Reprinted from Microelectronics Journal with permission from Elsevier)
13. N. Pandey, M. Gupta, K. Gupta, A PFSCL based configurable logic block, in *Proceeding of Annual IEEE India International Conference INDICON* (© 2016 IEEE, Reprinted with permission) (2015), pp. 1–4

Chapter 3
Differential CML Gates with Modified PDN

3.1 Introduction

The logic function is implemented in the PDN of a CML gate through a network of stacked source-coupled transistor pairs in accordance with the series-gating approach [1]. Many modifications in the PDN have been done to improve the performance of CML gates. These modifications include introduction of feedback transistors [2, 3], use of multi-threshold voltage transistors [4, 5], addition of an extra invalid logic level [6], and triple-tail cell-based design [7–11]. The feedback transistors result in speed improvement of the gate. The use of multi-threshold transistors lowers the minimum power supply value required by a CML gate and results in lower power consumption. The gates designed using this methodology are named as multi-threshold CMOS (MTCMOS) MOS current mode logic gates. The other method modifies the PDN by using an extra invalid logic level in addition to high and low logic levels of a conventional CML gate and is termed as triple-rail MOS current mode logic (Tr-MCML) style. The recent modification of the PDN is based on employing triple-tail cell concept to design of differential CML gates [7–11]. Out of all the available PDN modifications, the triple-tail cell-based design approach is the most promising since it reduces power as well as provides low-voltage CML gate topologies with improved speed in comparison to the conventional differential CML ones. An investigation on the different versions of triple-tail cell-based differential CML gate design is covered in the chapter.

3.2 Triple-Tail Cell-Based Approach

The structure of a conventional differential CML gate is a multi-level topology of stacked source-coupled transistor pairs obtained by following the series-gating approach. The approach has already been discussed in detail in Chap. 2. It is

© Springer Nature Singapore Pte Ltd. 2020
K. Gupta et al., *Model and Design of Improved Current Mode
Logic Gates*, https://doi.org/10.1007/978-981-15-0982-7_3

evident from the approach that the number of source-coupled transistor pair levels
(N) is equal to the number of inputs in the logic function. Additionally, the number
of these N levels decides the minimum power supply value for which all the PDN
transistors operate in the saturation region. To illustrate this, a generalized structure
of a two-level CML gate (Fig. 2.4) is revisited and is redrawn here as Fig. 3.1.
Assuming the inputs to the gate are such that current flows through $M1$, $M2$, and
$M4$, the expression for minimum power supply value [5, 7–11] of the conventional
structure $V_{DD\_MIN\_CON}$ can be written as

$$V_{DD\_MIN\_CON} = V_{DSAT\_1} + V_{DSAT\_2} + V_{GS\_4} \tag{3.1}$$

where V_{DSAT_1} and V_{DSAT_2} represent the drain-to-source saturation voltage of the
transistors $M1$ and $M2$, and V_{GS_4} is the gate-to-source voltage of $M4$. In general,
the drain-to-source saturation voltage and the gate-to-source voltage, for a transistor operating in saturation region [12], are expressed as:

$$V_{DSAT} = V_{GS} - V_T \tag{3.2}$$

$$V_{GS} = \sqrt{\frac{I_D}{k}} - V_T \tag{3.3}$$

where V_T is the threshold voltage of the transistor, I_D and k are the drain current and
the device transconductance of the transistor, respectively .

Using Eqs. (3.2) and (3.3), the minimum power supply voltage, $V_{DD\_MIN\_CON}$,
is calculated as:

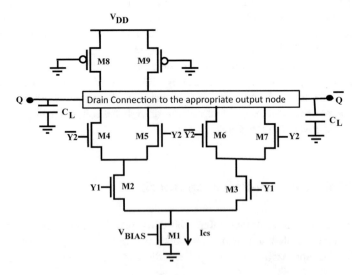

Fig. 3.1 A generalized two-level differential CML gate

$$V_{DD\_MIN\_CON} = \sqrt{\frac{I_{CS}}{K_1}} + \sqrt{\frac{I_{D\_M2}}{K_2}} + \sqrt{\frac{I_{D\_M4}}{K_4}} + V_{T\_4} \qquad (3.4)$$

where V_{T_4} is the threshold voltage of the upper-level transistor $M4$. For identical transistors $M2$ and $M4$ (i.e., $K_2 = K_4$), and assuming that the bias current I_{CS} completely flows through $M2$ and $M4$, the equation can be further simplified as:

$$V_{DD\_MIN\_CON} = \sqrt{I_{CS}}\left(\frac{1}{\sqrt{K_1}} + \frac{2}{\sqrt{K_2}}\right) + V_{T\_4} \qquad (3.5)$$

$$= \sqrt{K_1(V_{BIAS} - V_{T\_1})^2}\left(\frac{1}{\sqrt{K_1}} + \frac{2}{\sqrt{K_2}}\right) + V_{T\_4} \qquad (3.6)$$

$$= (V_{BIAS} - V_{T\_1})\left(1 + \frac{2\sqrt{K_1}}{\sqrt{K_2}}\right) + V_{T\_4} \qquad (3.7)$$

$$= 3\,V_{BIAS} - 3\,V_{T\_1} + V_{T\_4} \qquad (3.8)$$

where V_{T_i} is the threshold voltage of the ith transistor and V_{BIAS} is the bias voltage of transistor $M1$. Assuming same threshold voltage of all the transistors ($M1$–$M7$), the expression can be further simplified as:

$$V_{DD\_MIN\_CON} = 3\,V_{BIAS} - 2\,V_{T\_N} \qquad (3.9)$$

The above equation can be extended to a generalized CML gate with N source-coupled transistor-pair levels as:

$$V_{DD\_MIN\_CON} = (N+1)V_{BIAS} - NV_T \qquad (3.10)$$

As an example, for 0.18 μm CMOS technology, with $V_{T\_N} = 500\,mV$, and if $V_{BIAS} = 800\,mV$, the minimum supply voltage, $V_{DD\_MIN\_CON}$ for a two-level CML gate, is calculated as 1.4 V.

It is clear that the value of supply voltage varies with the number of source-coupled transistor pair levels. Hence, its value can be lowered by reducing these levels. This can be achieved by using triple-tail cell concept in function realization. A triple-tail cell has three source-coupled transistors ($M2$, $M3$, and $M4$)

Fig. 3.2 A triple-tail cell

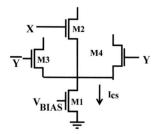

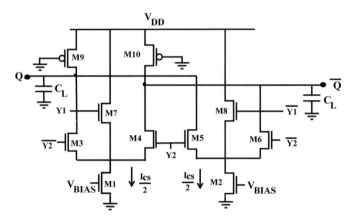

Fig. 3.3 A generalized triple-tail cell-based differential CML gate

as drawn in Fig. 3.2. The flow of bias current I_{CS} in transistor pair ($M3$–$M4$) is controlled by third transistor $M2$. The current flows in transistor pair ($M3$–$M4$) only when the transistor $M2$ is OFF ($M2$ is deactivated) otherwise entire current passes through $M2$ ($M2$ is activated).

The concept is further extended to CML gate design. As an illustration, a triple-tail cell-based structure of the generalized two-level differential CML gate is shown in Fig. 3.3. The circuit employs two triple-tail cells ($M3$, $M4$, and $M7$) and ($M5$, $M6$, and $M8$) biased by separate current sources of $I_{CS}/2$ value. The transistors $M7$ and $M8$ are driven by differential input $Y1$ and are connected between the power supply terminal and the common source terminal of transistor pairs ($M3$–$M4$) and ($M5$–$M6$), respectively. The differential input $Y2$ drives the two transistor pairs ($M3$–$M4$) and ($M5$–$M6$) as shown. For a high voltage on differential input $Y1$, transistor $M7$ is turned ON such that the transistor pair ($M3$–$M4$) is deactivated. At the same time, the transistor $M8$ turns OFF so that the transistor pair ($M5$–$M6$) generates the output according to the differential input $Y2$. Similarly, the transistor pair ($M3$–$M4$) gets activated for low voltage of differential input $Y1$, and the corresponding output is produced.

The value of minimum power supply voltage $V_{DD\_MIN\_TTC}$ for the circuit can be computed by using the same method as above. From the figure, by assuming that the inputs such that $M7$ and $M4$ are OFF and $M3$ is ON, the value of $V_{DD\_MIN\_TTC}$ can be expressed as:

$$V_{DD\_MIN\_TTC} = V_{DSAT\_1} + V_{GS\_3} \tag{3.11}$$

$$= \sqrt{\frac{I_{CS}}{K_1}} + \sqrt{\frac{I_{D\_M3}}{K_3}} + V_{T\_3} \tag{3.12}$$

where V_{T_3} is the threshold voltage of $M3$. The above equation can be expressed in terms of V_{BIAS} [7–9] as:

$$V_{DD\_MIN\_TTC} = 2V_{BIAS} - 2V_{T\_1} + V_{T\_3} \tag{3.13}$$

Assuming same threshold voltage of all the transistors, the expression can be simplified as:

$$V_{DD\_MIN\_TTC} = 2\,V_{BIAS\_N} - V_T \tag{3.14}$$

where V_T is the threshold voltage of transistors $M1$–$M6$ and V_{BIAS} is the bias voltage of transistor $M1$. For 0.18 μm CMOS technology, with $V_T = 500$ mV, and if $V_{BIAS} = 800$ mV, the minimum power supply voltage, $V_{DD\_MIN\_TTC}$ for two-level CML gate, is calculated as 1.1 V.

Thus, the triple-tail-based CML gates operate at reduced supply voltage in comparison to conventional ones. A careful examination of the generalized triple-tail cell-based differential CML gate reveals that if equal aspect ratio of all the transistors in the triple-tail cells is considered, then the transistors $M7$ and $M8$ will not be able to completely switch OFF the transistor pair $(M3–M4)$ and $(M5–M6)$. To illustrate this behavior, let us assume the value of differential input $Y2$ as low such that the transistors $M3$ and $M6$ are ON while the transistors $M4$ and $M5$ are OFF. Then, a high differential $Y1$ voltage turns ON transistor $M7$, and $M8$ is switched OFF. In this condition, the transistors $M3$ and $M7$ will draw equal currents as their gate–source voltages are same. Hence, the transistor $M7$ will not be able to completely deactivate the transistor pair $(M3–M4)$. Therefore, some modification needs to be done at transistor level for the complete deactivation of the transistor pairs. Two modifications have been done in this regard. The first modification makes the aspect ratio of transistors $M7$ and $M8$ greater than aspect ratio of other transistors by a factor M. The CML gates designed with this approach are referred to as triple-tail cell-1 (TTC-1)-based differential CML gates. The second one employs a low threshold voltage middle transistor in the triple-tail cell, and the corresponding CML gates are named as triple-tail cell-2 (TTC-2)-based cells. The effect of these modifications is analyzed by configuring them as a 2:1 multiplexer (MUX). A multiplexer is chosen for its versatility in realizing any arbitrary logic function by appropriately configuring its inputs.

3.3 Triple-Tail Cell (TT-1)-Based Differential CML Gates

The TT-1-based CML gates use triple-tail cell in which the aspect ratio of the third transistor is greater than the rest of the two by a factor M. The schematic of a MUX with select line (SEL) and two data lines $I0$ and $I1$ as the inputs [7] is shown in Fig. 3.4. The differential SEL signal drives transistors $M7$ and $M8$, while differential inputs $I0$ and $I1$ drive $(M3–M4)$ and $(M5–M6)$, respectively. A high voltage on differential SEL input deactivates the transistor pair $(M3–M4)$, but at the same time, the activated transistor pair $(M5–M6)$ generates the output according to the

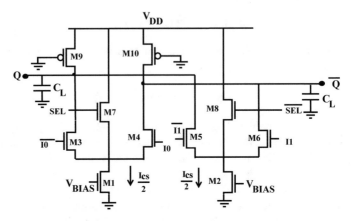

Fig. 3.4 TT-1-based differential CML MUX [7]

differential input $I1$ since $M8$ is OFF. Similarly, the transistor pair ($M3$–$M4$) produces output as $I0$ for low voltage of SEL input.

3.3.1 Analysis of TT-1-Based CML Gates

The behavior of MUX is analyzed in terms of voltage swing, small-signal voltage gain, noise margin, and delay parameters. To start the analysis, the load transistors $M9$ and $M10$ are first modeled by equivalent linear resistance, R_{LP}. The differential output of the gate can now be written as:

$$
\begin{aligned}
V_{\text{out\_d\_tt1}} &= V_Q - \overline{V_Q} \\
&= V_{\text{DD}} - R_{\text{LP}}(i_{D\_M3} + i_{D\_M5}) - [V_{\text{DD}} - R_{\text{LP}}(i_{D\_M4} + i_{D\_M6})] \quad (3.15)
\end{aligned}
$$

$$
= R_{\text{LP}}[(i_{D\_M4} + i_{D\_M6}) - (i_{D\_M3} + i_{D\_M5})] \quad (3.16)
$$

The voltage swing is determined by finding the current flow in the transistors for all the input conditions. As an example, let us assume that the data lines $I0$ and $I1$ are maintained at logic high and low levels, respectively. This condition makes $M4$ and $M5$ ON and keeps $M3$ and $M6$ OFF. Then a high-to-low transition on differential SEL input turns on $M8$ and deactivates the transistor pair ($M5$, $M6$). But since the transistors $M8$ and $M5$ have the same gate-source voltages, the currents flowing through $M5$ (i_{D_M5}) and $M8$ (i_{D_M8}) can be written as:

$$
i_{D\_M5} = \frac{I_{\text{CS}}}{2} \frac{1}{1+M} \quad (3.17)
$$

$$i_{D\_M8} = \frac{I_{CS}}{2} \frac{M}{1+M} \tag{3.18}$$

The current through $M5$ can be minimized by increasing factor M. This input condition produces minimum output voltage V_{OL} [7] as:

$$V_{OL} = V_Q - \overline{V_Q} = R_{LP}[(i_{D\_M4} + i_{D\_M6}) - (i_{D\_M3} + i_{D\_M5})] \tag{3.19}$$

$$= -\frac{R_{LP}I_{CS}}{2}\left(1 + \frac{1}{1+M}\right) \tag{3.20}$$

where $i_{D\_M3}, i_{D\_M4}, i_{D\_M5}, i_{D\_M6}$ are the currents through transistors $M3$, $M4$, $M5$, and $M6$, respectively. The differential output voltages for various input combinations are enlisted in Table 3.1. It can be observed from Table 3.1 that there are two values of both maximum output voltage V_{OH} and minimum output voltage V_{OL} for different input combinations. It can be found out that for the case when $I0$ and $I1$ are same, the voltage swing, V_{SWING1} [7], is expressed as:

$$V_{SWING1} = V_{OH1} - V_{OL1} = R_{LP}I_{CS}\left(1 + \frac{1}{1+M}\right) \tag{3.21}$$

Table 3.1 Output voltage levels for different input combinations for TT-1-based differential CML MUX [7]

Differential inputs			Currents through the transistors						Differential output ($V_Q - \overline{V_Q}$)	
SEL	$I0$	$I1$	$M3$	$M4$	$M5$	$M6$	$M7$	$M8$	Level	$R_{LP}[(i_{D\_M4} + i_{D\_M6}) - (i_{D\_M3} + i_{D\_M5})]$
L	L	L	$I1$	0	$I3$	0	0	$I2$	V_{OL1}	$-R_{LP}\frac{I_{CS}}{2}\left(1 + \frac{1}{1+M}\right)$
	L	H	$I1$	0	0	$I3$	0	$I2$	V_{OL2}	$-R_{LP}\frac{I_{CS}}{2}\left(\frac{M}{1+M}\right)$
	H	L	0	$I1$	$I3$	0	0	$I2$	V_{OH2}	$R_{LP}\frac{I_{CS}}{2}\left(\frac{M}{1+M}\right)$
	H	H	0	$I1$	0	$I3$	0	$I2$	V_{OH1}	$R_{LP}\frac{I_{CS}}{2}\left(1 + \frac{1}{1+M}\right)$
H	L	L	$I3$	0	$I1$	0	$I2$	0	V_{OL1}	$-R_{LP}\frac{I_{CS}}{2}\left(1 + \frac{1}{1+M}\right)$
	L	H	$I3$	0	0	$I1$	$I2$	0	V_{OH2}	$R_{LP}\frac{I_{CS}}{2}\left(\frac{1}{1+M}\right)$
	H	L	0	$I3$	$I1$	0	$I2$	0	V_{OL2}	$-R_{LP}\frac{I_{CS}}{2}\left(\frac{1}{1+M}\right)$
	H	H	0	$I3$	0	$I1$	$I2$	0	V_{OH1}	$R_{LP}\frac{I_{CS}}{2}\left(1 + \frac{1}{1+M}\right)$

where L/H = low/high differential input voltage, $I1 = \frac{I_{CS}}{2}$, $I2 = \frac{I_{CS}}{2}\left(\frac{M}{1+M}\right)$ and $I3 = \frac{I_{CS}}{2}\left(\frac{1}{1+M}\right)$

where V_{OH1} and V_{OL1} are maximum output voltage and minimum output voltage, respectively, for same differential inputs. The voltage swing, V_{SWING2}, for the different differential inputs ($I0$ and $I1$) can be expressed as:

$$V_{\text{SWING2}} = V_{\text{OH2}} - V_{\text{OL2}} = R_{\text{LP}} I_{\text{CS}} \left(\frac{M}{1+M} \right) \qquad (3.22)$$

where $V_{\text{OH2}}, V_{\text{OL2}}$ are maximum output voltage and minimum output voltage, respectively, for different differential inputs. As $V_{\text{SWING2}} < V_{\text{SWING1}}$, V_{SWING2} has been considered as the worst-case voltage swing. Therefore, the voltage swing V_{SWING} can be further approximated as:

$$V_{\text{SWING}} = V_{\text{OH}} - V_{\text{OL}} = R_{\text{LP}} I_{\text{CS}} \left(\frac{M}{1+M} \right) \qquad (3.23)$$

The small-signal voltage gain ($A_{v\_d\_\text{tt1}}$) and noise margin (NM) are computed by using the same method as followed for conventional differential CML gates as:

$$A_{v\_d\_\text{tt1}} = g_{m,n} R_{\text{LP}} = \frac{1+M}{M} \frac{V_{\text{SWING}}}{2} \sqrt{2\mu_{\text{eff},n} C_{\text{OX}} \frac{W_N}{L_N} \frac{1}{I_{\text{CS}}}} \qquad (3.24)$$

$$NM = \frac{V_{\text{SWING}}}{2} \left[1 - \frac{\sqrt{2}}{A_{v\_d\_\text{tt1}}} \right] \qquad (3.25)$$

where $\mu_{\text{eff},n}$, $g_{m,n}$, W_N and L_N are the effective electron mobility, the transconductance, the effective channel width and length of transistors $M3$–$M6$, respectively.

The delay expression for the MUX can be formulated by considering a high-to-low transition on the differential SEL input, the output switch by activating (deactivating) the transistor pair $M3$–$M4$ ($M5$–$M6$) abruptly, and the circuit thus reduces to a simple differential CML inverter. At the same time, the transistors

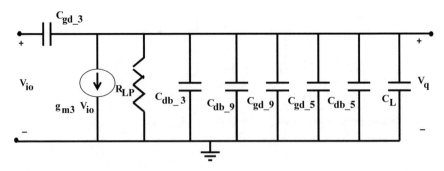

Fig. 3.5 Linear half circuit (with low value of differential input SEL)

$M5$–$M6$ are deactivated so that they affect the transient response through the parasitic capacitance. The equivalent linear half circuit is shown in Fig. 3.5, where C_{gd_i}, C_{db_i} represents the gate–drain capacitance and the drain–bulk junction capacitance of the ith ($i = 3, 5, 9$) transistor as discussed in Chap. 2.

The delay of TT-1-based differential CML MUX is evaluated as:

$$t_{PD\_TT1} = 0.69\, R_{LP}\left(C_{db\_3} + C_{gd\_3} + C_{gd\_9} + C_{db\_9} + C_{db\_5} + C_{gd\_5} + C_L\right)$$

$$(3.26)$$

with $C_{db\_3} = C_{db\_5}$, $C_{gd\_3} = C_{gd\_5}$ and, $R_{LP} = \frac{1+M}{M}\frac{V_{SWING}}{I_{CS}}$, Eq. (3.26) can be rewritten as:

$$t_{PD\_TT1} = 0.69\,\frac{1+M}{M}\frac{V_{SWING}}{I_{CS}}\left(2C_{db\_3} + 2C_{gd\_3} + C_{gd\_9} + C_{db\_9} + C_L\right) \quad (3.27)$$

It can be observed that the delay given in Eq. (3.27) is expressed in terms of the parasitic capacitances of various transistors, which in turn depend on their aspect ratio. In practical situations, the transistor aspect ratio must be set to meet the design specifications on noise margin, power, and delay. Therefore, the dependence of the delay on the aspect ratio should also be determined. To this end, a design procedure to size the transistors is worked out, and the delay model is revisited again for the purpose.

3.3.2 Design of TT-1-Based CML Gates

On the basis of the above analysis, a procedure to size the transistors in TT-1-based circuits is developed. Given a specified value of NM, factor M, bias current I_{CS}, and $A_{v\_d\_tt1}$ (≥ 1.4 for CML gate [13]), the voltage swing is calculated using Eq. (3.25) as:

$$V_{SWING} = \frac{2NM}{1 - \frac{\sqrt{2}}{A_{v\_d\_tt1}}} \quad (3.28)$$

The value of V_{SWING} obtained should be lower than the maximum value of $2V_T$. to ensure that transistors $M3$–$M6$ operate in saturation region. Since the bias current value I_{CS} is also specified, the required voltage swing can be achieved by sizing the load transistor having equivalent resistance $R_{LP}\left(= \frac{1+M}{M}\frac{V_{SWING}}{I_{CS}}\right)$. To find the aspect ratio of the load transistor ($M9$–$M10$), the bias current I_{HIGH} corresponding to the minimum-sized PMOS transistor with equivalent resistance, R_{LP_MIN}, is determined as:

$$I_{\text{HIGH}} = \frac{V_{\text{SWING}}}{R_{\text{LP\_MIN}}} \tag{3.29}$$

If the bias current I_{CS} is higher than I_{HIGH}, then R_{LP} is made less than $R_{\text{LP\_MIN}}$ by setting L_P to its minimum value, i.e., L_{MIN} and W_P which is calculated by solving Eqs. (2.7) and (2.8) as:

$$W_P = \frac{M}{1+M} \frac{I_{\text{CS}}}{V_{\text{SWING}}} \frac{L_{\text{MIN}}}{\mu_{\text{eff},p} C_{ox} \left(V_{\text{DD}} - |V_{\text{T,P}}|\right) \left\{ 1 - \frac{R_{\text{DSW}} 10^{-6}}{L_{\text{MIN}}} \left[\mu_{\text{eff},p} C_{ox} \left(V_{\text{DD}} - |V_{T,P}|\right) \right] \right\}} \tag{3.30}$$

Similarly, if the bias current I_{CS} is lower than I_{HIGH}, then R_{LP}. needs to be greater than $R_{\text{LP\_MIN}}$. The width W_P is set to its minimum value, i.e., W_{MIN} and L_P is calculated as:

$$L_P = W_{\text{MIN}} \, \mu_{\text{eff},p} C_{ox} \left(V_{\text{DD}} - |V_{\text{T,P}}|\right) \left(\frac{1+M}{M} \frac{V_{\text{SWING}}}{I_{\text{CS}}} - \frac{R_{\text{DSW}} 10^{-6}}{W_{\text{MIN}}} \right). \tag{3.31}$$

The width of transistors in the PDN ($M3$–$M6$) is determined by using small-signal voltage gain $(A_{v\_d\_\text{ttl}})$ given in Eq. (3.24). Assuming minimum channel length for these transistors, the width is computed as:

$$W_{\text{N}} = \frac{2}{\mu_{\text{eff},n} C_{ox}} \left(\frac{M}{1+M} \right)^2 \left(\frac{A_{v\_d\_\text{ttl}}}{V_{\text{SWING}}} \right)^2 I_{\text{CS}} L_{\text{MIN}} \tag{3.32}$$

Sometimes, there exist cases wherein the calculated value of W_N is smaller than the minimum channel width. This usually happens when the bias current is lower than the current of minimum-sized NMOS transistor, I_{LOW}. Using Eq. (3.24), I_{LOW} can be computed as:

$$I_{\text{LOW}} = \frac{1}{2} \left(\frac{1+M}{M} \right)^2 \frac{W_{\text{MIN}}}{L_{\text{MIN}}} \mu_{\text{eff},n} C_{ox} \left(\frac{V_{\text{SWING}}}{A_{v\_d\_\text{ttl}}} \right)^2 \tag{3.33}$$

So, in those cases W_N is also set to W_{MIN}. After calculation of the width, the width of transistors $M7$ and $M8$ is made M times greater than the width of transistors $M3$–$M6$ for proper switching.

The above design procedure has expressed the dimensions of the transistors in terms of bias and the voltage swing; therefore, the parasitic capacitances associated in the delay expressions can also be expressed in terms of these parameters. A capacitance C_{xy} connected between terminals x and y can be generalized as:

$$C_{xy} = \frac{a_{xy}}{(V_{\text{SWING}})^2} I_{\text{CS}} + b_{xy} \frac{V_{\text{SWING}}}{I_{\text{CS}}} + c_{xy} \tag{3.34}$$

Using design Eqs. (3.31) and (3.32), various capacitances in Eq. (3.37) for I_{CS} ranging from I_{LOW} to I_{HIGH} may be expressed as:

$$C_{\text{gd\_3}} = C_{\text{gdo}} W_3 = 2A^2_{v\_d\_ttl} C_{\text{gdo}} \left(\frac{M}{1+M}\right)^2 \frac{L_{\text{MIN}}}{\mu_{\text{eff},n} C_{\text{OX}}} \frac{I_{\text{CS}}}{(V_{\text{SWING}})^2} \tag{3.35}$$

$$C_{\text{db\_3}} = W_3 \left(K_{\text{jn}} C_{\text{jn}} L_{\text{dn}} + 2K_{\text{jswn}} C_{\text{jswn}}\right) + 2K_{\text{jswn}} C_{\text{jswn}} L_{\text{dn}} \tag{3.36}$$

$$= 2A^2_{v\_d\_ttl} \frac{L_{\text{MIN}}}{\mu_{\text{eff},n} C_{\text{OX}}} \left(\frac{M}{1+M}\right)^2 \left(K_{\text{jn}} C_{\text{jn}} L_{\text{dn}} + 2K_{\text{jswn}} C_{\text{jswn}}\right) \frac{I_{\text{CS}}}{(V_{\text{SWING}})^2}$$
$$+ 2K_{\text{jswn}} C_{\text{jswn}} L_{\text{dn}} \tag{3.37}$$

$$C_{\text{gd\_9}} = C_{\text{gdo}} W_{\text{MIN}} + \frac{3}{4} A_{\text{bulk,max}} W_{\text{MIN}} L_P C_{\text{ox}} \tag{3.38}$$

$$= C_{\text{gdo}} W_{\text{MIN}} + \frac{3}{4} A_{\text{bulk,max}} W_{\text{MIN}} C_{\text{ox}} \left\{ \mu_{\text{eff},p} C_{\text{ox}} W_{\text{MIN}} (V_{\text{DD}} - |V_{T,P}|) \left[\frac{1+M}{M} \frac{V_{\text{SWING}}}{I_{\text{CS}}} - \frac{R_{\text{DSW}} 10^{-6}}{W_{\text{MIN}}}\right]\right\} \tag{3.39}$$

$$C_{\text{db\_9}} = W_{\text{MIN}} \left(K_{\text{jp}} C_{\text{jp}} L_{\text{dp}} + 2K_{\text{jswp}} C_{\text{jswp}}\right) + 2K_{\text{jswp}} C_{\text{jswp}} L_{\text{dp}} \tag{3.40}$$

The coefficients a_{xy}, b_{xy} and c_{xy} of all the capacitances in Eq. (3.27) are summarized in Table 3.2.

Table 3.2 Coefficients of capacitances for TT-1 based differential CML MUX

NMOS coefficients	
a_{db3}	$\frac{2A^2_{v\_d\_ttl} L_{\text{MIN}}}{\mu_{\text{eff},n} C_{ox}} \left(\frac{M}{1+M}\right)^2 \left(K_{\text{jn}} C_{\text{jn}} L_{\text{dn}} + 2K_{\text{jswn}} C_{\text{jswn}}\right)$
a_{gd3}	$2A^2_{v\_d\_ttl} C_{\text{gdo}} \left(\frac{M}{1+M}\right)^2 \frac{L_{\text{MIN}}}{\mu_{\text{eff},n} C_{ox}}$
c_{db3}	$2K_{\text{jswn}} C_{\text{jswn}} L_{\text{dn}}$
$b_{\text{db3}}, b_{\text{gd3}}, c_{\text{gd3}}$	0
PMOS coefficients	
b_{gd9}	$\frac{3}{4} \left(\frac{1+M}{M}\right) A_{\text{bulk,max}} \mu_{\text{eff},p} C^2_{ox} W^2_{\text{MIN}} (V_{\text{DD}} - |V_{T,P}|)$
c_{gd9}	$C_{\text{gdo}} W_{\text{MIN}} - \frac{3}{4} A_{\text{bulk,max}} \mu_{\text{eff},p} C^2_{ox} W_{\text{MIN}} (V_{\text{DD}} - |V_{T,P}|) R_{\text{DSW}} 10^{-6}$
c_{db9}	$K_{\text{jp}} C_{\text{jp}} L_{\text{dp}} W_{\text{MIN}} + 2K_{\text{jswp}} C_{\text{jswp}} (L_{\text{dp}} + W_{\text{MIN}})$
$a_{\text{gd9}}, a_{\text{db9}}, b_{\text{db9}}$	0

where the symbols have their usual meaning

The various capacitances in the delay expression can now be substituted by their respective coefficients. The delay expression using Eqs. (3.35–3.40) can be written as:

$$t_{\text{PD\_TT1}} = 0.69 \frac{1+M}{M} V_{\text{SWING}} \left(\frac{a}{V_{\text{SWING}}^2} + b \frac{V_{\text{SWING}}}{I_{\text{CS}}^2} + \frac{c+C_L}{I_{\text{CS}}} \right) \qquad (3.41)$$

where

$$a = 2a_{\text{db3}} + 2a_{\text{gd3}} \qquad (3.42a)$$

$$b = b_{\text{gd9}} \qquad (3.42b)$$

$$c = 2c_{\text{db3}} + c_{\text{gd9}} + c_{\text{db9}} \qquad (3.42c)$$

The delay model can also be used for I_{CS} value outside the range $[I_{\text{LOW}}, I_{\text{HIGH}}]$. This is because for $I_{\text{CS}} > I_{\text{HIGH}}$, the capacitance coefficients of PMOS transistor in Eq. (3.41) differ as explained in design procedure. As the capacitive contribution of PMOS transistor is negligible for high values of I_{CS}, Eq. (3.41) can be used to predict the delay. Similarly, for $I_{\text{CS}} < I_{\text{LOW}}$, the capacitance coefficients of NMOS transistor differ. As the delay majorly depends on the capacitances of PMOS transistor for low values of I_{CS}, therefore, Eq. (3.47) is used to estimate the delay.

An example to elaborate the above design procedure, the design of a MUX for a $NM = 130$ mV, $A_{v\_d\_tt1} = 4$, $M = 5$, and $I_{\text{CS}} = 15$ μA for the 0.18 μm CMOS technology parameters is discussed. By following the design procedure, V_{SWING}, I_{HIGH}, I_{LOW}, L_P, and W_N are calculated as 335 mV, 18.75 μA, 2 μA, 0.272 μm, and 2.01 μm, respectively. As per the procedure, W_P and L_N are set to their minimum values. Using the coefficients in Table 3.2, the propagation delay is evaluated as 1.01 ns, while a delay of 1.2 ns is obtained through simulations.

The same procedure is followed to design TT-1-based differential CML MUX with a power supply of 1.1 V for wide range of operating conditions—voltage swing of 300 and 400 mV, small-signal voltage gain of 2 and 4, $M = 5$, and the bias current ranging from 10 to 100 μA. The accuracy of the static model is validated through SPICE simulations. The error plots in the simulated values of static parameters with respect to the predicted values for small-signal voltage gain of 2, 4 and voltage swing of 300 mV and 400 mV are shown in Figs. 3.6a–f [7]. It may be noted that maximum error in voltage swing, small-signal voltage gain, and noise margin are 11%, 13%, and 11%, respectively. An error plot of noise margin for small-signal voltage gain of 2 and 4, $M = 5$ and the voltage swing ranging from 0.2 to 0.7 V is plotted in Fig. 3.7. It may be observed that the maximum error in noise margin is 14%. It is found that there is a close agreement between the simulated and the predicted values of static parameters for all the operating conditions.

The delay is plotted as a function of M for $A_{v\_d\_tt1} = 4$, $NM = 130$ mV, $I_{\text{CS}} = 50$ μA, and $C_L = 50$ fF in Fig. 3.8. It is found out that the delay asymptotically reaches to value of 455 ps. However, a high value of M results in larger transistor sizes of M7, M8, thus increasing the input capacitance seen from input

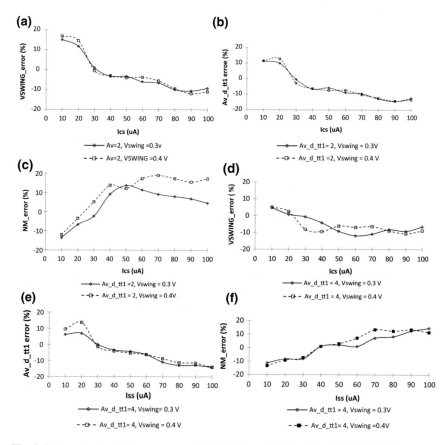

Fig. 3.6 Errors in the static parameters of the TT-1-based differential CML MUX [7]

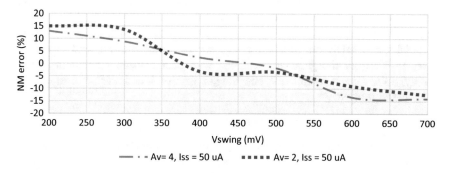

Fig. 3.7 Error in noise margin for different voltage swing values

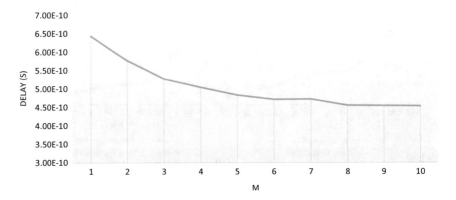

Fig. 3.8 Delay versus M of the TT-1-based differential CML MUX

SEL. Therefore, a good compromise between the two opposing requirements is to set $M = 5$ as after which improvement in speed is not significant. Similar results are obtained for other operating conditions.

The accuracy of the delay model is also validated through SPICE simulations for the same operating conditions with the load capacitance of 0 fF, 10 fF, 100 fF, 1 pF, and fan out of 4 (FO4). The simulated and the predicted delay in particular for $A_{V\_d\_tt1} = 4$, $V_{SWING} = 400\,\text{mV}$, with different load capacitances are plotted in Fig. 3.9. It is found that there is a close agreement between the simulated and the predicted delay for all the operating conditions. Similar plots for other operating conditions were also obtained. They have not been drawn for the sake of brevity.

3.3.3 Performance Comparison

In the previous subsections, the behavior of TT-1-based differential CML gate is modeled and design parameters are expressed as a function of bias current and voltage swing. Now, it is required to compare the performance of TT-1-based CML gates with conventional one. So, both the conventional and the TT-1-based differential CML MUX are design for high-speed, power-efficient, and low-power cases [7–9]. Both the gates are designed with their respective minimum power supply, noise margin of 130 mV, small-signal gain of 4, and a value of $M = 5$ (for TT-1-based design).

Design Case 1: High-Speed Design

For high-speed design, the delay of the gate has to be minimum. It is obvious from delay expression in Eq. (3.41) that the delay decreases with increasing I_{CS} values. It may be concluded that for $I_{CS} \rightarrow \infty$, the delay tends to an asymptotic minimum

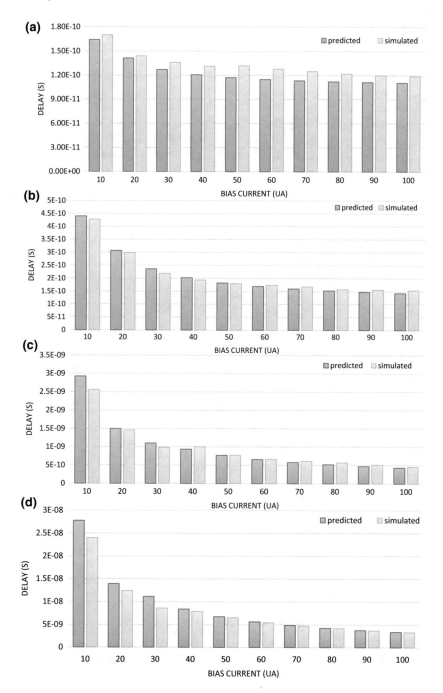

Fig. 3.9 Simulated and predicted delays of TT-1-based differential CML MUX versus I_{CS} with $A_{v\_d\_tt1} = 4$, $NM = 130$ mV for different C_L values: **a** 0 fF, **b** 10 fF, **c** 100 fF, **d** 1 pF, and **e** FO4

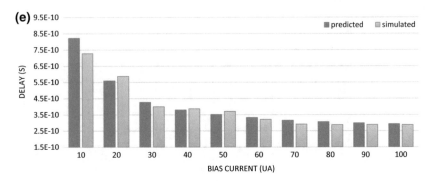

Fig. 3.9 (continued)

value of $0.69\frac{1+M}{M}\frac{a}{V_{\text{SWING}}}$. A substantial improvement in delay with increasing bias current is achieved if condition

$$\frac{a}{V_{\text{SWING}}^2} \geq b\frac{V_{\text{SWING}}}{I_{\text{CS}}^2} + \frac{c+C_L}{I_{\text{CS}}} \tag{3.43}$$

is satisfied. However, such a high value of bias current results in large transistor sizes. Therefore, the bias current is set to such a value after which the improvement in speed is not significant. If equality sign in Eq. (3.43) is considered, then the delay is close to its minimum value, and the use of high bias current is avoided. Therefore, this assumption leads to a bias current ($I_{\text{CS\_HS}}$) and delay ($t_{\text{PD\_MIN}}$) as:

$$I_{\text{CS\_HS}} = \frac{c+C_L}{2a}V_{\text{SWING}}^2\left(1 + \sqrt{1 + 4\frac{ab}{(c+C_L)^2}\frac{1}{V_{\text{SWING}}}}\right) \tag{3.44}$$

$$t_{\text{PD\_MIN}} = 2 \times 0.69\frac{1+M}{M}\frac{a}{V_{\text{SWING}}} \tag{3.45}$$

For a load capacitance of 50 fF, the bias current ($I_{\text{CS\_HS}}$) as expressed in Eq. (3.44) is calculated as 160 μA. A delay of 194 and 211 ps is obtained from Eq. (3.45) and simulations, respectively. On the contrary, the conventional MUX results in a delay of 528 ps. This indicates that TT-1-based MUX can achieve much higher speed than the conventional one.

Design Case 2: Power-Efficient Design

A power-efficient design requires bias current that results in minimum power-delay product (PDP). The power is calculated as the product of V_{DD} and I_{CS}. So, the PDP of the TT-1-based differential CML MUX is expressed as:

$$\text{PDP} = 0.69\, V_{DD} V_{SWING} \frac{1+M}{M} \left(\frac{a}{V_{SWING}^2} I_{CS} + b \frac{V_{SWING}}{I_{CS}} + c + C_L \right) \qquad (3.46)$$

Therefore, the current I_{CS_PDP} for minimum PDP may be given as:

$$I_{CS\_PDP} = \sqrt{\frac{b}{a}} (V\_SWING)^{\frac{3}{2}} \qquad (3.47)$$

Accordingly, the minimum PDP results to

$$\text{PDP} = 0.69\, V_{DD} V_{SWING} \frac{1+M}{M} \left(\frac{2\sqrt{ab}}{\sqrt{V_{SWING}}} + c + C_L \right) \qquad (3.48)$$

With a load capacitance of 50 fF, the bias current for minimum PDP (I_{CS_PDP}) is 5.8 μA. A PDP value of 32 fJ is obtained for the TT-1-based differential CML MUX. On the other hand, a conventional MUX results in a PDP value of 13 fJ. The result signifies that TT-1-based differential CML MUX has higher PDP value than the conventional one.

Design Case 3: Low-Power Design

In low-power designs, the bias current I_{CS} is set to low values so that the term $b \frac{V_{SWING}}{I_{CS}^2}$ is dominant in Eq. (3.41). Hence, the delay reduces to

$$t_{PD} = 0.69\, b \left(\frac{1+M}{M} \right) \left(\frac{V_{SWING}}{I_{CS}} \right)^2 \qquad (3.49)$$

The TT-1-based differential CML MUX with the load capacitance of 5 fF gives I_{CS} as 2 μA and has a power consumption of 2.2 μW, while the conventional one results in power consumption of 2.8 μW.

The performance comparison of the TT-1-based differential CML gates and conventional gates for different design cases is summarized in Table 3.3.

Table 3.3 Summary of the design cases for TT-1-based and conventional differential CML MUX [7–9]

Design case	Parameter	TT-1 based	Conventional
High speed	Delay	Low	High
Power efficient	Power-delay product	High	Low
Low power	Power	Low	High

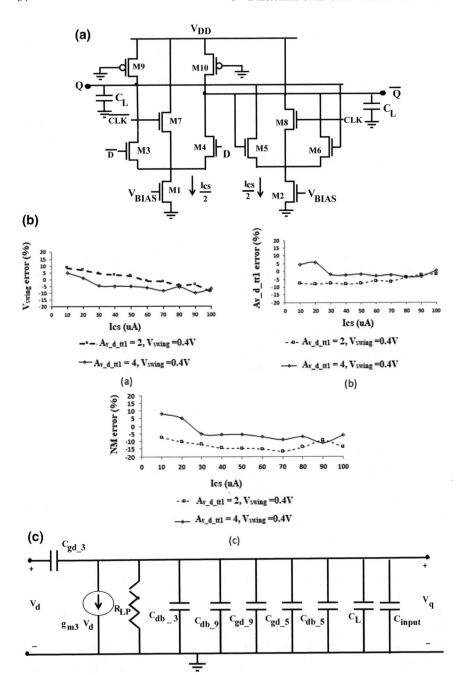

Fig. 3.10 TT-1-based differential CML D latch [9]—**a** circuit diagram, **b** errors in static model, **c** linear half circuit

Table 3.4 Differential output voltages of the TT-1-based D latch for various input combinations [9]

Inputs		Present state	Currents through the transistors						Next state differential output $(V_Q - \overline{V_Q})$	
CLK	D	Q	M3	M4	M5	M6	M7	M8	Level	$R_{LP}[(i_{D\_M4} + i_{D\_M6}) - (i_{D\_M3} + i_{D\_M5})]$
L	L	L	I3	0	I1	0	I2	0	V_{OL1}	$-R_{LP}\frac{I_{GS}}{2}\left(1+\frac{1}{1+M}\right)$
L	L	H	I3	0	0	I1	I2	0	V_{OH2}	$R_{LP}\frac{I_{GS}}{2}\left(\frac{M}{1+M}\right)$
L	H	L	0	I3	I1	0	I2	0	V_{OL2}	$-R_{LP}\frac{I_{GS}}{2}\left(\frac{M}{1+M}\right)$
L	H	H	0	I3	0	I1	I2	0	V_{OH1}	$R_{LP}\frac{I_{GS}}{2}\left(1+\frac{M}{1+M}\right)$
H	L	L	I1	0	I3	0	0	I2	V_{OL1}	$-R_{LP}\frac{I_{GS}}{2}\left(1+\frac{M}{1+M}\right)$
H	L	H	I1	0	0	I3	0	I2	V_{OL2}	$-R_{LP}\frac{I_{GS}}{2}\left(\frac{M}{1+M}\right)$
H	H	L	0	I1	I3	0	0	I2	V_{OH2}	$R_{LP}\frac{I_{GS}}{2}\left(\frac{M}{1+M}\right)$
H	H	H	0	I1	0	I3	0	I2	V_{OH1}	$R_P\frac{I_{GS}}{2}\left(1+\frac{M}{1+M}\right)$

where L/H = low/high differential input voltage, $I1 = \frac{I_{GS}}{2}$, $I2 = \frac{I_{GS}}{2}\left(\frac{M}{1+M}\right)$ and $I3 = \frac{I_{GS}}{2}\left(\frac{1}{1+M}\right)$

Table 3.5 Coefficients of the capacitances for the TT-1-based differential CML D latch [9]

NMOS coefficients	
a_{db3}	$\frac{2A_{v\_d\_tt1}^2 L_{MIN}}{\mu_{eff,n} C_{ox}} \left(\frac{M}{1+M}\right)^2 \left(K_{jn} C_{jn} L_{dn} + 2K_{jswn} C_{jswn}\right)$
a_{gd3}	$2A_{v\_d\_tt1}^2 C_{gdo} \left(\frac{M}{1+M}\right)^2 \frac{L_{MIN}}{\mu_{eff,n} C_{ox}}$
a_{input}	$\frac{4A_{v\_d\_tt1}^2}{3\mu_{eff,n}} \left(\frac{M}{1+M}\right)^2 L_{MIN}^2$
c_{db3}	$2K_{jswn} C_{jswn} L_{dn}$
$b_{db3}, b_{gd3}, c_{gd3}$	0
PMOS coefficients	
b_{gd9}	$\frac{3}{4} \left(\frac{1+M}{M}\right) A_{bulk,max} \mu_{eff,p} C_{ox}^2 W_{MIN}^2 \left(V_{DD} - |V_{T,P}|\right)$
c_{gd9}	$C_{gdo} W_{MIN} - \frac{3}{4} A_{bulk,max} \mu_{eff,p} C_{ox}^2 W_{MIN} \left(V_{DD} - |V_{T,P}|\right) R_{DSW} 10^{-6}$
c_{db9}	$K_{jp} C_{jp} L_{dp} W_{MIN} + 2K_{jswp} C_{jswp} \left(L_{dp} + W_{MIN}\right)$
$a_{gd9}, a_{db9}, b_{db9}$	0

where the symbols have their usual meaning

3.3.4 Extension to D Latch Design

So far, MUX design is considered, the same topology is further extended to design of sequential circuits. A D latch is chosen to represent them. The TT-1-based topology for a D latch with differential inputs D and CLK is shown in Fig. 3.10a. It consists of two triple-tail cells (M3, M4, M7) and (M5, M6, M8) biased by separate current sources of $I_{CS}/2$ value [9]. The transistors M7 and M8 are driven by the differential CLK input. A high value of differential CLK signal turns ON M8 and deactivates the transistor pair (M5–M6). But at the same time, M7 turns OFF allowing transistor pair (M3–M4) to generate the output according to the differential input D. This explains the working of D latch in transparent state. Similarly, for low value of differential CLK signal, the D latch operates in the hold state by preserving its previous output due to the activation of the transistor pair (M5–M6).

The behavior of D latch is analyzed in similar manner as explained for the MUX. The differential output voltages for various input combinations in a D latch are enlisted in Table 3.4. It can be observed that there are two values of maximum output voltage (V_{OH}) and minimum output voltage (V_{OL}). Therefore, the worst-case voltage swing is found to be same as Eq. (3.23). Similarly, the expressions for small-signal voltage gain ($A_{v\_d\_tt1}$) and noise margin (NM) remain the same as computed for MUX.

The accuracy of the static model is validated through SPICE simulations. The TT-1-based differential CML D latch was designed with a power supply of 1.1 V and simulated for wide range of operating conditions—voltage swing of 300 and 400 mV, small-signal voltage gain of 2 and 4, M = 5, and the bias current ranging from 10 to 100 μA. The error in simulated and theoretical values for voltage swing, small-signal voltage gain, and noise margin are plotted in Fig. 3.10b. It may be noted that maximum error in voltage swing, small-signal voltage gain, and noise margin are 10%, 8%, and 14%, respectively.

In terms of delay, the expression differs due to additional input capacitance which gets added at the output node because of the presence of the feedback connection in D latch. The half circuit of the D latch is drawn in Fig. 3.10c. Thus, the delay of D latch is equal to that of MUX loaded by a capacitance equal to the sum of the external capacitance C_L and the input capacitance of the source-coupled pair $M5$–$M6$.

The additional input capacitance C_{input} for the transistor $M5$ is expressed as:

$$C_{input} = \frac{2}{3} C_{ox} L_{MIN} W_5 = \frac{4}{3\mu_{eff,n}} \left(\frac{M}{1+M}\right)^2 \left(\frac{A_{v\_d\_tt1}}{V_{SWING}}\right)^2 I_{CS} L_{MIN}^2 \qquad (3.50)$$

The coefficients a_{xy}, b_{xy}, and c_{xy} of all the capacitances are summarized in Table 3.5. The delay of the D latch can be written as:

$$t_{PD\_TT1} = 0.69 \frac{1+M}{M} V_{SWING} \left(\frac{a}{V_{SWING}^2} + b\frac{V_{SWING}}{I_{CS}^2} + \frac{c+C_L}{I_{CS}}\right) \qquad (3.51)$$

where

$$a = 2a_{db3} + 2a_{gd3} + a_{input} \qquad (3.52a)$$

$$b = b_{gd9} \qquad (3.52b)$$

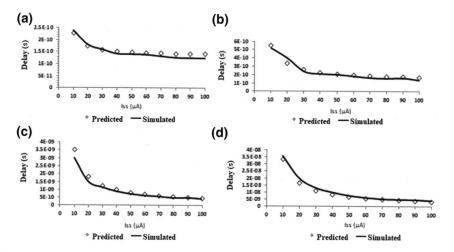

Fig. 3.11 Simulated and predicted delays of TT-1-based differential CML D latch versus I_{CS} with $A_{v\_d\_tt1} = 4$, $NM = 130$ mV for different C_L values [9], **a** 0 fF, **b** 10 fF, **c** 100 fF, **d** 1 pF

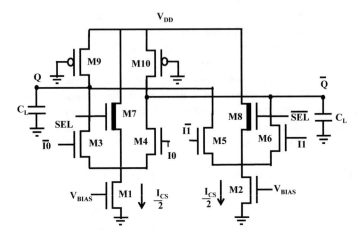

Fig. 3.12 Schematic of TT-2-based differential CML MUX [11]

$$c = 2c_{db3} + c_{gd9} + c_{db9} \qquad (3.52c)$$

To verify the accuracy of the delay model, the D latch was designed for wide range of operating conditions—voltage swing of 300 and 400 mV, small-signal voltage gain of 2 and 4, the bias current ranging from 10 to 100 μA, $M = 5$, and load capacitance of 0 fF, 10 fF, 100 fF, and 1 pF. The simulated and the predicted delay in particular for $NM = 130$ mV, $A_{v\_d\_tt1} = 4$, and with different load capacitances are plotted in Fig. 3.11. It is found that there is a close agreement between the simulated and the predicted values for all the operating conditions

3.4   Triple-Tail Cell (TT-2)-Based Differential CML Gates

The TT-2-based realization of MUX differs from TT-1-based realization by keeping the aspect ratio of all the transistors in the triple-tail cell equal and achieving the activation/deactivation of the triple-tail cell by employing low threshold voltage middle transistor. In TT-2-based design, the threshold voltage of middle transistors is lowered by a factor of δ than other transistors [11].

The schematic of TT-2-based MUX is shown in Fig. 3.12. The low threshold voltage middle transistors are differentiated by bold lines. The circuit operates in similar manner as the TT-1-based MUX.

3.4.1 Analysis of TT-2 Based CML Gates

The analysis differs due to difference in the manner by which activation/deactivation of triple-tail cell is attained. To illustrate this, the currents flowing through these (i_{D_M4} and i_{D_M7}) for high values of the differential inputs SEL and $I0$ are written as [11]:

$$i_{D\_M4} = \frac{\mu_{\text{eff},n} C_{ox}}{2} \frac{W_N}{L_N} \left(V_{GS} - V_{T,N}\right)^2 \tag{3.53}$$

$$i_{D\_M7} = \frac{\mu_{\text{eff},n} C_{ox}}{2} \frac{W_N}{L_N} \left(V_{GS} - \frac{V_{T,N}}{\delta}\right)^2 \tag{3.54}$$

where the symbols have their usual meaning. From Fig. 3.12, it is evident that the sum of the drain currents of M4 (i_{D_M4}) and M7 (i_{D_M7}) should be equal to $\frac{I_{CS}}{2}$. Using this, the above equations can be solved as [11]:

$$i_{D\_M4} = \frac{I_{CS}}{4} - \frac{\sqrt{\frac{\mu_{\text{eff},n} C_{ox}}{2} \frac{W_N}{L_N} V_{T,N}^2 \left(\frac{\delta-1}{\delta}\right)^2}}{2} \sqrt{I_{CS} - \frac{\mu_{\text{eff},n} C_{ox}}{2} \frac{W_N}{L_N} V_{T,N}^2 \left(\frac{\delta-1}{\delta}\right)^2} \tag{3.55}$$

$$i_{D\_M7} = \frac{I_{CS}}{4} + \frac{\sqrt{\frac{\mu_{\text{eff},n} C_{ox}}{2} \frac{W_N}{L_N} V_{T,N}^2 \left(\frac{\delta-1}{\delta}\right)^2}}{2} \sqrt{I_{CS} - \frac{\mu_{\text{eff},n} C_{ox}}{2} \frac{W_N}{L_N} V_{T,N}^2 \left(\frac{\delta-1}{\delta}\right)^2} \tag{3.56}$$

By substituting $x = \left(\frac{\mu_{\text{eff},n} C_{ox}}{2} \frac{W_n}{L_n} V_{T,N}^2 \left(\frac{\delta-1}{\delta}\right)^2\right)$, the Eqs. (3.55–3.56) can be simplified as:

$$i_{D\_M4} = \frac{I_{CS}}{4} - \frac{\sqrt{x}}{2} \sqrt{I_{CS} - x} \tag{3.57}$$

$$i_{D\_M7} = \frac{I_{CS}}{4} + \frac{\sqrt{x}}{2} \sqrt{I_{CS} - x} \tag{3.58}$$

By using the above current equations, the values of the high (V_{OH}) and the low output differential voltage (V_{OL}) can now be determined. As an example, let the differential voltages on the inputs SEL, $I0$, and $I1$ be low, high, and low, respectively. This input condition produces a high differential output [11] which can be computed as:

Table 3.6 Differential output for various input combinations of TT-2-based differential CML MUX [11]

Differential inputs			Currents through the transistors						Differential output $(V_Q - \overline{V_Q})$	
SEL	$I0$	$I1$	M3	M4	M5	M6	M7	M8	Level	$R_{LP}[(i_{D\_M4}+i_{D\_M6})-(i_{D\_M3}+i_{D\_M5})]$
L	L	L	I_1	0	I_3	0	0	I_2	V_{OL1}	$-\frac{R_{LP}}{2}\left(\frac{3I_{CS}}{2}-\sqrt{x}\sqrt{I_{CS}-x}\right)$
	L	H	I_1	0	0	I_3	0	I_2	V_{OL2}	$-\frac{R_{LP}}{2}\left(\frac{I_{CS}}{2}+\sqrt{x}\sqrt{I_{CS}-x}\right)$
	H	L	0	I_1	I_3	0	0	I_2	V_{OH2}	$\frac{R_{LP}}{2}\left(\frac{I_{CS}}{2}+\sqrt{x}\sqrt{I_{CS}-x}\right)$
	H	H	0	I_1	0	I_3	0	I_2	V_{OH1}	$\frac{R_{LP}}{2}\left(\frac{3I_{CS}}{2}-\sqrt{x}\sqrt{I_{CS}-x}\right)$
H	L	L	I_3	0	I_1	0	I_2	0	V_{OL1}	$-\frac{R_{LP}}{2}\left(\frac{3I_S}{2}-\sqrt{x}\sqrt{I_{CS}-x}\right)$
	L	H	I_3	0	0	I_1	I_2	0	V_{OH2}	$\frac{R_{LP}}{2}\left(\frac{I_{CS}}{2}+\sqrt{x}\sqrt{I_{CS}-x}\right)$
	H	L	0	I_3	I_1	0	I_2	0	V_{OL1}	$-\frac{R_{LP}}{2}\left(\frac{I_{CS}}{2}+\sqrt{x}\sqrt{I_{CS}-x}\right)$
	H	H	0	I_3	0	I_1	I_2	0	V_{OH1}	$\frac{R_{LP}}{2}\left(\frac{3I_{CS}}{2}-\sqrt{x}\sqrt{I_{CS}-x}\right)$

$$V_{OH} = V_Q - \overline{V_Q} = R_{LP}[(i_{D\_M4}+i_{D\_M6})-(i_{D\_M3}+i_{D\_M5})] \tag{3.59}$$

$$= \frac{R_{LP}}{2}\left(\frac{I_{CS}}{2}+\sqrt{x}\sqrt{I_{CS}-x}\right) \tag{3.60}$$

where i_{D_Mj} is drain current flowing through transistor $Mj(j = 3, 4, 5, 6)$ and R_{LP} is the equivalent load resistance. Based on this, the expressions of the differential output voltage for different input combinations are listed in Table 3.6. On closer examination of the results, it is found that there are two values of V_{OH} and V_{OL} as obtained in case of TT-1. The worst-case voltage swing of the circuit can be expressed as:

$$V_{SWING} = V_{OH} - V_{OL} = R_{LP}\left(\frac{I_{CS}}{2}+\sqrt{x}\sqrt{I_{CS}-x}\right) \tag{3.61}$$

Here $I_1 = \frac{I_{CS}}{2}$, $I_2 = \frac{I_S}{4} + \frac{\sqrt{x}}{2}\sqrt{I_{CS}-x}$ and $I_3 = \frac{I_{CS}}{4} - \frac{\sqrt{x}}{2}\sqrt{I_{CS}-x}$, where $x = \frac{\mu_{eff,n}C_{ox}}{2}\frac{W}{L}V_{T1}^2\left(\frac{\delta-1}{\delta}\right)^2$.

Also, the small-signal voltage gain $(A_{v\_d\_tt2})$ and noise margin (NM) for TT-2-based gate are expressed as:

$$A_{v\_d\_tt2} = g_{m,n}R_{LP} = \frac{V_{SWING}}{2}\left(\frac{1}{\frac{1}{2}+\frac{\sqrt{x}}{I_{CS}}\sqrt{I_{CS}-x}}\right)\sqrt{2\mu_{eff,n}C_{OX}\frac{W_N}{L_N}\cdot\frac{1}{I_{CS}}} \tag{3.62}$$

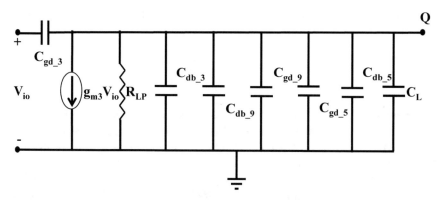

Fig. 3.13 Linear half circuit of TT-2-based differential CML MUX [11]

$$NM = \frac{V_{\text{SWING}}}{2}\left[1 - \frac{\sqrt{2}}{A_{v\_d\_tt2}}\right] \tag{3.63}$$

where $g_{m,n}$ is the transconductance of transistors $M3$–$M6$.

After this, to determine the delay of TT-2-based MUX, the effects of the parasitic capacitances associated with the transistors as well as output load capacitance are considered. A high-to-low transition on differential input SEL is assumed which causes switching at the output by activating (deactivating) the transistor pair $M3$–$M4$ ($M5$–$M6$). The circuit reduces to a simple CML inverter. The equivalent linear half circuit is shown in Fig. 3.13. By using the open-circuit time constant method, the delay [11] is evaluated as:

$$t_{\text{PD\_TT2}} = 0.69\,R_{\text{LP}}\left(C_{\text{db\_3}} + C_{\text{gd\_3}} + C_{\text{gd\_9}} + C_{\text{db\_9}} + C_{\text{db\_5}} + C_{\text{gd\_5}} + C_L\right) \tag{3.64}$$

By assuming $C_{\text{db\_3}} = C_{\text{db\_5}}$, $C_{\text{gd\_3}} = C_{\text{gd\_5}}$ and substituting $R_{\text{LP}} = \dfrac{V_{\text{SWING}}}{\left(\frac{I_{\text{CS}}}{2} + \sqrt{x}\sqrt{I_{\text{CS}} - x}\right)}$, Eq. 3.64 can be rewritten [11] as:

$$t_{\text{PD\_TT2}} = 0.69\,\frac{V_{\text{SWING}}}{\left(\frac{I_{\text{CS}}}{2} + \sqrt{x}\sqrt{I_{\text{CS}} - x}\right)}\left(2C_{\text{db\_3}} + 2C_{\text{gd\_3}} + C_{\text{gd\_9}} + C_{\text{db\_9}} + C_L\right) \tag{3.65}$$

3.4.2   Design of TT-2-Based CML Gates

In this section, the design procedure based on the static model is derived [11]. For a given value of noise margin, and the small-signal voltage gain (≥ 1.4 for CML

[13]), the voltage swing of the TT-2-based differential CML MUX [11] is calculated as:

$$V_{\text{SWING}} = \frac{2NM}{1 - \frac{\sqrt{2}}{A_{v\_d\_tt2}}} \tag{3.66}$$

It may be noted that V_{SWING} should be lower than the maximum value of $2V_{T,N}$ so as to ensure that transistors $M3$–$M6$ operate in saturation region. Using Eq. (3.61), for a specified value of the bias current I_{CS}, the resistance of the load transistor R_{LP} [11] is given as:

$$R_{LP} = \frac{V_{\text{SWING}}}{\left(\frac{I_{\text{CS}}}{2} + \sqrt{x}\sqrt{I_{\text{CS}} - x}\right)} \tag{3.67}$$

To determine the aspect ratio of the load transistors $M9$–$M10$, equivalent resistance of the minimum-sized PMOS, $R_{\text{LP\_MIN}}$, is determined first. Then, for the required voltage swing, the bias current I_{HIGH} [11] is determined as

$$I_{\text{HIGH}} = \frac{V_{\text{SWING}}}{R_{\text{LP\_MIN}}} \tag{3.68}$$

If the bias current is higher than I_{HIGH}, then R_{LP} should be less than $R_{\text{LP\_MIN}}$ and to achieve this, L_P is set to its minimum value, i.e., L_{MIN} and W_P [11], which is calculated as:

$$W_P = \frac{\left(\frac{I_{\text{CS}}}{2} + \sqrt{x}\sqrt{I_{\text{CS}} - x}\right)}{V_{\text{SWING}}}$$
$$* \frac{L_{\text{MIN}}}{\left[\mu_{\text{eff},p} C_{ox} \frac{W_P}{L_P} \left(V_{\text{DD}} - |V_{T,P}|\right)\right]\left[1 - \frac{(R_{\text{DSW}}*10^{-6})}{L_{\text{MIN}}} \mu_{\text{eff},p} C_{ox} \frac{W_P}{L_P} \left(V_{\text{DD}} - |V_{T,P}|\right)\right]} \tag{3.69}$$

Similarly, for the bias current values lower than I_{HIGH}, R_{LP} is made be greater than $R_{\text{LP\_MIN}}$. This requires W_P to be minimum, i.e., W_{MIN} and L_P [11] to be calculated as:

$$L_P = \mu_{\text{eff},p} C_{ox} W_{\text{MIN}} \left(V_{\text{DD}} - |V_{T,P}|\right) \left(\frac{V_{\text{SWING}}}{\left(\frac{I_{\text{CS}}}{2} + \sqrt{x}\sqrt{I_{\text{CS}} - x}\right)} - \frac{R_{\text{DSW}} * 10^{-6}}{W_{\text{MIN}}}\right) \tag{3.70}$$

For sizing the transistors $M3$–$M6$, the small-signal voltage gain $A_{v\_d\_tt2}$ [Eq. (3.62)] is used. The width of the transistors [11] by assuming minimum channel length is computed as:

$$W_N = 2\left(\frac{A_{v\_d\_tt2}}{V_{SWING}}\right)^2 \left(\frac{1}{2} + \frac{\sqrt{x}}{I_{CS}}\sqrt{I_{CS} - x}\right)^2 \frac{L_{MIN}I_{CS}}{\mu_{eff,n}C_{ox}} \tag{3.71}$$

It is found in some cases that for bias current values lower than the current of the minimum-sized NMOS transistor (I_{LOW}), the above equation results in W_N value lower than the minimum channel width. Therefore in such situations, the W_N is made equal to W_{MIN}. The I_{LOW} [11] can be evaluated by using Eq. (3.62) as:

$$I_{LOW} = \frac{1}{2}\left(\frac{V_{SWING}}{A_{v\_d\_tt2}}\right)^2 \frac{W_{MIN}}{L_{MIN}} \frac{1}{\left(\frac{1}{2} + \frac{\sqrt{x}}{I_{CS}}\sqrt{I_{CS} - x}\right)^2} \mu_{eff,n}C_{ox} \tag{3.72}$$

It may be noted that the above design expressions (Eqs. 3.69–3.72) relate the dimensions of the transistor to the bias current and the voltage swing. Hence, these are further used to express the capacitances used in the delay equation (Eq. 3.65) in order to establish the dependency of the delay on the bias current and voltage swing.

For the bias current I_{CS} ranging from I_{LOW} to I_{HIGH} and using Eqs. (3.69–3.72), various capacitances in (Eq. 3.65) are expressed as:

$$C_{gd\_3} = C_{gd0}W_3 = 2A_{v\_d\_tt2}^2 C_{gd0}\left(\frac{1}{2} + \frac{\sqrt{x}}{I_{CS}}\sqrt{I_{CS} - x}\right)^2 \frac{L_{MIN}}{\mu_{eff,n}C_{ox}}\frac{I_{CS}}{(V_{SWING})^2} \tag{3.73}$$

$$C_{db\_3} = W_3\left(K_{jn}C_{in}L_{dn} + 2K_{jswn}C_{jswn}\right) + 2K_{jswn}C_{jswn}L_{dn} \tag{3.74}$$

$$= 2A_{v\_d\_tt2}^2 \frac{L_{MIN}}{\mu_{eff,n}C_{ox}}\left(\frac{1}{2} + \frac{\sqrt{x}}{I_{CS}}\sqrt{I_{CS} - x}\right)^2 \left(K_{jn}C_{in}L_{dn} + 2K_{jswn}C_{jswn}\right)\frac{I_{CS}}{(V_{swing})^2} + 2K_{jswn}C_{jswn} \tag{3.75}$$

$$C_{gd\_9} = C_{gd0}W_{MIN} + \frac{3}{4}A_{bulk,max}W_{MIN}L_PC_{ox} \tag{3.76}$$

$$= C_{gd0}W_{MIN} + \frac{3}{4}A_{bulk,max}W_{MIN}C_{ox}\left\{\mu_{eff,p}C_{ox}W_{MIN}(V_{DD} - |V_{TP}|)\left(\frac{V_{SWING}}{\left(\frac{I_{CS}}{2} + \sqrt{x}\sqrt{I_{CS} - x}\right)} - \frac{R_{DSW} * 10^{-6}}{W_{MIN}}\right)\right\} \tag{3.77}$$

$$C_{db\_9} = W_{MIN}\left(K_{jp}C_{jp}L_{dp} + 2K_{jswp}C_{jswp}\right) + 2K_{jswp}C_{jswp}L_{dp} \tag{3.78}$$

Table 3.7 Coefficients of the capacitances for the TT-2-based differential CML MUX [11]

NMOS coefficients	
a_{db3}	$\dfrac{2A^2_{v\_d\_tt2}L_{MIN}}{\mu_{eff,n}C_{ox}}\left(K_{jn}C_{jn}L_{dn}+2K_{jswn}C_{jswn}\right)$
a_{gd3}	$2A^2_{v\_d\_tt2}C_{gd0}\dfrac{L_{MIN}}{\mu_{eff,n}C_{ox}}$
c_{db3}	$2K_{jswn}C_{jswn}L_{dn}$
$b_{db3},\ b_{gd3}$ and c_{gd3}	0
PMOS coefficients	
b_{gd9}	$\frac{3}{4}A_{bulk,max}\mu_{eff,p}C^2_{ox}W^2_{MIN}\left(V_{DD}-|V_{T,P}|\right)$
c_{gd9}	$C_{gd0}W_{MIN}-\frac{3}{4}A_{bulk,max}\mu_{eff,p}C^2_{ox}W_{MIN}\left(V_{DD}-|V_{T,P}|\right)R_{DSW}*10^{-6}$
c_{db9}	$K_{jp}C_{jp}L_{dp}W_{MIN}+2K_{jswp}C_{jswp}\left(L_{dp}+W_{MIN}\right)$
$a_{gd9},\ a_{db9}$ and b_{db9}	0

where the symbols have their usual meaning

Therefore, the capacitances may be expressed in terms of the bias current and the voltage swing as:

$$C_{xy}=\frac{a_{xy}}{\left(V_{swing}\right)^2}p^2I_{CS}+\frac{b_{xy}V_{swing}}{pI^2_{CS}}+c_{xy} \qquad (3.79)$$

where $p=\frac{1}{2}+\frac{\sqrt{x}}{I_{CS}}\sqrt{I_{CS}-x}$ has been substituted. The expressions of the coefficients a_{xy}, b_{xy}, and c_{xy} in all the capacitances in Eq. (3.79) are summarized in Table 3.7.

Using Eqs. (3.73–3.79), Eq. (3.65) can be written as:

$$t_{PD\_TT2}=0.69\,V_{swing}\left(\frac{ap}{V^2_{swing}}+b\frac{V_{swing}}{p^2\,I^2_{CS}}+\frac{c+C_L}{pI_{CS}}\right) \qquad (3.80)$$

where

$$a=2a_{db3}+2a_{gd3} \qquad (3.81a)$$

$$b=b_{gd9} \qquad (3.81b)$$

$$c=2c_{db3}+c_{gd9}+c_{db9} \qquad (3.81c)$$

For the completeness of the delay model, it is necessary to discuss its validity for I_{LOW} to I_{HIGH}. For $I_{CS}>I_{HIGH}$, it can be observed that the capacitance coefficients of PMOS transistor in Eqs. (3.69) and (3.70) differ. But it may be noted that for such values of I_{CS}, the capacitive contribution of PMOS transistor is negligible; therefore, Eq. (3.80) can predict the delay. Similarly, for $I_{CS}<I_{LOW}$, the delay majorly depends on the capacitances of PMOS transistor; therefore, the capacitance

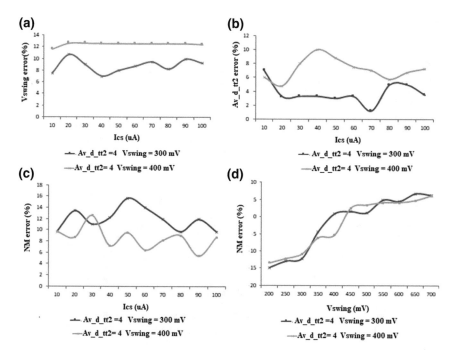

Fig. 3.14 Errors in the static model of the TT-2-based differential CML MUX [11]

coefficients of NMOS transistor do not affect the delay. So, the delay expression represented in (Eq. 3.80) can estimate the delay.

The accuracy of the static and the delay models is validated through SPICE simulations by using 0.18 μm CMOS technology parameters and with a power supply of 1.1 V. The TT-2-based differential CML MUX was designed and simulated for wide range of operating conditions: voltage swing of 300 and 400 mV, small-signal voltage gain of 2 and 4, $\delta = 1.5$, and the bias current ranging from 10 to 100 μA. The plots displaying the errors in the simulated and the predicted values of the static parameters for small-signal voltage gain of 4 and voltage swing of 300 and 400 mV are shown in Fig. 3.14a–c. A close inspection of the plots reveals that for the simulation condition with $V_{swing} = 300$ mV, $A_{v\_d\_tt2} = 4$, the maximum, minimum errors in V_{SWING}, NM, and $A_{v\_d\_tt2}$ are, respectively, (13%, 16%, 7%), (11%, 6%, 1%) with average errors of (12%, 4%, 11%) showing maximum variation of ±5% around the average values. Similarly, for $V_{swing} = 400$ mV, $A_{v\_d\_tt2} = 4$, the maximum, minimum, and average error in V_{SWING}, NM, and $A_{v\_d\_tt2}$ are, respectively, (11%, 13%, 11%), (7%, 5%, 5%), and (9%, 9%, 8%) with a maximum variation of ±4% around the average values. Therefore, it can be stated that the presented models will show a maximum variation of ±5% around the average values in static parameters. The dependence of the noise margin on the voltage swing is evaluated, and an error plot of noise margin by varying the voltage swing from 0.2 to 0.7 V is shown in Fig. 3.14d. It may be observed that the

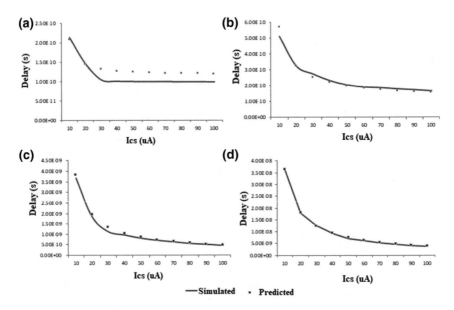

Fig. 3.15 Simulated and predicted delays of TT-2-based differential CML MUX versus I_{CS} with $A_{v\_d\_tt2} = 4$, $NM = 130$ mV for different C_L values: **a** 0 fF, **b** 10 fF, **c** 100 fF, and **d** 1 pF [11]

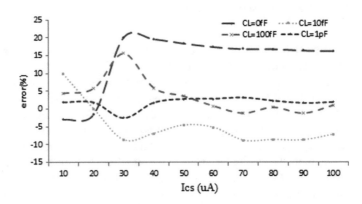

Fig. 3.16 Error summary for the TT-2-based differential CML MUX [11]

maximum error in noise margin is 14.8%. The delay is also noted for the above conditions; the simulated and the predicted delay values in particular for $V_{swing} = 400$ mV, $A_{v\_d\_tt2} = 4$, and the load capacitances of 0 fF, 10 fF, 100 fF, and 1 pF are plotted in Fig. 3.15. The error of (Eq. 3.80) with respect to simulations under the same load conditions is shown in Fig. 3.16. The maximum, minimum, and average errors in gate delay having load capacitance of 0 fF, 10 fF, 100 fF, and 1 pF are (22%, −3%, 9.5%), (10%, −10%, 0%), (16%, 5%, 10.5%), and (4%, −3%, 0.5%), respectively. It is worth noting that the error is maximum for the zero load

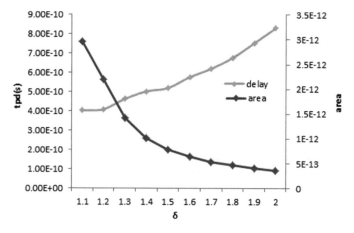

Fig. 3.17 Propagation delay and area vs. δ [11]

capacitance which is strongly an unrealistic case. Finally, the inspection of Fig. 3.15 indicates that the error tends to settle to a constant value for high values of the bias current.

After the verification of the models, it is necessary to determine the optimum value of the scaling factor. To find out the value, the TT-2-based differential CML MUX is designed for $A_{v\_d\_tt2} = 4$, $NM = 130\,\text{mV}$, $I_{CS} = 50\,\mu\text{A}$, and the propagation delay and the implementation area are plotted in Fig. 3.17 as a function of δ. It is observed that the delay increases with the increase in δ, whereas an opposite trend is noted in implementation area. The area reduction may be attributed to the fact that a high value of δ lowers the threshold voltage of $M7$ and $M8$ and results in small-sized $M3$–$M8$, thereby lowering the overall area. Therefore, an increase in area can be viewed as a trade-off for delay reduction as demonstrated by the plot. On closer examination, the value of $δ = 1.3$ is the optimum choice in terms of both delay and area.

3.4.3 Performance Comparison

In this section, the implementation area of the TT-2-based differential CML MUX and the available MUX is estimated and compared [11]. Thereafter, the performance of the TT-2-based differential CML MUX and the available MUXs is compared by designing them for different design cases. In all the simulations, the MUX is designed with minimum power supply, noise margin of 130 mV, small-signal gain of 4, and load capacitance of 50 fF. The values of $M(=5)$ and $δ(=1.3)$ are taken for designing TT-1- and TT-2-based differential CML MUX gate, respectively.

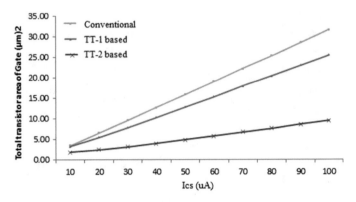

Fig. 3.18 Total transistor area required to design the differential CML MUX: **a** conventional, **b** TT-1 based and **c** TT-2 based [11]

Area Comparison

It is difficult to find out exact area without layout; therefore, preliminary area estimation is done on the basis of multiplying length and width of individual transistor employed in the circuit [14]. The area is computed for the conventional, TT-1-, and TT-2-based differential CML MUX for bias current ranging from 10 μA and 100 μA while keeping the simulation conditions described in the beginning of the current section. The findings are reported in Fig. 3.18 which identifies that the TT-2-based topology occupies least area among all. Further, at lower bias currents the area is almost half of the both TT-1 and the conventional MUX topologies while at higher bias currents, it is around one-third.

Design Cases

The performance of TT-2-based MUX is compared with the available ones for the different design cases. In literature, three design cases, namely high speed, power efficient and low power, have been considered. Therefore, for the sake of fair comparison, the TT-2-based MUX is designed for different performance. In high-speed design case, the basic aim is to design the MUX topologies with minimum delay. For the TT-2-based MUX, a bias current of 121.5 μA is obtained for high-speed performance. The delay of 492.426, 269.714, and 242.375 ps is obtained for the conventional, TT-1-, and TT-2-based differential CML MUX, respectively, through simulations. This indicates that the TT-2-based differential CML MUX can achieve higher speed than the conventional and TT-1-based differential CML MUX.

For power-efficient design, the minimization of the power-delay product (PDP) is considered. The MUX under this design case results in PDP values of 21.58, 19.53, and 23.38 fJ for the conventional, TT-1-, and TT-2-based differential CML MUX, respectively. The result indicates that the TT-2-based differential

Table 3.8 Comparison of differential CML MUX topologies [11]

Design cases	Performance parameter		TT-2 based	Conventional	TT-1 based
High speed	Delay	Value	242.375 ps	492.426 ps	269.714 ps
		Improvement	50.7%	–	45.22%
		Analysis	fastest	–	faster
Power efficient	PDP	Value	23.38 fJ	21.58 fJ	19.53 fJ
		Improvement	7.6%	–	16.4%
		Analysis	lesser	–	least
Low power	Power	Value	2.2 μW	2.8 μW	2.2 μW
		Improvement	21.4%	–	21.4%
		Analysis	low	–	low

CML MUX results in higher PDP values than the conventional and TT-1-based differential CML MUX.

In low-power designs, the motive is to achieve a low value of bias current for reducing the power consumption of the gate. The low-power TT-2-based MUX gives the value of I_{CS} as 2 μA. The low-power MUX gives a power consumption of 2.8, 2.2, and 2.2 μW for the conventional, TT-1-, and TT-2-based differential CML MUX topologies. The comparison for different design cases is summarized in Table 3.8.

3.5   Summary

In this chapter, differential CML gate based on triple-tail cell concept is elucidated. The number of source-coupled levels in triple-tail cell-based PDN design is reduced by one which leads to reduction in the minimum power supply. Two approaches to design triple-tail cell-based differential CML gates are presented. The first approach uses triple-tail wherein the aspect ratio of the transistors differs for proper activation/deactivation of the cell. In contrast, the use of multiple threshold voltage transistors is suggested as the second approach. A MUX is chosen as a test case to illustrate the concept. Mathematical formulations for analysis of static parameters are presented first followed by the design procedure which relates design parameters to bias current. The performance of the triple-tail-based CML gates is compared with its conventional counterpart for high-speed, power-efficient, and low-power cases.

References

1. M. Alioto, G. Palumbo, *Model and Design of Bipolar and MOS Current-Mode logic (CML, ECL and SCL Digital Circuits)* (Kluwer Academic Publications, 2005)
2. A. Tanabe, M. Umetani, I. Fujiwara, T. Ogura, K. Kataoka, M. Okihara, H. Sakuraba, T. Endoh, F. Masuoka, 0.18-μm CMOS 10-Gb/s multiplexer/demultiplexer ICs using current mode logic with tolerance to threshold voltage fluctuation. IEEE J. Solid-State Circ. **36**(6), 988–996 (2001)
3. A. Tanabe, M. Umetani, I. Fujiwara, T. Ogura, K. Kataoka, M. Okihara, H. Sakuraba, T. Endoh, F. Masuoka, A 10-Gb/s multiplexer/demultiplexer IC in 0.18 μm CMOS using current mode logic with tolerance to threshold voltage fluctuation, in *Proceedings of IEEE International Conference on Solid-State Circuits* (San Francisco, 2000), pp. 62–63
4. H. Hassan, M. Anis, M. Elmasry, Low power multi-threshold MCML: analysis, design and variability. Microelectr. J. **37**(10), 1097–1104 (2006)
5. H. Hassan, M. Anis, M. Elmasry, Analysis and design of low-power multi-threshold MCML, in *Proceedings of the IEEE International Conference on System-on-Chip* (2004), pp. 25–29
6. K. Zhou, S. Chen, A. Rucinski, J.F. McDonald, T. Zhang, Self-timed triple-rail MOS current mode logic pipeline for power-on-demand design, in *Proceedings of IEEE International Symposium on Circuits and Systems* (2005), pp. 1394–1397
7. K. Gupta, N. Pandey, M. Gupta, Low-voltage MOS current mode logic multiplexer. Radio Eng. **22**(1), 259–268 (2013)
8. K. Gupta, N. Pandey, M. Gupta, Analysis and design of MOS current mode logic exclusive-OR gate using triple-tail cells, Copyright (2013) (with permission from Elsevier, vol. 44, no. 6) (Reprinted from Microelectronics Journal), pp. 561–567
9. K. Gupta, N. Pandey, M. Gupta, MCML D-latch using triple-tail cells: analysis and design. Active Passive Electr. Comp. **2013**, 9 (2013) (Article ID. 217674)
10. K. Gupta, N. Pandey, N. Saxena, S. Dutta, Implementation and performance comparison of a four-bit ripple-carry adder using different MOS current mode logic topologies. *In the proceedings of International Conference on Computational Science and Its Applications—ICCSA* (2017), pp. 299–313
11. N. Pandey, K. Gupta, Garima Bhatia, Bharat Choudhary, MOS current mode logic exclusive-OR gate using multi-threshold triple-tail cells, vol. 57. Copyright (2016), with permission from Elsevier (Reprinted from Microelectronics Journal), pp. 13–20
12. B. Razavi, *Design of analog CMOS integrated circuits* (Tata McGraw Hill Edition, 2007)
13. H. Hassan, M. Anis, M. Elmasry, MOS current mode circuits: analysis, design, and variability. IEEE Trans Very Large Scale Integr (VLSI) Syst **13**(8), 885–898 (2005)
14. H. Ng, D. Allstot, CMOS current steering logic for low-voltage mixed-signal integrated circuits. IEEE Trans. VLSI Syst. **5**(3), 301–308 (1997)

Chapter 4
CML Gates with Modified Current Source

4.1 Introduction

The basic structure of a CML gate is derived from a differential amplifier which is an essential component in almost all analog applications. The amplifier usually has a constant current source to minimize its dependence on common-mode voltage. But in CML gates, the advantage of employing current source is to suppress switching noise, a major requirement for providing an analog-friendly environment in mixed-signal circuits. Its presence results in static power consumption restricting its usage in portable applications. Different approaches to reduce the static power consumption by modifying the current source section are suggested in the literature [1–6]. The first approach removes bias voltage from current source and allows current source operation for short durations. A pulse generator is required for the purpose. It generates short duration pulses corresponding to the transitions in the inputs which further drives the current source, giving rise to a self-timed MCML (ST-MCML) style [1]. Another approach uses an additional sleep transistor to isolate the current source from the rest of the circuit in sleep mode, thus lowering the overall power consumption [2, 3]. Both of these approaches are unattractive as additional circuitry is needed in ST-MCML gate for each input which will increase with the fan-in. Also, the CML gate using sleep transistor consumes same power as a differential CML gate while operating in active mode. Thus, like CMOS circuits, the concept of dynamic circuits is explored in CML gates [4–6]. The suitability of dynamic CML gate for low-power applications is investigated in this chapter.

© Springer Nature Singapore Pte Ltd. 2020
K. Gupta et al., *Model and Design of Improved Current Mode Logic Gates*, https://doi.org/10.1007/978-981-15-0982-7_4

4.2   Dynamic CML Gates

In the previous chapters, all the CML gates studied so far generate the output corresponding to the applied input voltages and preserve the output voltage as long as the power supply is provided. This class of CML gates falls in the category of static CML gates. There exists another class of CML gates named as dynamic CML gates which presents a low-power alternative to static CML gates for portable applications [4–6]. Their operation is based on the temporary storage of charge on a soft node and periodically updating the voltage levels, since stored charge in a capacitor cannot be retained indefinitely. Therefore, a dynamic CML gate uses a periodic clock signal (CLK) to control refreshing of charge on the soft node. Consequently, a dynamic CML gate has two operating phases, namely precharge phase and evaluation phase. The precharge phase refreshes the charges stored on the node while the evaluation phase generates the output according to the logic function implemented by the gate.

With this discussion, it is now clear that output is available in only evaluation phase and remains precharged to supply voltage otherwise. Therefore, there is a need to modify the structure of basic CML gate to achieve dynamic operation. It requires a mechanism that allows the charging of the output load capacitance as well as inhibits inputs to cause any change at the output node during the precharge phase and allows the logic function evaluation in the other phase. To fulfill these requirements, the load and current source sections of static CML gate are required to be modified so that their operation depends on CLK signal. A full-swing periodic CLK signal is used for the purpose. For low value of CLK signal, the circuit must exhibit precharge phase implying that the output load capacitance should be pre-charged to V_{DD} and gate inputs should not have affected the voltage level at the output node. Alternatively, for high CLK value, the output capacitance gets dis-connected from the power supply and the gate is evaluated in accordance with the inputs. To this end, the PMOS load transistors ($M1$, $M2$) are driven by CLK and are now termed as precharge transistors. The constant current source is replaced by a dynamic current source. A basic schematic of a dynamic CML (D-CML) gate is shown in Fig. 4.1 [4]. The dynamic current source is designed to exhibit the fol-lowing two characteristics. It must isolate the output load capacitance from ground during precharge phase. Secondly, the gate shall attain the required low voltage level in the evaluation phase. Two circuit implementations with the required characteristic are discussed in the following text.

NN-Dynamic Current Source

The NN-dynamic current source is depicted in Fig. 4.2a. Its name is derived from the fact that it uses two stacked NMOS transistors ($M1$, $M2$) [4]. The CMOS inverter I_1 is used to provide signal for controlling the switching of NMOS tran-sistors. For CLK = '0', transistor $M2$ is ON, so capacitor C_1 is discharged to ground potential. The connection to ground does not exist for CLK = '1', and capacitor C_1 attains a value depending upon node Y voltage.

Fig. 4.1 Basic structure of a D-CML gate

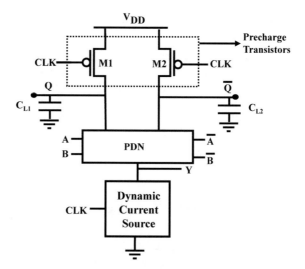

Fig. 4.2 Dynamic current sources: **a** NN-type and **b** NP-type

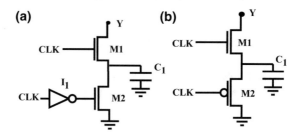

NP-Dynamic Current Source

The NN-dynamic current source employs a CMOS inverter I_1 to generate the complement of the CLK signal that drives the transistor $M2$. Since a CMOS inverter generates large switching noise, it is not suited in mixed-signal environments. Hence, a dynamic current source realization that avoids the use of CMOS inverter is used. The NMOS transistor $M2$ in NN-dynamic current source is replaced by a PMOS transistor. The PMOS is now driven by CLK signal as shown in Fig. 4.2b and avoids the use of CMOS inverter.

Either of the two dynamic current sources can be used for realizing dynamic CML gate. The analysis of both differential and PFSCL dynamic CML gates is explored.

4.3   Dynamic Differential CML Gates

Two types of differential dynamic CML gates based on the dynamic current source being used are designed and studied. A basic schematic of the gates is drawn in Fig. 4.3. The schematic in Fig. 4.3a uses NN-dynamic current source and is referred to as Dy-DCML-NN gates. Similarly, NP-dynamic current source is used in Fig. 4.3b and is referred to as Dy-DCML-NP gates. The section first discusses the operation, design, and power analysis of Dy-DCML-NN gates and, thereafter, presents Dy-DCML-NP gates.

4.3.1   Dy-DCML-NN Gates

The schematic of a Dy-DCML-NN inverter [4] is shown in Fig. 4.4a. The PDN is realized in similar manner as in static CML gates. The periodic CLK signal drives the precharge transistors as well as the dynamic current source.

4.3.1.1   Operation of a Dy-DCML-NN Inverter

For low values of CLK signal, the transistors $M2$, $M5$, and $M6$ are ON and the transistor $M1$ is OFF. The circuit operates in precharge phase, wherein both the

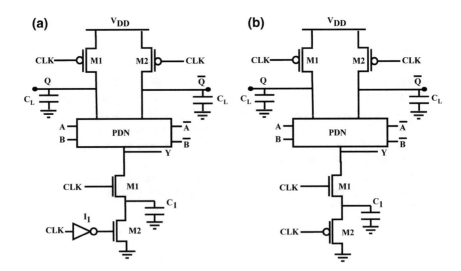

Fig. 4.3 Basic structure of **a** Dy-DCML-NN gate and **b** Dy-DCML-NP gate

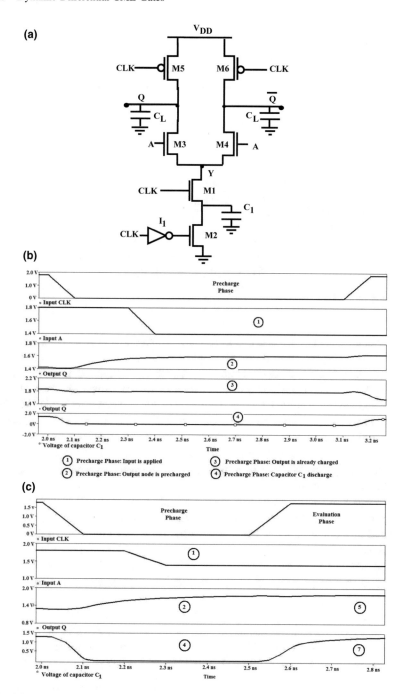

Fig. 4.4 a Dy-DCML-NN inverter, **b** operation in precharge phase, **c** operation for low input, **d** operation for high input

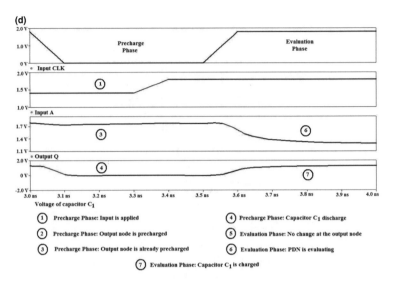

Fig. 4.4 (continued)

output nodes Q and $\overline{Q}$ are charged to the high voltage level ($V_{OH} = V_{DD}$) through $M5$ and $M6$, respectively. Also, the capacitor C_1 is discharged to the ground potential via transistor $M2$ in dynamic current source. The applied differential input A does not cause any change in the output level as the precharge transistors $M5$, $M6$ are ON and the transistor $M1$ is OFF. To illustrate this, a differential Dy-DCML-NN inverter is simulated with a power supply, voltage swing, and load capacitance of 1.8 V, 400 mV, and 100 fF, respectively. Corresponding voltage waveforms at various nodes are depicted in Fig. 4.4b. It can be observed that both the output nodes (Q and $\overline{Q}$) are charged to a high level in the precharge phase and are not affected by the applied input.

The circuit enters the evaluation phase for high value of the CLK signal. In this case, transistor $M1$ is ON while transistors $M2$, $M5$, and $M6$ are OFF. The output is evaluated depending on the value of differential input. For low value of differential input A, $M3$ is OFF and output node Q remains high ($V_Q = V_{DD}$). On the other hand, as $M4$ is ON charge transfer from load capacitor C_L to capacitor C_1 gets initiated such that the voltage of output node $\overline{Q}$ starts to decrease. The charge transfer continues to take place until both the capacitors are at same voltage level. It is worth mentioning that the attainment of the required low logic level requires proper design of C_1 which is discussed later. Similarly, for high value of differential input A, the transistor $M3$ is ON and $M4$ is OFF. The potential of the output node Q decreases to a low level ($V_Q = V_{DD} - V_{SWING}$), whereas the output node $\overline{Q}$ remains at high $\left(V_{\overline{Q}} = V_{DD} \right)$ potential. This functionality can be verified through the simulation waveforms shown in Fig. 4.4c, d for the low and high values of the input, respectively.

4.3.1.2 Design of a Dy-DCML-NN Inverter

In the evaluation phase, the logic function is evaluated due to the formation of a conduction path between C_L and C_1 depending on the inputs. The transfer of charge from the C_L to C_1 takes place resulting in a decrease in the output node potential. The charge transfer continues till both the capacitors attain equal potential. Thus, it is necessary to ensure that charge transfer ceases only when the potential of the output node is reduced by V_{SWING}. This can be accomplished by proper sizing of capacitor C_1. By using charge conservation principle, we can write

$$V_{DD}C_{OUT} = (C_1 + C_{OUT})(V_{DD} - V_{SWING}) \tag{4.1}$$

where C_{OUT} is the sum of the load capacitance C_L at the output node and the parasitic capacitances of the transistors [7]. By rearranging Eq. (4.1), C_1 can be expressed as:

$$C_1 = \frac{V_{SWING}C_{OUT}}{V_{DD} - V_{SWING}} \tag{4.2}$$

In integrated circuits, a capacitor is generally realized by a MOSFET with its source and drain terminals connected together. Therefore, by substituting, $C_1 = W_{C_1} \times L_{C_1} \times C_{ox}$, and for a given value of L_{C_1}, the width W_{C_1} of transistor is calculated as:

$$W_{C_1} = \frac{V_{SWING}C_L}{L_{C_1}C_{ox}(V_{DD} - V_{SWING})} \tag{4.3}$$

where W_{C_1} and L_{C_1} are the width and length of transistor for C_1.

4.3.1.3 Power Consumption of Dy-DCML-NN Gates

The static differential CML inverter shows static power consumption due to the constant current flow maintained in the circuit. However, in the Dy-DCML-NN inverter, a direct path between power supply and ground is not established since the transistor pairs $M1$ and $M2$ (Fig. 4.4a) never turns ON simultaneously. This is due to the fact that these transistors are driven by CLK and its complement signal. As a consequence, the static power is negligible, but these gates consume dynamic power due to the presence of capacitors. The power consumption of Dy-DCML-NN inverter is given as:

$$P_{dyn} = C_{OUT}V_{DD}V_{SWING}f_{CLK} + P_{CMOS\_INV} \tag{4.4}$$

where f_{CLK} represents the frequency of the CLK signal, and P_{CMOS_INV} is the power consumption of the CMOS inverter I_1 [8].

4.3.1.4 Design Examples

This section details the design of a Dy-DCML-NN inverter with power supply V_{DD}, voltage swing, and load capacitance C_L of 1.8 V, 400 mV, and 100 fF, respectively. A clock frequency of 1 GHz is applied. All the transistors are assumed to be minimum sized. The parasitic capacitance of the transistor approximates to 2 fF. Therefore, by using design equation in Eq. 4.3, the value of C_1 is calculated as 29 fF. Further, the amount of power consumed by the inverter is calculated by using Eq. 4.4 which evaluates to 79 μW. Alternatively, simulation results indicate the power consumption of 83 μW resulting in a percentage error of 4.8%.

The design of two-level Dy-DCML-NN is also considered for the sake of completeness. A 2:1 multiplexer (MUX) is selected. The circuit diagram of Dy-DCML-NN MUX is shown in Fig. 4.5. The total parasitic capacitance of all the minimum-sized transistors at the output node capacitance is 6 fF. Therefore, by using the design equation, the value of C_1 is found out as 31 fF. The theoretical and simulated power consumption values with the same simulating condition above are 83 and 86 μW with an error of 3.4%.

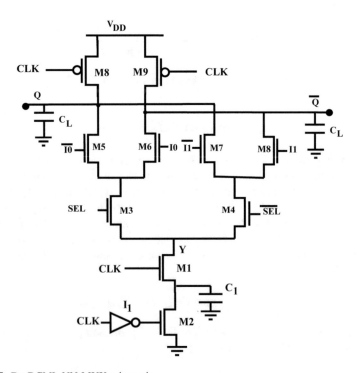

Fig. 4.5 Dy-DCML-NN MUX schematic

4.3.2 Dy-DCML-NP Gates

The schematic of a Dy-DCML-NP inverter is shown in Fig. 4.6a. The PDN has a source-coupled transistor pair ($M3$–$M4$) driven by a differential input A. The precharge and the dynamic current source are driven by periodic CLK signal.

4.3.2.1 Operation of a Dy-DCML-NP Inverter

In the precharge phase, low value of CLK signal turns ON transistors $M2$, $M5$, and $M6$ while transistor $M1$ is OFF. The two output nodes Q and $\overline{Q}$ are precharged to a high voltage level ($V_{OH} = V_{DD}$). Simultaneously, capacitor C_1 is discharged to a voltage level which is one threshold voltage above the ground potential through $M2$. The capacitor C_1 is not discharged to ground potential due to the inherit characteristic of PMOS transistor $M2$ in Dy-DCML-NN inverter for transferring low voltage levels. The applied inputs during this phase cause no change at the output node since both the precharge transistors $M5$, $M6$ are ON, and the transistor $M1$ is OFF.

In the evaluation phase, CLK goes high and makes transistor $M1$ ON, while transistors $M2$, $M5$, and $M6$ are switched OFF. The output is evaluated depending on the value of differential input A. For a low value of differential input A, $M3$ is OFF and $M4$ is ON, and the output node Q remains high ($V_Q = V_{DD}$) while potential of output node $\overline{Q}$ decreases to low level $\left(V_{\overline{Q}} = V_{DD} - V_{SWING} \right)$ due to the charge transfer from load capacitor C_L to capacitor C_1. Similarly, for a high value of the differential input A, the transistor $M3$ is ON and $M4$ is OFF. The potential of the output node Q decreases to a low level ($V_Q = V_{DD} - V_{SWING}$), whereas the output node $\overline{Q}$ remains at high $\left(V_{\overline{Q}} = V_{DD} \right)$ potential. It is clear now that the attainment of low logic level requires proper design of C_1 for a particular voltage swing value.

The behavior is elaborated by simulating a differential Dy-DCML-NP inverter with a power supply, voltage swing, and load capacitance of 1.8 V, 400 mV, and 100 fF, respectively. The voltage waveforms at different nodes of the inverter are shown in Fig. 4.6b, c. It can be observed that both the output nodes (Q and $\overline{Q}$) are charged to a high level in the precharge phase and are not affected by the applied input. Also, the voltage of C_1 discharges to one threshold voltage above the ground potential during the precharge phase. In the evaluation, either of the two output node discharges to low logic level depending upon the input maintaining the differential nature at the output nodes of the gate.

4.3.2.2 Design of Dy-DCML-NP Inverter

As explained for Dy-DCML-NN gates, the required voltage swing V_{SWING} for Dy-DCML-NP gates is achieved by properly sizing capacitor C_1 such that the

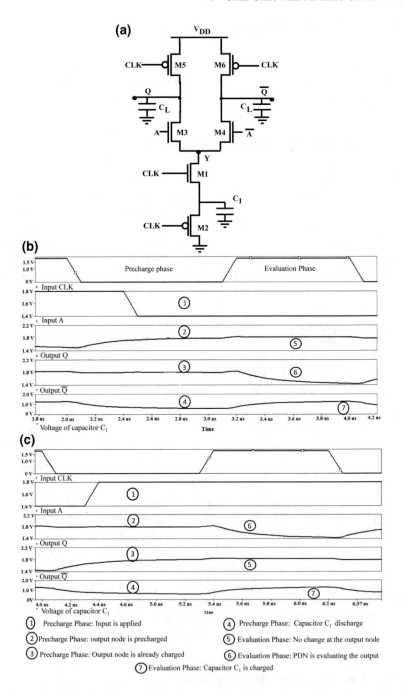

Fig. 4.6 a Dy-DCML-NP inverter, **b** inverter operation for low input, **c** inverter operation for high input

output is discharged to low level ($V_{DD} - V_{SWING}$) during the evaluation phase. Using the charge conservation principle, we can write

$$V_{DD}C_{OUT} + C_1|V_{T,P}| = (C_1 + C_{OUT})(V_{DD} - V_{SWING}) \qquad (4.5)$$

where C_{OUT} is the total load capacitance at the output node including the parasitic capacitances of the transistors [7]. Further, C_1 can be expressed as:

$$C_1 = \frac{V_{SWING}C_{OUT}}{V_{DD} - V_{SWING} - |V_{T,P}|} \qquad (4.6)$$

If capacitor is realized through a MOSFET with its source and drain terminals connected together, then the width W_{C_1} of transistor is calculated as:

$$W_{C_1} = \frac{V_{SWING} \times C_{OUT}}{L_{C_1}C_{ox}(V_{DD} - V_{SWING} - |V_{T,P}|)} \qquad (4.7)$$

where W_{C_1} and L_{C_1} are the width and length of transistor substituted for C_1.

4.3.2.3   Power Consumption of Dy-DCML-NP Gates

The power consumption of Dy-DCML-NP gates is dynamic in nature due to the presence of capacitors. These gates similar to Dy-DCML-NN gates do not consume static power as a direct path between power supply and ground is not established since the transistor pairs $M1$ and $M2$ (Fig. 4.6a) in dynamic current source never turns ON simultaneously. Therefore, the power consumption of Dy-DCML-NP gate is given as:

$$P_{dyn} = C_{OUT}V_{DD}V_{SWING}f_{CLK} \qquad (4.8)$$

where f_{CLK} represents the frequency of the CLK signal. It is to be noted that since Dy-DCML-NP gates do not use CMOS inverter, their power consumption is further reduced in comparison to Dy-DCML-NN gates.

4.3.2.4   Design Examples

The design of a Dy-DCML-NP inverter on the basis of the above theoretical proposition is illustrated first. The inverter is designed to operate with a power supply value, $V_{DD} = 1.8$ V for a voltage swing of 400 mV, having load capacitance $C_L = 100$ fF. A clock frequency of 1 GHz is applied. All the transistors are assumed to be minimum sized. The parasitic capacitance of the transistor approximates to 2 fF. Therefore, by using design equation in Eq. (4.7), the value of C_1 is calculated as 46 fF. Further, the amount of power consumed by the inverter is

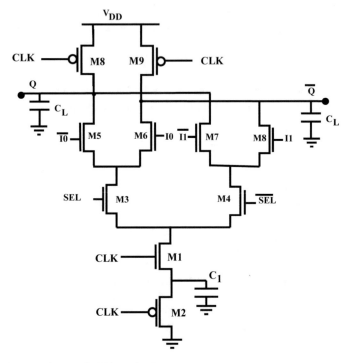

Fig. 4.7 Schematic of Dy-DCML-NP MUX

calculated by using Eq. (4.8) which evaluates to 73 µW. Alternatively, simulation results indicate the power consumption of 80 µW resulting in a percentage error of 8.75%.

The design of a two-level Dy-DCML-NP gate is also considered for the sake of completeness. A 2:1 MUX is selected as taken for Dy-DCML-NN gate. The circuit diagram of Dy-DCML-NP MUX is shown in Fig. 4.7. The total parasitic capacitance of all the minimum-sized transistors at the output node capacitance is 6 fF. Therefore, by using the design equation, the value of C_1 is found out as 47 fF. The theoretical and simulated power consumption values with the same simulating condition above are 76 and 82 µW with an error of 7.3%.

4.3.3   General Discussion on Dynamic Differential CML Gate

Based on the above discussion on the dynamic differential CML gates, some of the important characteristics can be drawn as:

1. The size of the precharge transistors $M5$, $M6$ does not determine the voltage swing of the gate as in conventional differential CML gates.
2. The capacitor C_1 is always discharged/charged in precharge/evaluation phases irrespective of the input.
3. The performance of the gates is affected by the charge sharing effect and charge leakage. These can be overcome by adding a latch in parallel to the precharge transistors.

4.4 Dynamic PFSCL Gates

The static PFSCL gates are transformed into dynamic PFSCL gates by applying the same principles as followed for differential CML gates. The constant current source and load transistors are replaced by dynamic current source and the precharge transistors. Depending on the type of dynamic current source, the basic schematic of the two types of dynamic PFSCL gates is shown in Fig. 4.8. The circuit in Fig. 4.8a employs NN-dynamic current source therefore named as Dy-PFSCL-NN gates. Alternatively, the other circuit shown in Fig. 4.8b has NP-dynamic current source and is referred to as Dy-PFSCL-NP gates. The PDN is implemented in the similar manner as in conventional PFSCL gates.

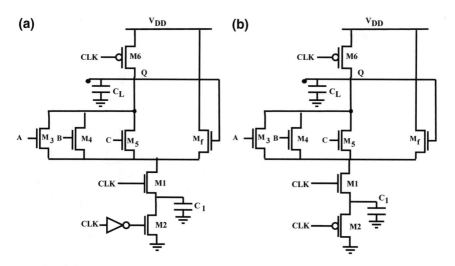

Fig. 4.8 Basic structure of dynamic PFSCL gates: **a** Dy-PFSCL-NN gate and **b** Dy-PFSCL-NP gate

4.4.1   Dy-PFSCL-NN Gates

The schematic of a Dy-DCML-NN inverter [6] is shown in Fig. 4.9. The PDN is realized in similar manner as in static PFSCL gates. The periodic CLK signal drives the precharge transistors as well as the dynamic current source.

4.4.1.1   Operation of a Dy-PFSCL-NN Inverter

The operation of Dy-PFSCL-NN gates can be illustrated through an inverter. It works on precharge–evaluation logic depending on the CLK signal value. For low values of CLK, the transistors $M2$ and $M5$ are ON and the transistor $M1$ is OFF. The circuit operates in precharge phase, wherein the output node Q is charged to high voltage level ($V_{OH} = V_{DD}$) through $M5$. Also, the capacitor C_1 is discharged to the ground potential via transistor $M2$ in dynamic current source. The applied input A does not cause any change in the output level as the precharge transistors $M5$ is ON and the transistor $M1$ is OFF. In the evaluation phase, the CLK goes high and makes the transistor $M1$ ON, and the transistors $M2$ and $M5$ are OFF. The output is evaluated depending on the value of input A. For a low value of input A, the transistor $M3$ is OFF and the inverter output remains high ($V_{OH} = V_{DD}$) as no path exists to transfer the charge stored on load capacitor C_L to capacitor C_1. However, the positive feedback makes the transistor $M4$ ON and the capacitor C_1 gets charged from the power supply through transistor $M1$. For a high value of the input A, the

Fig. 4.9 Dy-PFSCL-NN inverter

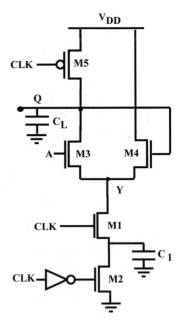

transistor $M3$ is ON, and the potential of the output node Q decreases to low level ($V_{OL} = V_{DD} - V_{SWING}$) as the result of the charge transfer from the load capacitor C_L to capacitor C_1.

The functioning of Dy-PFSCL-NN inverter in the evaluation phase is demonstrated through simulations with a power supply of 1.8 V. The inverter is simulated for a voltage swing of 500 mV and load capacitance of 100 fF. The simulation waveform for low and high values of input A is shown in Fig. 4.10 [6]. It is

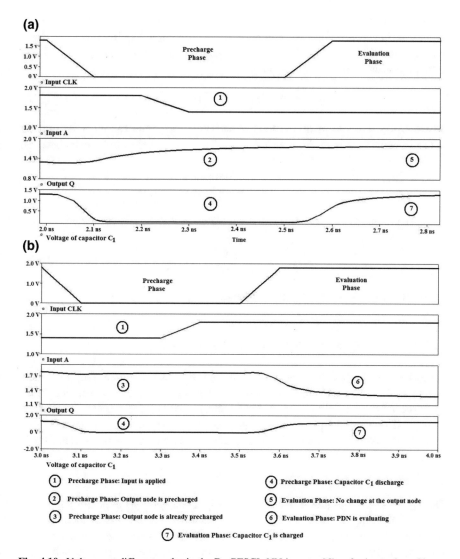

Fig. 4.10 Voltages at different nodes in the Dy-PFSCL-NN inverter [6], **a** for low value of input A and **b** for high value of input A

observed in Fig. 4.10a that for low value of input A, the output node remains at the high level as no charge transfer takes place and the capacitor C_1 gets charged through the power supply since $M1$ is ON due to the high output voltage being feedback. In Fig. 4.10b for high value of the input A, there is charge transfer from C_L to C_1 and the output node Q attains low logic level.

4.4.1.2   Design of Dy-PFSCL-NN Gates

As it is evident that charging of capacitor C_1 should continue till the required voltage drop ($V_{DD} - V_{SWING}$) is attained at the output this requires proper sizing of the capacitor C_1. Therefore, by using the charge conservation principle, the charge transfer process can be summarized by

$$V_{DD} C_{OUT} = (C_{OUT} + C_1)(V_{DD} - V_{SWING}) \qquad (4.9)$$

where C_{OUT} is the sum of the load capacitance C_L at the output node and the parasitic capacitances of the transistors [9]. The value of C_1 can be calculated as:

$$C_1 = \frac{V_{SWING} C_{OUT}}{V_{DD} - V_{SWING}} \qquad (4.10)$$

If C_1 is replaced by MOSFET, the equivalent width W_{C_1} is computed as:

$$W_{C_1} = \frac{V_{SWING} C_{OUT}}{L_{C_1} C_{ox}(V_{DD} - V_{SWING})} \qquad (4.11)$$

where W_{C_1} and L_{C_1} are the width and length of the transistor for C_1.

4.4.1.3   Power Consumption of a Dy-PFSCL-NN Gate

Since Dy-PFSCL-NN gates do not use a constant current source, they have negligible static power consumption however, consumes dynamic power due to the presence of the capacitors. The power consumption of these gates differs from Dy-DCML-NN counterparts and is found to be data dependent. To elaborate this, an in-depth analysis of inverter is performed and is then extended to N-input PFSCL gate.

Case 1: when the output is low

During the precharge phase, the capacitor C_L is charged by the power supply via $M5$. The charging of capacitor C_1 could not take place as no current path between the power supply and capacitor C_1 can be established since the transistor $M1$ is OFF. In the precharge phase it is worthnoting that a low to high transition will occur at the output only if the output node was discharged during the preceeding evaluation phase. In the evaluation phase for high value of input, the output becomes low due to charge transfer from C_L to C_1. Therefore, the power consumption of Dy-PFSCL-NN inverter for low output value is computed as:

$$P_{dyn,0} = 0.5 C_{OUT} V_{DD} V_{SWING} f_{CLK} + P_{CMOS\_INV} \quad (4.12a)$$

where the first term refers to the component of power accounting for low to high transition in the preceeding evaluation phase, P_{CMOS_INV} is the power consumption of the CMOS inverter I_1 [8] and rest of the symbols have their usual meaning.

Case 2: when the output is high

This case corresponds to the condition when input is low. Since $M3$ is OFF, the charge transfer from output node will not take place. But since the output is maintained at high level, M4 is ON due to positive feedback, the capacitor C_1 is charged from power supply via transistors $M1$ and $M4$. Therefore, the power consumption of a Dy-PFSCL-NN inverter for high value of the output is given as:

$$P_{dyn,1} = 0.5 \left(C_{OUT} V_{DD} V_{SWING} + C_1 V_{DD} (V_{DD} - V_{T,N}) \right) f_{CLK} + P_{CMOS\_INV} \quad (4.12b)$$

The same can be extended to a generic Dy-PFSCL-NN gate by computing the low-to-high transition probability of the output node. As it is evident, the output node makes a low-to-high transition during the precharge phase, only if the output was discharged during the preceding evaluation phase. By assuming uniformly distributed inputs, the low-to-high transition probability for an N-input gate [8] is given as:

$$\alpha_{L \to H} = \frac{N_0}{2^N} \quad (4.13)$$

where N_0 is the number of zero entries in the truth table of the logic function.

Thus, the power consumption of an N-input Dy-PFSCL-NN gate with transition probability $\alpha_{L \to H}$ is given as

$$P_{dyn,0} = \alpha_{L \to H} C_{OUT} V_{DD} V_{SWING} f_{CLK} + P_{CMOS\_INV} \quad \text{(for case 1)} \quad (4.14a)$$

$$P_{dyn,1} = (1 - \alpha_{L \to H}) \left(C_{OUT} V_{DD} V_{SWING} + C_1 V_{DD} (V_{DD} - V_{T,N}) \right) f_{CLK} + P_{CMOS\_INV}$$
$$\text{(for case 2)}$$

$$(4.14b)$$

4.4.1.4 Design Examples

The above discussion on Dy-PSFCL-NN gate design is first applied to inverter and then extended to the design of other gates. The inverter is designed to operate with a power supply value, $V_{DD} = 1.8$ V for a voltage swing of 400 mV, having load capacitance $C_L = 100$ fF. A clock frequency of 1 GHz is to be applied. All the transistors are assumed to be minimum sized. The parasitic capacitance of all the transistors approximates to 4 fF. Therefore, by using design equation in Eq. (4.11), the value of C_1 is calculated as 30 fF. Further, the amount of power consumed by the inverter is calculated for the two cases depending on the output logic level. For the case when output is low, a power consumption of 44 μW is calculated by using (Eq. 4.12a) while from simulation the value is 48 μW showing a percentage error of 8.5%. Alternatively, the theoretical and simulated values when output is at high logic level are 73.84 μW and 79 μW, respectively.

After this, the design of a three-input Dy-PFSCL-NN NOR gate is considered. The schematic is shown in Fig. 4.11. The total parasitic capacitance of all the minimum-sized transistors at the output node is 6 fF. Therefore, by using the design equation, the value of C_1 is found out as 31 fF. With the same simulating condition as for the inverter, when the output is low and substituting $\alpha_{L\rightarrow H} = 7/8$ in Eq. (4.14a), the theoretical power consumption value of 73.26 μW is obtained. The simulated value for the case is 80 μW; thus, an error of 8.4% exhibited. Conversely, the theoretical (using Eq. 4.14b) and simulated power consumption values when the output is high are 30 μW and 36 μW, respectively, showing an error of 16%.

4.4.2 Dy-PFSCL-NP Gates

This section presents Dy-PFSCL-NP gates. To develop an understanding, a detailed analysis for the inverter is presented here. The schematic of a Dy-PFSCL-NP

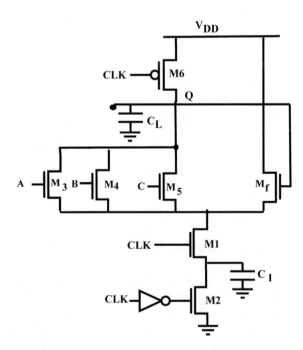

Fig. 4.11 Schematic of a three-input Dy-PFSCL-NN NOR gate

Fig. 4.12 Dy-PFSCL-NP
inverter

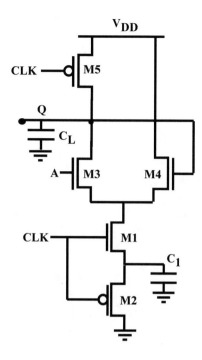

inverter is shown in Fig. 4.12. The PDN consists of source-coupled transistor pair ($M3$, $M4$). The precharge transistor $M5$ and the dynamic current source ($M1$, $M2$, C_1) are driven by a clock signal (CLK).

4.4.2.1 Operation of Dy-PFSCL-NP Inverter

The circuit operates in the precharge and evaluation phases according to the CLK signal value. The circuit operation in the precharge phase is same as described for Dy-DCML-NP inverter. With a low to high transition on CLK, the circuit enters evaluation phase. The precharge transistor $M5$ and transistor $M2$ of dynamic current source get turned off. The output is evaluated depending on the value of input A as $M1$ is ON. For a low value of input, the transistor $M3$ is OFF and the inverter output remains high ($V_{OH} = V_{DD}$) as no charge transfer could take place. However, the capacitor C_1 gets charged through transistor $M1$ and $M4$. Conversely, for a high value of input A, the potential of output node Q decreases to low level ($V_{OL} = V_{DD} - V_{SWING}$) as the result of the charge transfer from the C_L to C_1 through $M3$.

The functioning of Dy-PFSCL-NP inverter is demonstrated through simulations conducted with a power supply, voltage swing, and load capacitance of 1.8 V, 500 mV, and 100 fF, respectively. The voltage waveforms at different nodes of the inverter are shown in Fig. 4.13. For low value of input A in Fig. 4.13a, the output

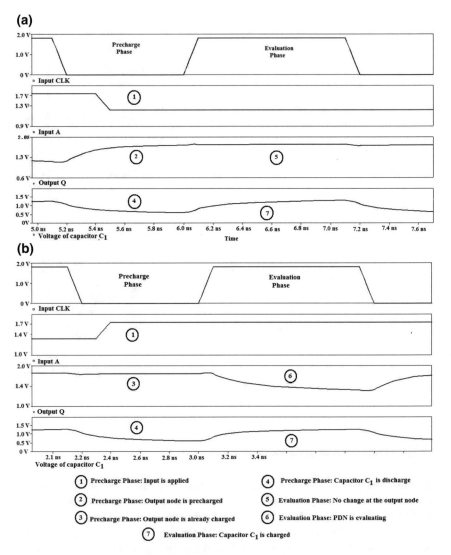

Fig. 4.13 Voltages at different nodes in the Dy-PFSCL-NP inverter, **a** for low value of input *A* and **b** for high value of input *A*

node remains at the high level as no charge transfer take place and the capacitor C_1 gets charged due to the positive feedback. In Fig. 4.13b for high value of the input *A*, there is a charge transfer from C_L to C_1 and the output node *Q* attains low level.

4.4.2.2 Design of Dy-PFSCL-NP Inverter

An appropriate value of capacitor C_1 is used in order to achieve the required voltage swing V_{SWING} during evaluation. Using the charge conservation principle, the charge transfer process can be modeled as:

$$V_{DD}C_{OUT} + C_1 |V_{T,P}| = (C_{OUT} + C_1)(V_{DD} - V_{SWING}) \quad (4.15)$$

where C_L is the total load capacitance at the output node which include the parasitic capacitances of the transistors. The value of capacitor C_1 can be evaluated as:

$$C_1 = \frac{V_{SWING}C_{OUT}}{V_{DD} - V_{SWING} - |V_{T,P}|} \quad (4.16)$$

By substituting, $C_1 = W_{C_1}L_{C_1}C_{ox}$, the width W_{C_1} of transistor is calculated as:

$$W_{C_1} = \frac{V_{SWING}C_{OUT}}{L_{C_1}C_{ox}(V_{DD} - V_{SWING} - |V_{T,P}|)} \quad (4.17)$$

where W_{C_1} and L_{C_1} are the width and length of transistor for C_1.

4.4.2.3 Power Consumption of Dy-PFSCL-NP Gates

The static power consumption of the Dy-PFSCL-NP inverter is negligible as the transistors $M1$ and $M2$ will never turn ON simultaneously. The inverter has dynamic power consumption due to the capacitors in the circuit. The power consumption of Dy-PFSCL-NP inverter is found to be data dependent. To elaborate this, the operation of an inverter is examined during high and low output cases and the dynamic power consumption is computed.

Case 1: when the output is low

During the precharge phase, the output capacitor C_L is charged by the power supply if the output was discharged during the preceeding evaluation phase. The charging of capacitor C_1 does not take place since the transistor $M1$ is OFF and no current path exists between the power supply and the capacitor C_1. Also, in the evaluation phase for high input value, the output is low and the charge from C_L is shared with capacitor C_1. Thus, the power consumption is given as:

$$P_{dyn,0} = 0.5C_{OUT}V_{DD}V_{SWING}f_{CLK} \quad (4.18)$$

where the symbols have their usual meanings.

Case 2: when the output is high

In this case, during the precharge phase the C_L will be charged by the power supply. The charging of capacitor C_1 will not take place since the transistor $M1$ is OFF in precharge phase. But, in the evaluation phase for low input value, the output is high; thus, the capacitor C_1 is charged from the power supply through the transistors $M1$ and $M4$. Therefore, the power consumption when the output is high is computed as:

$$P_{dyn,1} = 0.5\left(C_{OUT}V_{DD}V_{SWING} + C_1 V_{DD}\left(V_{DD} - V_{T,N} - |V_{T,P}|\right)\right)f_{CLK} \qquad (4.19)$$

where the symbols have their usual meanings.

In general for an N-input Dy-PFSCL-NP gate with transition probability $\alpha_{L\rightarrow H}$, the dynamic power consumption corresponding to the above two cases can be expressed as:

$$P_{dyn,0} = \alpha_{L\rightarrow H}C_{OUT}V_{DD}V_{SWING}f_{CLK} \quad (\text{case 1}) \qquad (4.20a)$$

$$P_{dyn,1} = (1 - \alpha_{L\rightarrow H})\left(C_{OUT}V_{DD}V_{SWING} + C_1\left(V_{DD} - V_{T,N} - |V_{T,P}|\right)\right)f_{CLK} \quad (\text{case 2})$$
$$\qquad (4.20b)$$

4.4.2.4 Design Examples

The above theoretical propositions for Dy-PSFCL-NP gate design are first applied to inverter and then extended to the design of other gates. The inverter is designed to operate with a power supply value, $V_{DD} = 1.8$ V for a voltage swing of 400 mV, having load capacitance $C_L = 100$ fF. A clock frequency of 1 GHz is to be applied. All the transistors are assumed to be minimum sized. The parasitic capacitance of all the transistors approximates to 4 fF. Therefore, by using design equation in Eq. 4.17, the value of C_1 is calculated as 52 fF. Further, the amount of power consumed by the inverter is calculated for the two cases depending on the output logic level. For the case when output is low, a power consumption of 38 fF μW is calculated by using Eq. 4.19, while from simulation the value is 42 μW showing a percentage error of 11%. Alternatively, the theoretical and simulated values when output is at high logic level are 84.2 μW and 96 μW, respectively.

After this, the design of a three-input Dy-PFSCL-NN NOR gate is considered. The schematic is shown in Fig. 4.14. The total parasitic capacitance of all the minimum-sized transistors at the output node is 6 fF. Therefore, by using the design equation, the value of C_1 is found out as 53 fF. With the same simulating condition as for the inverter, when the output is low and substituting $\alpha_{L\rightarrow H} = 7/8$ in Eq. (4.20a), the theoretical power consumption value of 66.78 μW is obtained. The simulated value for the case is 75 μW; thus, an error of 12.3% exhibited. Conversely, the theoretical (using Eq. 4.20b) and simulated power consumption values when the output is high are 23 μW and 27 μW, respectively, showing an error of 17.4%.

Fig. 4.14 Schematic of a three-input Dy-PFSCL-NP NOR gate

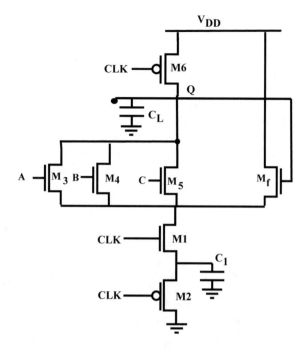

4.4.3 General Discussion on Dy-PFSCL Gates

The important characteristics of Dy-PFSCL gates are summarized as:

1. The size of the precharge transistor does not determine the voltage swing of the circuit as in PFSCL style.
2. The capacitor C_1 is always discharged to one threshold voltage above the ground potential in the precharge phase.
3. The charging and discharging of capacitors C_1 take place in every clock cycle.
4. The performance of Dy-PFSCL gates is not affected by charge sharing effect of dynamic circuits as they employ a single level of source-coupled transistors in their PDN.
5. The Dy-PFSCL gates exhibit charge leakage during the evaluation phase because of the leakage currents. This can be compensated by driving the pre-charge transistor $M5$ with a signal that makes it to remain in near cut-off during the evaluation phase as suggested in [9].

4.5 Multi-stage Applications

The circuits which have been studied so far in this chapter are limited to the design of single-stage dynamic gate. But in practice, gates are generally cascaded to realize multi-stage architecture for complex circuit realizations. In these cases, the D-CML gates have restrictions. To elaborate this issue, consider a cascade of two Dy-DCML-NN inverters, as depicted in Fig. 4.15a. During the precharge phase, the outputs of both the inverters are high. Assuming the input of the first stage as logic high, the output makes a high-to-low-level transition in the evaluation phase. Since the evaluation of the second stage is simultaneously started with the first stage, the

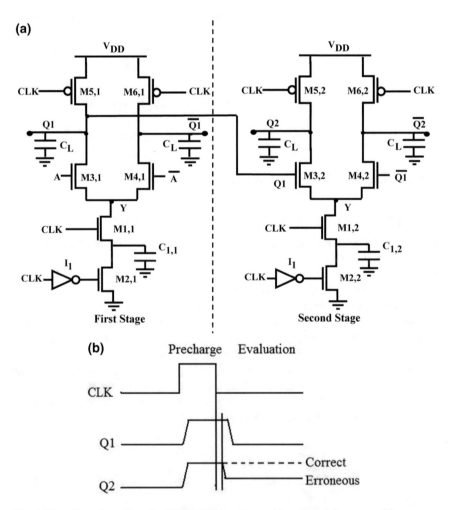

Fig. 4.15 **a** Cascading of two Dy-DCML-NN inverters and **b** output of the stages with respect to the common CLK signal [6]

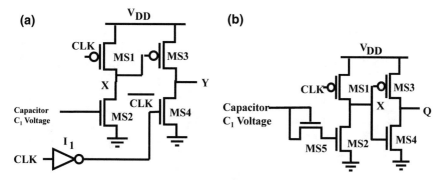

Fig. 4.16 Schematic of self-timed buffer: **a** STB-1 and **b** STB-2

potential of the output nodes in the second-stage inverter reduces by some amount. This is due to the fact both the input transistors ($M3,2$ and $M4,2$) of the second stage are driven by high voltage and are ON at the start of the evaluation phase. This behavior is explained in Fig. 4.15b and cannot be corrected. Therefore, it is evident that the D-CML gates cannot be cascaded directly.

The problem in cascading two D-CML inverters is due to the fact that both stages are evaluating simultaneously and the output nodes of the first stage are at high potential. This situation can be practically avoided by delaying the evaluation in the second stage until the first stage completes the evaluation. A circuit that allows the evaluation of the second stage only after the complete evaluation of the second stage is required. The required circuit shown in Fig. 4.16 when inserted between the D-CML gates serves the purpose. It is named as self-timed buffer and converts the voltage stored on capacitor C_1 in dynamic current source to a full-swing output which is used as clock input by the next stage. There are two circuit implementations available for self-timed buffer and are drawn in Fig. 4.16. The first circuit referred to as STB-1 is a cascade of two clocked inverters and requires the usage of both CLK signal and its complement [4]. The other circuit uses only CLK signal and is denoted as STB-2. Their usage in realizing multi-stage dynamic CML circuits is described further.

4.5.1 Multi-stage D-CML Design Using STB-1

In this section, the multi-stage D-CML design using STB-1 is described by considering the cascade of two Dy-DCML-NN inverters. The complete schematic with STB-1 inserted between the stages is shown in Fig. 4.17. The CLK signal is applied to the first stage only. The voltage stored on the capacitor $C_{1,1}$ of the first Dy-DCML-NN stage serves as an input to the first inverter of STB-1. During the precharge phase, the output of the first stage is charged to a high level and the capacitor $C_{1,1}$ gets discharged simultaneously. Since CLK is low, transistors MS1

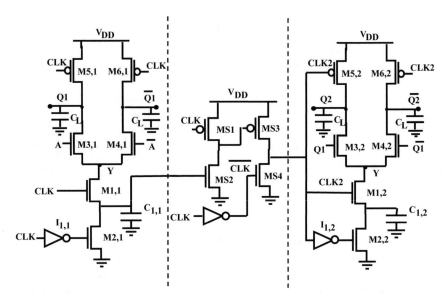

Fig. 4.17 Illustration of the use of STB-1 to cascade two Dy-DCML-NN inverters

and MS4 are ON while transistor MS2 is OFF. The intermediate node is at high level such that transistor MS3 is OFF. This condition ensures that the output of the buffer is at low level and the subsequent stage is also in the precharge phase.

In the evaluation phase, CLK makes a low-to-high transition, the first stage gets evaluated. The capacitor $C_{1,1}$ gets charged, and the transistors MS1 and MS4 are OFF in this condition. The intermediate node is discharged since MS2 is ON and a high level is obtained at the output of STB-1. This transition initiates the evaluation of the subsequent stage and resolves the issue in realizing multi-stage applications by using dynamic CML gates.

The STB-1 uses a clock and its complement generated which restricts its usage in employing it to design multi-stage applications with Dy-DCML-NP and Dy-PFSCL-NP gates. Therefore, in such cases STB-2 is used. Therefore, STB-2 is used to implement in such conditions.

4.5.2   Multi-stage D-CML Design Using STB-2

A cascade of two Dy-DCML-NP inverters with STB-2 in-between them is shown in Fig. 4.18. As discussed in the previous method, CLK signal is applied to the first stage only. During the precharge phase, the output of the first stage is precharged to a high level and the capacitor $C_{1,1}$ gets discharged to one threshold voltage above the ground potential. The MS5 in the configuration further lowers this potential and drives the inverters in the buffer. Since CLK is low, the transistors MS1 is ON and

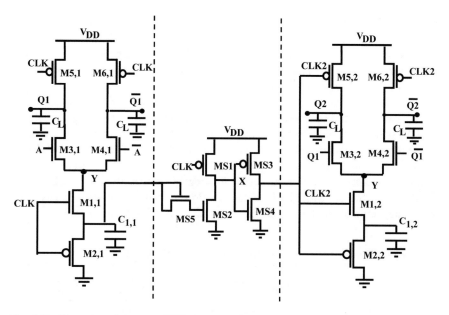

Fig. 4.18 Illustration of the use of STB-2 to cascade two Dy-DCML-NP inverters

MS2 is OFF via MS5. The intermediate node X is charged to a high logic level making STB-2 output as low. This condition ensures that the subsequent stage is also in precharge phase. Conversely, for high value of CLK, C_1 is charged such that the transistors MS5 and MS2 are turned ON. The intermediate node attains a low logic level, consequently making buffer output at high logic level. This satisfies our requirement by allowing the evaluation in the second phase only after the complete evaluation of the preceding stage.

4.6 Performance Comparison with Static Gates

In this section, the performance of the D-CML gates is compared with their static CML counterparts. The performance parameters such as power consumption, propagation delay high-to-low transition (t_{PHL}), propagation delay low-to-high transition (t_{PLH}), and precharge time (t_{pre}) are noted.

4.6.1 Performance Comparison of Differential CML Gates

A set of logic gates is considered for comparing the performance of the Dy-DCML-NP style, Dy-DCML-NN style, and static differential CML style. The

Dy-DCML-NN gates and the Dy-DCML-NP gates are designed for a $V_{SWING} = 400$ mV and load capacitance of 100 fF. The static differential CML circuits maintain a bias current of 100 μA and are designed using the approach described in Chap. 2. The simulation results of the gates are summarized in Table 4.1 and are discussed with respect to the performance parameter.

The examination of power results reveals that out of the three styles, Dy-DCML-NP gates consume the lowest power and offer a maximum power saving of 71% with respect to the static differential CML gates. The simulation results for different timing parameters show that both Dy-DCML-NP and Dy-DCML-NN gates have almost similar precharge time due to the fact that the precharge transistors with same dimensions are taken in simulations. Regarding the high-to-low delay (t_{PHL}), the Dy-MCML-NP gates are slower than the Dy-DCML-NN gates since they employ higher value capacitor C_1 that adds to the delay. Also for

Table 4.1 Performance comparison of the logic gates in differential CML styles

Style	Gate			
	Inverter	2-input NAND	2-input NOR	2-input XOR
Power consumption (μW)				
Static differential CML	252	120	120	120
Dy-DCML-NN	100	101	100	108
Dy-DCML-NP	72	76.8	80	84
Propagation delay high-to-low transition, t_{PHL} *(ps)*				
Static differential CML	520	486	450	500
Dy-DCML-NN	165	175	263	370
Dy-DCML-NP	256	276	300	450
Propagation delay low-to-high transition, t_{PLH} *(ps)*				
Static differential CML	330	388	255	410
Dy-DCML-NN	0	0	0	0
Dy-DCML-NP	0	0	0	0
Precharge time t_{pre} *(ps)*				
Static differential CML	–	–	–	–
Dy-DCML-NN	132	135	131	139
Dy-DCML-NP	130	134	134	138
Improvement in parameters for Dy-DCML-NP gates				
Power saving (%)				
w. r. t. static differential CML	71	36	33	30
w. r. t. Dy-DCML-NN	28	23.4	20	22.2
Propagation delay high-to-low transition, t_{PHL} *(ps) reduction (%)*				
w. r. t. static differential CML	50	44	33	10
w. r. t. Dy-DCML-NN	−55	−59	−14	−21
Precharge time reduction (%)				
w. r. t. Dy-DCML-NN	1.5	0.7	−2.2	−0.7

dynamic circuits, the value of propagation delay low-to-high transition (t_{PLH}) is zero as the output is high at the beginning of evaluation period and no switching at the output takes place for low values of the inputs. Therefore, the results pertaining to propagation delay which is computed as the average of low-to-high transition (t_{PLH}) and low-to-high transition (t_{PHL}) indicate lower value for the Dy-DCML-NN gates in comparison to the static differential CML and Dy-DCML-NP gates. These results confirm the better performance of differential D-CML gates in comparison to the static differential CML gates.

4.6.2 Performance Comparison of PFSCL Gates

The performance of Dy-PFSCL-NN gates and Dy-PFSCL-NP gates is compared with their conventional static PFSCL counterparts. The Dy-PFSCL-NN gates and Dy-PFSCL-NP gates are designed for a $V_{SWING} = 400$ mV and load capacitance of 100 fF. The static PFSCL circuits are designed with a bias current of 100 μA by using the approach outlined in Chap. 2. The simulation results of the gates based on the three logic styles are listed in Table 4.2.

The simulation results are discussed on the basis of performance parameters as done in case of differential CML gates. It can be observed that a power saving of 11–78.5% and 29–79.3% with respect to the static PFSCL style is obtained by using Dy-PFSCL-NN and Dy-PFSCL-NP styles, respectively. Thus, a significant reduction in power consumption can be achieved by adopting the Dy-PFSCL style over static one. The results pertaining to t_{PHL} indicate that the Dy-PFSCL-NN gates show the lowest value as it does not require any additional switching for low input as in static PFSCL gates, as well as use low value capacitor C_1 in comparison to Dy-PFSCL-NN gates.

Table 4.2 Performance comparison of the logic gates in PFSCL styles

Style	Gate				
	Inverter	2-input NOR	3-input NOR	2-input XOR	3-input XOR
Power consumption (μW)					
PFSCL	252	120	120	600	1200
DY-PFSCL-NN	54	96	107	480	960
DY-PFSCL-NP	52	79	85	395	790
Propagation delay high-to-low transition, t_{PHL} (ps)					
PFSCL	518	473	445	1235	1290
DY-PFSCL-NN	93	145	132	450	496
DY-PFSCL-NP	109	186	135	458	501

(continued)

Table 4.2 (continued)

Style	Gate				
	Inverter	2-input NOR	3-input NOR	2-input XOR	3-input XOR
Propagation delay low-to-high transition, t_{PLH} (ps)					
PFSCL	329	371	254	1135	1210
DY-PFSCL-NN	0	0	0	0	0
DY-PFSCL-NP	0	0	0	0	0
Precharge time t_{pre} (ps)					
PFSCL	–	–	–	–	–
DY-PFSCL-NN	111	112	118	250	296
DY-PFSCL-NP	111	111	118	252	298
Improvement in parameters w. r. t. PFSCL gates					
Power saving (%)					
DY-PFSCL-NN	78.5	20	11	20	20
DY-PFSCL-NP	79.3	34.16	29	34	34
Propagation delay high-to-low transition, t_{PHL} (ps) reduction (%)					
DY-PFSCL-NN	82	69.3	70.3	63.5	61.5
DY-PFSCL-NP	78.9	54.9	56.1	60.4	60.2

4.7 Summary

In this chapter, another variant of CML gates namely dynamic CML gates (D-CML) is discussed. The D-CML gate uses dynamic current source instead of constant current source and results in reduced power consumption. Two variants of dynamic current source are available and employ either two NMOS transistors in series (NN) or an NMOS and a PMOS in series (NP) along with a capacitor. For proper operation, NN-dynamic current source uses an additional CMOS inverter that mitigates the advantage of power saving. The NP-dynamic current source does not require CMOS inverter. Differential CML and PFSCL gates are designed using dynamic current sources.

An in-depth analysis of the power consumption is also presented. It is found that the power consumption of dynamic PFSCL gates is data dependent. Dynamic CML digital logic gates are implemented, and their performance is compared with static CML gates through simulations. It is found that the dynamic CML gates show a significant reduction in power consumption. For multi-stage applications with D-CML gates, self-timed buffer is an essential component and its internal structure is different for NN-dynamic and NP-dynamic current sources. Its use in the design of multi-stage applications is elaborated.

References

1. M.H. Anis, M.I. Elmasry, Self-timed MOS current mode logic for digital applications, in Proceedings of IEEE International Symposium on Circuits and Systems (2002), pp. 113–116
2. J.B. Kim, Low-power MCML circuit with sleep-transistor, in Proceedings of IEEE International Conference on Application-Specific Integrated Circuits (2009), pp. 25–28
3. K. Zou, J. Hu, A power-gating scheme for MOS current mode logic circuits. Telkomnika **11** (10), 6111–6119 (2013)
4. M.W. Allam, M.I. Elmasry, Dynamic current mode logic (DyMCML): a new low-power high performance logic style. IEEE J. Solid-State Circuits **36**(3), 550–558 (2001)
5. G. Caruso, D. Sclafani, Analysis of compressor architectures in MOS current-mode logic, in Proceedings of IEEE International Conference on Electronics, Circuits, and Systems, Athens (2010), pp. 13–16
6. K. Gupta, N. Pandey, M. Gupta, Dynamic positive-feedback source-coupled logic (D-PFSCL). Int. J. Electron. **103**(10), 1626–1638 (2016). Taylor and Francis, reprinted by permission of the publisher (Taylor and Francis Ltd., http://www.tandfonline.com)
7. M. Alioto, G. Palumbo, *Model and Design of Bipolar and MOS Current-Mode logic (CML, ECL and SCL Digital Circuits)* (Kluwer Academic Publications, 2005)
8. J.M. Rabaey, A. Chandrakasan, B. Nikolic, *Digital Integrated Circuits*, 2nd edn. (Pearson Education, 2003)
9. M. Alioto, L. Pancioni, S. Rocchi, V. Vignoli, Modeling and evaluation of positive-feedback source-coupled logic. IEEE Trans. Circuits Syst.-I, Regul. Pap. **51**(4), 2345–2355 (2004)

Chapter 5
CML Gates with Modified Load

5.1 Introduction

The proliferation of efficient telecommunication networks, high-speed microprocessors, and memories has rekindled interest in electronics devices and systems. High-capacity channels and high-speed digital transceiver circuits are needed in communication system designs. CML gates, since the early days of digital integrated circuits, are used to implement high-speed digital circuits. However, to meet the increasing rate of data transmission, it is necessary to improve the speed of CML gates. The load section in a CML gate plays an important role in determining the speed and is therefore worked upon. In this chapter, a brief description on available loads for CML gate is presented and out of them the one which is most suited for high-speed applications is studied and an in-depth analysis is carried out. Its usage and benefits are explored for both differential CML and PFSCL gates. The mathematical formulations are put forward to model their behavior. Basic digital logic gates are implemented and the improvement in performance is compared with the other loads.

5.2 Available Loads

The load section in a CML gate performs the current-to-voltage conversion and determines the speed of the circuit. Conventionally, a passive resistor as shown in Fig. 5.1a is employed as load but due to the large implementation area requirement, the use of active loads is preferred. A MOS transistor operating in saturation or linear region can be used as load [1]. A diode-connected NMOS transistor and PMOS current source, as drawn in Fig. 5.1b, c, are few loads that operate in saturation region. These loads are not suited for high-speed digital circuits due to their large resistance leading to large propagation delay values. Alternatively, a

© Springer Nature Singapore Pte Ltd. 2020
K. Gupta et al., *Model and Design of Improved Current Mode Logic Gates*, https://doi.org/10.1007/978-981-15-0982-7_5

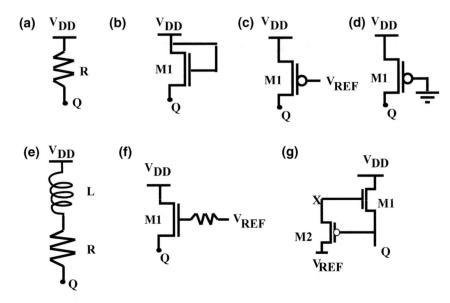

Fig. 5.1 Available loads for a CML gate **a** passive resistor, **b** diode-connected transistor, **c** current source, **d** transistor in linear region, **e** series-connected passive inductor and resistor, **f** active inductor, and **g** NP-load

PMOS transistor operating in linear region shown in Fig. 5.1d is generally used as load in CML gates. Its gate is connected to the ground potential to ensure operation in linear region for all output range. Additionally, the resistance is independent of substrate bias effect [2].

Besides the above conventional loads, other options can also be explored. To fulfil the purpose, it is recollected that the basic building block of a CML gate is a differential amplifier. The techniques developed to improve the circuit performance of a differential amplifier are reviewed. It is found that shunt-peaking technique is used in differential amplifier to improve its bandwidth. It places a passive inductor in series with the resistor for the purpose (Fig. 5.1e) [3]. This technique when applied to CML gate results in speed improvement. Several restrictions such as large component size and lengthier design process are imposed due to passive inductor; therefore, use of active inductor (Fig. 5.1f) is recommended. This active inductor realization employs a NMOS transistor with its gate connected to separate supply via passive resistor [4–10]. However, the passive resistor in this arrangement makes it unattractive from integrated circuit viewpoint. An alternate load employing a NMOS transistor $M1$ and a PMOS transistor $M2$ as shown in Fig. 5.1g is suggested in [11–13]. It is referred to as NP-load and is suitable for integrated circuit design as it does not involve any passive component. The CML gates using the NP-load are designed and analyzed in the chapter. A discussion on differential CML gates having NP-load is first presented which is followed by the PFSCL gates designed using the NP-load.

5.3 NP-Load

The configuration of NP-load having an NMOS transistor $M1$ and a PMOS transistor $M2$ [12, 13] is shown in Fig. 5.1g. The drain and the source terminals of transistor $M1$ are connected to the power supply and node Q, respectively. The gate of transistor $M2$ is connected to node Q, whereas its source terminal is connected to a reference voltage source V_{REF}. The voltage of the reference source V_{REF} is made one threshold voltage greater than the power supply V_{DD}. The load exhibits capacitive coupling during the transition at node Q. The mathematical formulation about the capacitive coupling phenomenon and the resistance offered by NP-load are derived.

5.3.1 Analysis of NP-Load

The NP-load is analyzed by identifying the transistor parasitic capacitances. The load along with the associated capacitances [12, 13] is shown in Fig. 5.2 where C_{gd_i}, C_{db_i}, and C_{gs_i} represent the gate-to-drain capacitance, drain–bulk capacitance, and gate-to-source capacitance of the ith ($i = 1, 2$) transistor, respectively. To simplify the analysis, the capacitances between node Q and intermediate node X is represented as coupling capacitance C_C. From the figure, it is clear that it is expressed as the sum of gate-to-source capacitance of $M1$ (C_{gs_1}) and gate-to-drain capacitance of $M2$ (C_{gd_2}). The capacitances between node X and ground is represented as intermediate node capacitance C_X and can be expressed as sum of gate-to-drain capacitance of $M1$ (C_{gd_1}) and drain–bulk capacitance of $M2$ (C_{db_2}).

Now, assuming that node Q makes a low-to-high transition, the voltage changes at node Q gets coupled to node X through the coupling capacitance C_C. Let i_{C_C} and i_{C_X} be the transient currents flowing through C_C and C_X, respectively. By applying

Fig. 5.2 Parasitic capacitances in NP-load [12, 13]

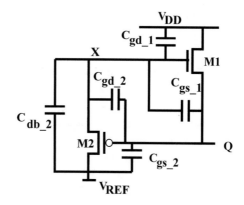

KCL and assuming that negligible current flows in transistor $M2$, the current equation at node X can be written as:

$$i_{C_C} - i_{C_X} \approx 0 \tag{5.1}$$

Substituting the current values,

$$C_X \frac{dV_X}{dt} \approx C_C \frac{d(V_Q - V_X)}{dt} \tag{5.2}$$

where V_Q and V_X represent the voltages of the nodes Q and X, respectively. Equation (5.2) can be rearranged as:

$$\frac{dV_X}{dt} = \frac{C_C}{C_C + C_X} \frac{dV_Q}{dt} \tag{5.3}$$

The above equation verifies the observed phenomenon that changes in voltage of node X follows the change in the node Q voltage. The solution [12] of Eq. (5.3) can be found by integrating both the sides as:

$$\int_{V_{REF}}^{V_X(t)} dV_X = \left(\frac{C_C}{C_C + C_X} \right) \int_{V_Q(0)}^{V_Q(t)} dV_Q dt \tag{5.4}$$

The evaluation of the integral yields

$$V_X(t) = V_{REF} + m[V_Q(t) - V_Q(0)] \tag{5.5}$$

where $m = \frac{C_C}{C_C + C_X}$ represents the capacitance ratio and $V_{REF} = V_{DD} + V_{T,N}$ [12]. The above equation expresses the voltage of node X in terms of voltage transitions on node Q. It can be also be inferred that for a rising transition at node Q, the intermediate node X will have voltage greater than V_{REF} since $V_Q(t) > V_Q(0)$. Analogously, for falling transitions at node Q as $(V_Q(t) < V_Q(0))$, node X potential will be lower than V_{REF}.

5.3.2 Resistance of NP-Load

After an insight to the capacitive coupling phenomenon in NP-load, it is now necessary to evaluate its resistance for further analysis. A basic CML gate employing the NP-load is shown in Fig. 5.3. It is clear that the output nodes makes a transition from V_{DD} to $V_{DD} - 0.5V_{SWING}$ or $V_{DD} - 0.5V_{SWING}$ to V_{DD}, i.e., $V_{DD} > V_Q > V_{DD} - 0.5V_{SWING}$ where $V_{SWING} \leq 2V_{T,N}$. Due to capacitive coupling phenomenon, the voltage of node X exceeds the power supply voltage atleast by

Fig. 5.3 Differential
CML-CC inverter

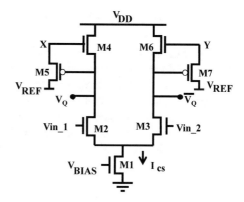

$V_{T,N}$; therefore, the transistor $M1$ operates in the linear region. Thus, the resistance of the NP-load is calculated by using the standard BSIM3v3 MOSFET model parameters as:

$$R_{\mathrm{NP}} = \frac{R_{\mathrm{int}}}{1 - \frac{(R_{\mathrm{DSW}}10^{-6})/W_N}{R_{\mathrm{int}}}} \tag{5.6}$$

where R_{DSW} is the empirical model parameter, W_N is the effective channel width of transistor $M1$, and the parameter R_{int} is the intrinsic resistance of the NMOS transistor in the linear region and is given as:

$$R_{\mathrm{int}} = \left[\mu_{\mathrm{eff},n} C_{\mathrm{ox}} \frac{W_N}{L_N} \left(V_{\mathrm{REF}} - V_{\mathrm{DD}} + 0.5 V_{\mathrm{SWING}} - V_{T,N} \right) \right]^{-1} \tag{5.7}$$

where the parameters $V_{T,N}$ and L_N are the threshold voltage and the effective channel length of transistor $M1$, respectively. The NP-load is used to design differential CML and PFSCL gates and the corresponding gates are referred to as differential CML-CC and PFSCL-CC gates. The suffix CC represents the underlying capacitive coupling phenomenon.

5.4 Differential CML Gates with NP-Load (CML-CC)

The schematic of a differential CML-CC inverter [12] is shown in Fig. 5.3. The PDN ($M2$–$M3$) and the current source ($M1$) are the same as used in conventional CML inverter. The transistor ($M4$, $M5$) and ($M6$, $M7$) forms the NP-load. The operation, analysis, and design of the differential CML-CC inverter are described below.

5.4.1   Operation of Differential CML-CC Inverter

As explained in Sect. 5.3.2, the NP-load behaves as a resistor, and therefore, the differential CML-CC inverter operates in the same manner as a conventional differential CML inverter. However, the benefit of NP-load is visible during the switching event at the output nodes. For a low-to-high transition at the output node Q, the charges are coupled to node X due to capacitive coupling which produces a larger gate-to-source voltage at node X than if it is biased at fixed potential in accordance with Eq. (5.5). This accelerates the charging process and results in the speed improvement.

5.4.2   Analysis of Differential CML-CC Inverter

The differential CML-CC inverter is analyzed in terms of static and delay parameters. For an inverter (Fig. 5.3), the differential input (v_{in_d}) and output (v_{out_d}) voltages are defined as:

$$v_{in\_d} = v_{in\_1} - v_{in\_2} \tag{5.8a}$$

$$v_{out\_d} = v_Q - \overline{v_Q} = R_{NP}(i_{D\_M3} - i_{D\_M2}) \tag{5.8b}$$

5.4.2.1   Static Model

The static behavior is modeled in terms of voltage swing, small-signal voltage gain, noise margin, and power. The output voltage corresponding to high and low values of differential input voltage are first derived. For the case, when differential input voltage v_{in_d} is high, i.e., when $v_{in\_1} > v_{in\_2}$, the bias current I_{CS} flows through $M2$. Therefore, by substituting $i_{D\_M2} = I_{CS}$ and $i_{D\_M3} = 0$ in Eq. (5.8b), low differential output voltage $(v_{out\_d} = V_{OL})$ is derived as:

$$V_{OL} = -I_{CS}R_{NP} \tag{5.9}$$

Similarly, for low value of differential input $v_{in\_1} < v_{in\_2}$, the bias current I_{CS} gets steered to transistor $M3$. This condition yields a high differential output voltage $(v_{out\_d} = V_{OH})$ whose expression is found by substituting $i_{D\_M2} = 0$ and $i_{D\_M3} = I_{CS}$ in Eq. (5.8b)

$$V_{OH} = I_{CS}R_{NP} \tag{5.10}$$

The above equations are verified through VTC of differential CML-CC inverter plotted in Fig. 5.4. It is to be noted that the characteristic is symmetrical around a logic threshold voltage $V_{LT} = 0$.

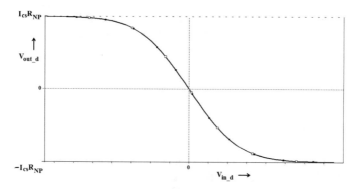

Fig. 5.4 Voltage transfer characteristic of a differential CML inverter

From the above two expressions, the voltage swing (V_{SWING}) is found as:

$$V_{\text{SWING}} = V_{\text{OH}} - V_{\text{OL}} = 2I_{\text{CS}}R_{\text{NP}} \quad (5.11)$$

The small-signal voltage gain (A_{v_cc}) is the gain evaluated around the logic threshold voltage. As the differential CML-CC gate is symmetric and has fully differential inputs therefore in accordance with half circuit concept, A_{v_cc} around the logic threshold voltage is computed as:

$$A_{v\_cc} = g_{m,n}R_{\text{NP}} = R_{\text{NP}}\sqrt{2\mu_{\text{eff},n}C_{\text{ox}}\frac{W_N}{L_N}\frac{I_{\text{CS}}}{2}} \quad (5.12)$$

where $g_{m,n}$ is defined as the transconductance and is substituted as $\sqrt{\mu_{\text{eff},n}C_{\text{ox}}\frac{W_N}{L_N}I_{\text{CS}}}$.

Using Eq. (5.11), to replace R_{NP}, we get the resulting expression of A_{v_cc} as:

$$A_{v\_cc} = \frac{V_{\text{SWING}}}{2}\sqrt{\mu_{\text{eff},n}C_{\text{ox}}\frac{W_N}{L_N}\frac{1}{I_{\text{CS}}}} \quad (5.13)$$

The VTC of CML-CC inverter is symmetric; therefore, the noise margin (NM) for low and high signal value (NM_L and NM_H) are equal [14]. By following the same procedure as conventional differential CML inverter, NM is calculated as:

$$\text{NM} = \frac{V_{\text{SWING}}}{2}\left(1 - \frac{\sqrt{2}}{A_{v\_cc}}\right) \quad (5.14)$$

Further, the present constant current source results in static power consumption which is computed as the product of bias current I_{CS} and the power supply voltage V_{DD}.

$$P = V_{DD}I_{CS} \tag{5.15}$$

5.4.2.2   Delay Model

The delay of the differential CML-CC inverter is computed by solving the state equation of the output node in the time domain [14]. The half circuit of the CML-CC inverter with the parasitic capacitances of the transistors is shown in Fig. 5.5a where C_{out} represents the output capacitance that includes the interconnect capacitance and the input capacitance of the subsequent stage. The total capacitance at the output node C_{L_CML} is shown in Fig. 5.5b which is computed as:

$$C_{L\_CML} = C_{gd\_2} + C_{db\_2} + C_{gs\_5} + C_{gd\_5} + C_{gs\_4} + C_{out} \tag{5.16}$$

where C_{gd_i}, C_{db_i}, and C_{gs_i} represent the gate-to-drain capacitance, drain–bulk capacitance, and gate-to-source capacitance of the ith ($i = 2, 4, 5$) transistor [12]. The current through capacitor C_{L_CML} is computed as the difference of drain currents flowing through the transistors $M4$ and $M2$ and may be written as:

$$C_{L\_CML} \frac{dV_Q}{dt} = i_{C_{L\_CML}} = i_{D\_M4} - i_{D\_M2} \tag{5.17}$$

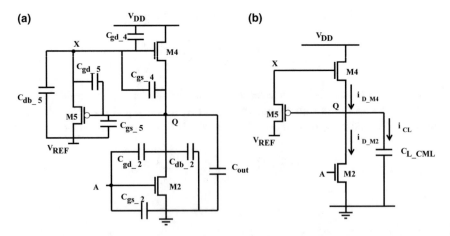

Fig. 5.5 Half circuit of the differential CML-CC inverter [12] **a** with all parasitic capacitances and **b** with total capacitance, C_{L_CML}

When the input switches from high-to-low logic level, the current through transistor $M2$ reduces to zero which allows C_{L_CML} to be charged through transistor $M4$. Thus, Eq. (5.17) reduces to

$$C_{L\_CML} \frac{dV_Q}{dt} = i_{D\_M4} \qquad (5.18)$$

The rising output voltage initiates the process of capacitive coupling in the load circuit. It is clear from Eq. (5.5) that the gate potential of $M4$ remains greater than or equal to V_{REF} during the charging process; hence, transistor $M4$ operates in linear region throughout the switching process. Therefore, the delay t_{PD} [12] may be calculated by solving Eq. (5.18) as:

$$t_{PD} = \int_{t_0}^{t_1} dt = C_{L\_CML} \int_{V_0}^{V_1} \left(\frac{1}{i_{D\_4}} \right) dV_Q \qquad (5.19)$$

Substituting i_{D_M4} results in

$$t_{PD} = \frac{2C_{L\_CML}}{k_{n,4}} \int_{V_0}^{V_1} \left(\frac{1}{\left[2(V_X - V_Q - V_{T,N})(V_{DD} - V_Q) - (V_{DD} - V_Q)^2 \right]} \right) dV_Q \qquad (5.20)$$

where $k_{n,4}$ is the device transconductance of transistor $M4$.

Substituting V_X from Eq. (5.5), the delay expression becomes

$$t_{PD} = \frac{2\,C_{L\_CML}}{k_{n,4}} \int_{V_0}^{V_1} \left(\frac{1}{(V_{DD} - V_Q)[V_{DD} + (2m - 1)V_Q - 2m\,V_Q(0)]} \right) dV_Q \qquad (5.21)$$

Evaluating the integral yields

$$t_{PD} = \frac{C_{L\_CML}}{2k_{n,4}} \frac{1}{m(V_{DD} - V_0)} \ln \frac{V_{DD} + 2m(V_1 - V_0) - V_1}{V_{DD} - V_1} \qquad (5.22)$$

5.4.3 Design of Differential CML-CC Inverter

The inverter is designed for a given value of bias current I_{CS} and noise margin NM. For a specified value of NM, and assuming $A_{v\_cc}(\geq 1.4)$, the voltage swing is calculated using Eq. (5.14) as:

$$V_{\text{SWING}} = \frac{2NM}{1 - \frac{\sqrt{2}}{A_{v\_cc}}} \tag{5.23}$$

The voltage swing obtained from Eq. (5.23) requires sizing of the transistor $M4$, $M6$ with equivalent resistance $R_{\text{NP}}\left(= \frac{V_{\text{SWING}}}{2I_{\text{CS}}}\right)$. For this, the equivalent resistance, $R_{\text{NP\_MIN}}$, for the minimum-sized NMOS transistor is determined first and then the bias current I_{HIGH} for the required voltage swing is determined as:

$$I_{\text{HIGH}} = \frac{V_{\text{SWING}}}{2R_{\text{NP\_MIN}}} \tag{5.24}$$

If the bias current is higher than I_{HIGH}, then R_{NP} should be less than $R_{\text{NP\_MIN}}$, and this is achieved by setting L_N to its minimum value, i.e., L_{MIN}. The width W_N can therefore is calculated by solving Eqs. (5.6) and (5.7) as:

$$W_N = \frac{2I_{\text{CS}}}{V_{\text{SWING}}} \frac{L_{\text{MIN}}}{\mu_{\text{eff},n}C_{\text{ox}}(V_{\text{REF}} - V_{\text{DD}} + 0.5V_{\text{SWING}} - V_{T,N})\left\{1 - \frac{R_{\text{DSW}}10^{-6}}{L_{\text{MIN}}}\left[\mu_{\text{eff},n}C_{\text{ox}}(V_{\text{REF}} - V_{\text{DD}} + 0.5V_{\text{SWING}} - V_{T,N})\right]\right\}} \tag{5.25}$$

Similarly, if the bias current is lower than I_{HIGH}, then R_{NP} is made greater than $R_{\text{NP\_MIN}}$. This requires setting W_N to its minimum value, i.e., W_{MIN} and to determine L_N by solving Eqs. (5.6) and (5.7) as:

$$L_N = W_{\text{MIN}}\mu_{\text{eff},n}C_{\text{ox}}(V_{\text{REF}} - V_{\text{DD}} + 0.5V_{\text{SWING}} - V_{T,N})\left(\frac{V_{\text{SWING}}}{2I_{\text{CS}}} - \frac{R_{\text{DSW}}10^{-6}}{W_{\text{MIN}}}\right) \tag{5.26}$$

The dimensions of transistor $M5$ is set by following the simulation-based approach for the given specification. The small-signal voltage gain (A_{v_cc}) given in Eq. (5.13) decides the size of transistors $M2$, $M3$. Assuming minimum channel length for the said transistors, the width is computed as:

$$W_N = \frac{4}{\mu_{\text{eff},n}C_{\text{ox}}}\left(\frac{A_{v\_cc}}{V_{\text{SWING}}}\right)^2 I_{\text{CS}}L_{\text{MIN}} \tag{5.27}$$

Equation (5.27) sometimes results in a value of W_N smaller than the minimum channel width. In all these cases also, W_N is set to W_{MIN}. This happens when the bias current is lower than the current of the minimum-sized NMOS transistor, I_{LOW} Using Eq. (5.13), I_{LOW} is given as:

$$I_{\text{LOW}} = \frac{1}{4}\frac{W_{\text{MIN}}}{L_{\text{MIN}}}\mu_{\text{eff},n}C_{\text{ox}}\left(\frac{V_{\text{SWING}}}{A_{v\_cc}}\right)^2 \tag{5.28}$$

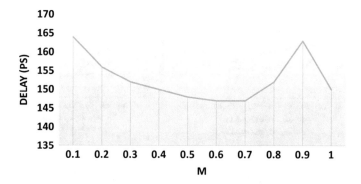

Fig. 5.6 Propagation delay versus m for differential CML-CC inverter

The theoretical propositions are validated through SPICE simulations with a power supply of 1.8 V. The differential CML-CC inverter is designed for $A_{v\_cc} = 2$, NM = 130 mV, $I_{CS} = 100$ μA, and $C_{L\_CML} = 50$ fF. A plot of the simulated delay for various values of m is shown in Fig. 5.6. It is found out that the value of m = 0.6 results in minimum delay and therefore is chosen as the optimum value.

The behavior of differential CML-CC inverter during the switching is verified through simulations for the above conditions. The simulated waveforms for the input A, node X, and output Q are shown in Fig. 5.7. It can be observed that a low-to-high transition at the output node Q subsequently results in an increased voltage of node X. This confirms the relation Eq. (5.5) between voltages at node Q and X.

The accuracy of the analytical model is verified by designing and simulating the differential CML-CC inverter for wide range of operating conditions—voltage swing of 400 and 800 mV, small-signal voltage gain of 2 and 4, and the bias current

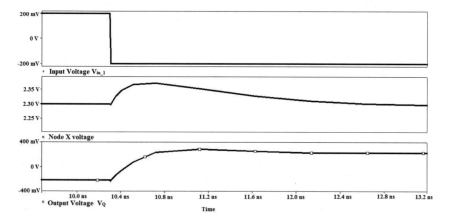

Fig. 5.7 Simulation waveforms at different nodes of differential CML-CC inverter

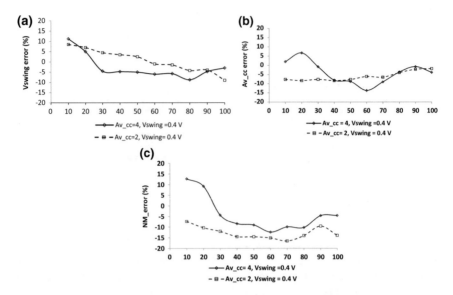

Fig. 5.8 Errors in the static parameters of the CML-CC inverter **a** voltage swing, **b** small-signal voltage gain, and **c** noise margin

ranging from 10 to 100 µA. The error plots in the simulated values of static parameters with respect to the predicted values in particular for small-signal voltage gain of 2 and voltage swing of 400 mV are shown in Figs. 5.8a–c. It may be noted that maximum error in voltage swing, small-signal voltage gain, and noise margin are 11%, 13%, and 13%, respectively. It is found that there is a close agreement between the simulated and the predicted values of static parameters for all the operating conditions.

The accuracy of the delay model is validated for load capacitance of 0, 10, and 100 fF. The simulated and the predicted delay in particular for NM = 130 mV, A_{v_cc} = 2, and with different load capacitances are plotted in Fig. 5.9. A close agreement between the simulated and the predicted delay for all the operating conditions is witnessed.

5.4.4   Performance Comparison

Several logic gates such as inverter, two input AND/NAND, 2:1 MUX, full adder, and a D latch are implemented in the differential CML-CC style and the differential CML style with resistor, PMOS and the inductor (passive and the active inductor) as loads. All the gates operate with a power supply, bias current, noise margin, and small-signal gain of 1.8 V, 100 µA, 130 mV, and 4, respectively. It may be noted that since all the circuits are implemented with the same supply voltage and bias

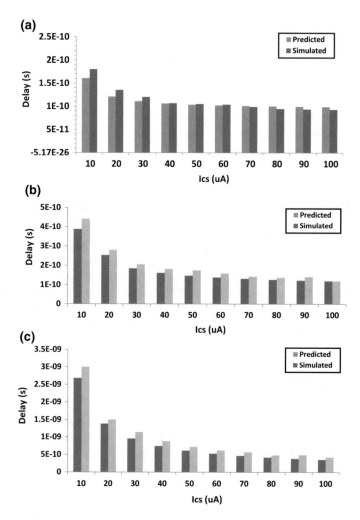

Fig. 5.9 Simulated and predicted delays of the differential CML-CC inverter versus Ics with NM = 130 mV, $A_{v\_cc} = 2$ for different C_{L_CML} values **a** 0 fF, **b** 10 fF, **c** 100 fF

current, all of these consume same static power computed as the product of the supply voltage and bias current [12]. The simulated values for the delay are listed in Table 5.1. It can be observed that the passive inductor topology shows the maximum improvement in delay, followed by the CML-CC topology. The CML-CC gates show a maximum delay improvement of 21% with respect to the conventional CML inverter having PMOS load.

Table 5.1 Comparison in propagation delay (ps) of differential CML circuits with different loads

Circuit		Load				
		Resistor	PMOS	Spiral inductor	Active inductor	NP-load
Inverter		142	148	122	140	135
AND/NAND		150	158	128	145	142
2:1 MUX		175	193	149	169	153
Full adder	Sum	327	367	289	301	295
	Carry	332	381	290	322	301
D latch		195	225	161	191	181

5.5   PFSCL Gates with Modified NP-Load (PFSCL-CC)

The basic structure of PFSCL-CC gates remains the same as that of conventional PFSCL gates. The difference exists only in terms of the load. The schematic of a PFSCL-CC inverter [13] is shown in Fig. 5.10. The PDN ($M2$–$M3$) and the current source ($M1$) are same as in conventional PFSCL inverter. The transistors ($M4$, $M5$) in NP-load replace the PMOS load used in conventional one. The operation, analysis, and design of the PFSCL-CC inverter are discussed below.

5.5.1   Operation of PFSCL-CC Inverter

The behavior of PFSCL-CC inverter remains the same as that of a conventional PFSCL inverter since NP-load behaves as a resistor as explained in Sect. 5.3.2. However, the benefit of NP-load is visible during the switching event at the output node. For a low-to-high transition at the output node, the capacitive coupling occurs

Fig. 5.10 PFSCL-CC
inverter [13]

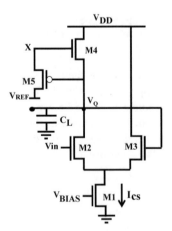

and a larger gate-to-source voltage is produced at node X than if the gate was connected to a fixed potential thus confirming the relation depicted in Eq. (5.5). The increase in gate voltage accelerates the charging process and results in the speed improvement.

5.5.2 Analysis of PFSCL-CC Inverter

The behavior of the PFSCL-CC inverter is analyzed in terms of static and delay model and is presented below.

5.5.2.1 Static Model

The static behavior is modeled in terms of voltage swing, small-signal voltage gain, noise margin, and power. The voltage transfer characteristics of the PFSCL-CC inverter is plotted in Fig. 5.11 and is found to be symmetrical around the logic threshold voltage $V_{LT} = V_{DD} - R_{NP}I_{CS}/2$. In accordance with the operation of the inverter, the high (V_{OH}) and low (V_{OL}) output voltages can be expressed as:

$$V_{OH} = V_{DD} \tag{5.29a}$$

$$V_{OL} = V_{DD} - I_{CS}R_{NP} \tag{5.29b}$$

From the above two expressions, the voltage swing (V_{SWING}) is calculated as:

$$V_{SWING} = V_{OH} - V_{OL} = I_{CS}R_{NP} \tag{5.30}$$

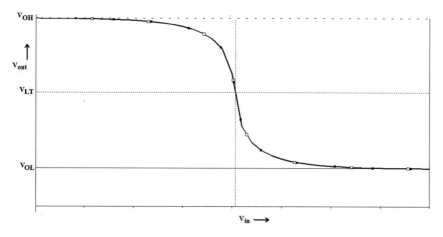

Fig. 5.11 Voltage transfer characteristic of a PFSCL-CC inverter

The small-signal voltage gain $(A_{v\_p\_cc})$ is evaluated around the logic threshold voltage. By following the superposition theorem, the value of $A_{v\_p\_cc}$ around the logic threshold voltage is computed as:

$$A_{v\_p\_cc} = \frac{g_{m,n}R_{NP}/2}{1 - g_{m,n}R_{NP}/2} \tag{5.31}$$

where $g_{m,n}$ is the transconductance of the NMOS transistor computed around the logic threshold as $\sqrt{\mu_{\mathrm{eff},n} C_{\mathrm{ox}} \frac{W_N}{L_N} I_{CS}}$.

The noise margin (NM) by considering $g_{m,n}R_{NP}/2 < 1$ is computed as:

$$\mathrm{NM} = \frac{V_{\mathrm{SWING}}}{2}\left(1 - \frac{1}{A_{v\_p\_cc}}\right) \tag{5.32}$$

Further, the presence of constant current source results in static power consumption which is computed as the product of bias current I_{CS} and the power supply voltage V_{DD} and can be written as:

$$P = V_{DD}I_{CS} \tag{5.33}$$

5.5.2.2 Delay Model

As followed for differential CML-CC gates, the delay of PFSCL-CC inverter is computed by solving the state equation of the output node in the time domain [14]. The total capacitance at the output node C_{L_PFSCL} is shown in Fig. 5.12 and is computed as:

$$C_{L\_PFSCL} = C_{gd\_2} + C_{db\_2} + C_{gs\_4} + C_{gd\_5} + C_{gs\_5} + C_{gd\_3} + 0.5C_{gs\_3} + C_{\mathrm{out}} \tag{5.34}$$

where C_{gd_i}, C_{db_i}, and C_{gs_i} represent the gate-drain capacitance, drain–bulk capacitance, and gate-source capacitance of the ith (i = 2, 3, 4, 5) transistor, respectively, and C_{out} accounts for the interconnect capacitance and the input capacitance of the subsequent stage. By neglecting the gate currents of transistor $M3$ and $M5$, the current through capacitor C_{L_PFSCL} may be written as:

$$C_{L\_PFSCL}\frac{dV_Q}{dt} = i_{C_{L\_PFSCL}} = i_{D\_M4} - i_{D\_M2} \tag{5.35}$$

where i_{D_Mi} represents the drain current of ith transistor.

To simplify the analysis, the condition when the input switches from high-to-low logic level is examined. The current through transistor $M2$ becomes zero such that

Fig. 5.12 PFSCL-CC
inverter with load
capacitance, C_{L_PFSCL}

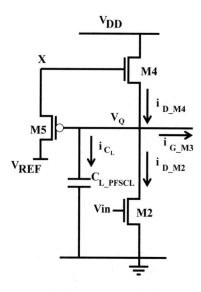

C_{L_PFSCL} begins to charge through the load transistor $M4$. Thus, Eq. (5.35) reduces to

$$C_{L\_PFSCL} \frac{dV_Q}{dt} = i_{D\_M4} \qquad (5.36)$$

The rising output voltage initiates the process of capacitive coupling in the load circuit. It is clear from Eq. (5.5) that the gate potential of $M4$ remains greater than or equal to V_{REF} during the charging process, and hence, $M4$ operates in linear region throughout the switching process. Therefore, the delay t_{PD} may be calculated by solving Eq. (5.36) as:

$$t_{PD} = \int_{t_0}^{t_1} dt = C_{L\_PFSCL} \int_{V_0}^{V_1} \left(\frac{1}{i_{D\_M4}} \right) dV_Q \qquad (5.37)$$

Substituting i_{D_M4} results in

$$t_{PD} = \frac{2\,C_{L\_PFSCL}}{k_{n,4}} \int_{V_0}^{V_1} \left(\frac{1}{\left[2(V_X - V_Q - V_T)(V_{DD} - V_Q) - (V_{DD} - V_Q)^2 \right]} \right) dV_Q \qquad (5.38)$$

where $k_{n,4}$ is the device transconductance parameter of transistor $M4$. Evaluating the integral by substituting V_X from Eq. (5.5) yields

$$t_{PD} = \frac{C_{L\_PFSCL}}{2k_{n,4}} \frac{1}{m(V_{DD} - V_0)} \ln \frac{V_{DD} + 2m(V_1 - V_0) - V_1}{V_1 - V_0} \tag{5.39}$$

5.5.3   Design of PFSCL-CC Inverter

The PFSCL-CC inverter is designed for a given values of the bias current I_{CS} and noise margin NM. In this design procedure, the value of $g_{m,n}R_{NP}/2$ is set to unity, i.e., $g_{m,n}R_{NP}/2 = 1$. For a specified value of NM, the voltage swing is calculated using Eqs. (5.31) and (5.32) as:

$$V_{SWING} = 2NM \tag{5.40}$$

The voltage swing obtained from Eq. (5.40) requires sizing of the load transistor with equivalent resistance $R_{NP}\left(= \frac{V_{SWING}}{I_{CS}}\right)$. To this end, the equivalent resistance, R_{NP_MIN}, for the minimum-sized NMOS transistor is first determined and then the bias current I_{HIGH} for the required voltage swing is determined as:

$$I_{HIGH} = \frac{V_{SWING}}{R_{NP\_MIN}} \tag{5.41}$$

If the bias current is higher than I_{HIGH}, then R_{NP} should be less than R_{NP_MIN} and this is achieved by setting L_N to its minimum value, i.e., L_{MIN} and W_N which is calculated by solving Eqs. (5.6) and (5.7) as:

$$W_N = \frac{I_{CS}}{V_{SWING}} \frac{L_{MIN}}{\mu_{eff,n} C_{ox} (V_{REF} - V_{DD} + 0.5V_{SWING} - V_{T,N}) \left\{1 - \frac{R_{DSW}10^{-6}}{L_{MIN}} \left[\mu_{eff,n} C_{ox} (V_{REF} - V_{DD} + 0.5V_{SWING} - V_{T,N})\right]\right\}}. \tag{5.42}$$

Similarly, if the bias current is lower than I_{HIGH}, then R_{NP} should be greater than R_{NP_MIN} and this is achieved by setting W_N to its minimum value, i.e., W_{MIN} and L_N which is calculated by solving Eqs. (5.6) and (5.7) as:

$$L_N = W_{MIN}\mu_{eff,n} C_{ox} (V_{REF} - V_{DD} + 0.5V_{SWING} - V_{T,N}) \left(\frac{V_{SWING}}{I_{CS}} - \frac{R_{DSW}10^{-6}}{W_{MIN}}\right) \tag{5.43}$$

Assuming minimum channel length for the said transistors, $g_{m,n}R_{NP}/2 = 1$ and using Eq. (5.27), the width is computed as:

$$W_N = \frac{4}{\mu_{\text{eff},n} C_{\text{ox}}} \frac{I_{\text{CS}} L_{\text{MIN}}}{V_{\text{SWING}}^2} \tag{5.44}$$

Sometimes Eq. (5.44) results in a value of W_N smaller than the minimum channel width. Therefore, in such cases, W_N is also set to W_{MIN}. This happens when the bias current is lower than the current of the minimum-sized NMOS transistor, I_{LOW}. Using Eq. (5.44), I_{LOW} is given as:

$$I_{\text{LOW}} = \frac{1}{4} \frac{W_{\text{MIN}}}{L_{\text{MIN}}} \mu_{\text{eff},n} C_{\text{ox}} V_{\text{SWING}}^2 \tag{5.45}$$

The theoretical propositions are validated through SPICE simulations with a power supply of 1.8 V. The PFSCL-CC inverter is designed for $A_{\text{v\_p\_cc}} = 0.9$, $V_{\text{SWING}} = 400$ mV, $I_{\text{CS}} = 100$ μA, and $C_L = 50$ fF. A plot of the simulated delay for various values of m is shown in Fig. 5.13. It is found out that the value of $m = 0.7$ results in minimum delay and therefore is chosen as the optimum value.

The behavior of PFSCL-CC inverter is verified for capacitive coupling during the switching event through simulation for the above condition. The simulated waveforms for the input A, node X, and output Q are shown in Fig. 5.14. It can be observed that the voltage of node X increases for a low-to-high transition at the output node Q thus confirming the relation expressed in Eq. (5.5).

The accuracy of the analytical model is verified by designing and simulating inverter for wide range of operating conditions—voltage swing of 300 and 400 mV, small-signal voltage gain of 0.9 and 0.95, and the bias current ranging from 10 to 100 μA. The error plots in the simulated values of static parameters with respect to the predicted values in particular for small-signal voltage gain of 0.9, 0.95, and voltage swing of 0.4 V are shown in Fig. 5.15a–c. It may be noted that maximum error in voltage swing, small-signal voltage gain, and noise margin are 12%, 14%, and 13%, respectively. It is found that there is a close agreement between the

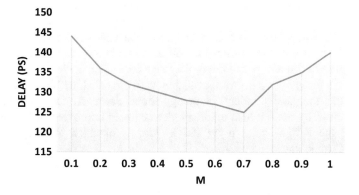

Fig. 5.13 Propagation delay versus m for the PFSCL-CC inverter

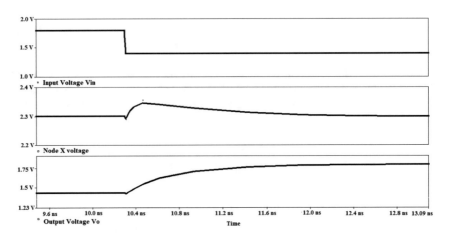

Fig. 5.14 Simulation waveforms of PFSCL-CC inverter

simulated and the predicted values of static parameters for all the operating conditions.

The accuracy of the delay model for PFSCL-CC inverter is validated with load capacitance of 0, 10, and 100 fF. The simulated and the predicted delay in particular for NM = 130 mV, $A_{v\_p\_cc} = 0.95$ and with different load capacitances are plotted in Fig. 5.16. It is found that there is a close agreement between the simulated and the predicted delay for all the operating conditions.

5.5.4   Performance Comparison

Several logic gates such as inverter, 2-input NOR, 3-input NOR, 2-input XOR, and 3-input XOR gates are implemented in the PFSCL-CC style and conventional PFSCL style with a resistive, PMOS and the inductor (passive and the active inductor) loads. All the gates maintain a bias current of 100 μA and voltage swing of 0.4 V. The supply voltage of 1.8 V and a load capacitance of 50 fF are taken for simulations. It may be noted that since all the circuits are implemented with the same supply voltage and bias current, they consume equal static power. The simulated delays for various gates with available loads are listed in Table 5.2. It can be observed that the passive inductor topology shows the maximum delay improvement, followed by the NP-load topology. A maximum improvement of 25% with respect to the PFSCL gates using PMOS load is obtained in delay by using PFSCL-CC logic gates.

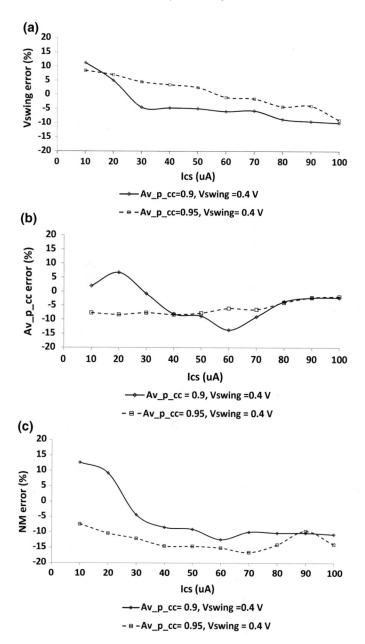

Fig. 5.15 Errors in the static parameters of the PFSCL-CC inverter **a** voltage gain, **b** small-signal voltage gain, **c** noise margin

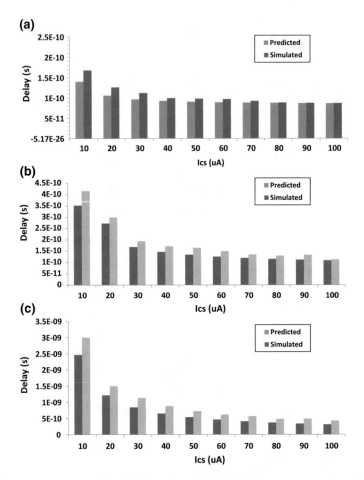

Fig. 5.16 Simulated and predicted delay values of PFSCL-CC inverter versus I_{CS} with NM = 130 mV, $A_{v\_p\_cc}$ = 0.95 for different C_{L_PFSCL} values **a** 0 fF, **b** 10 fF, **c** 100 fF

Table 5.2 Comparison in propagation delay (ps) of PFSCL circuits with different loads

Circuit	Load				
	Resistor	PMOS	Spiral inductor	Active inductor	NP-load
Inverter	132	148	102	127	115
2-input NOR	143	158	108	135	122
3-input NOR	149	162	112	140	128
2-input XOR	163	193	139	159	144
3-input XOR	311	367	289	307	300

5.6   Summary

The load section in a CML gate is responsible for deciding its speed. Existing loads have been discussed in this chapter with an emphasis on an active load that is suitable for high-speed operation. This active load comprises of an NMOS and a PMOS transistor and is referred as NP-load. The load exhibits capacitive coupling which is prime reason for speed improvement. As NP-load may be used in differential CML as well as PFSCL gates; the mathematical formulation for analysis of static parameters as well as delay is presented. The design procedure is also outlined. The models are functionally verified through simulations. Some circuit examples using NP-load are also included and are compared with other loads. The comparison clearly show that the NP-load outperform the other load.

References

1. B. Razavi, *Design of Analog CMOS Integrated Circuits* (Tata McGraw Hill Edition, 2007)
2. S.M. Masood, *Active Loads in Current-Mode Logic (CML) Topology* (Technical University of Denmark, 2006)
3. A. Worapishet, M. Thamsirianunt, An NMOS inductive loading technique for extended operating frequency CMOS ring oscillators, in Proceedings of IEEE Midwest Symposium on Circuits and Systems (2002), pp. 116–119
4. H.T. Bui, Y. Savaria, 10 GHz PLL using active shunt-peaked MCML gates and improved frequency acquisition XOR phase detector in 0.18 µm CMOS, in Proceedings of the IEEE International Workshop SOC for Real-Time Applications (2004), pp. 115–118
5. S.S. Mohan, M. del Mar Hershenson, S.P. Boyd, T.H. Lee, Bandwidth extension in CMOS with optimized on-chip inductors. IEEE J. Solid-State Circuits 35(3), 346–354 (2000)
6. H.T. Bui, Y. Savaria, Shunt-peaking of MCML gates using active inductors, in Proceedings of IEEE Northeast Workshop on Circuits and Systems (2004), pp. 361–364
7. K. Gupta, N. Pandey, M. Gupta, A novel active shunt-peaked MCML array multiplier. J. Multi Disciplinary Eng. Technol. 6(2) (2012)
8. K. Gupta, N. Pandey, M. Gupta, A new active shunt-peaked MCML based high performance 1:8 demultiplexer for serial communication. Int. J. Eng. Technol. 2(10), 4632–4639 (2010)
9. K. Gupta, N. Pandey, M. Gupta, A novel active shunt-peaked MOS current mode logic C-element for asynchronous pipelines, in Proceedings of IEEE International Conference on Multimedia, Signal Processing and Communication Technologies (2011), pp. 122–125
10. K. Gupta, N. Pandey, M. Gupta, Shunt-peaking in MCML memory element design in 0.18 µm CMOS technology, in Proceedings of Annual IEEE India Conference (INDICON) (2010), pp. 1–4
11. F. Yuan, CMOS Active Inductors and Transformers: Principle, Implementation and Applications (Springer, 2008)
12. K. Gupta, N. Pandey, M. Gupta, MOS current mode logic with capacitive coupling. ISRN Electron. 2012, 7 (2012). Article ID 473257
13. K. Gupta, N. Pandey, M. Gupta, Performance improvement of PFSCL gates through capacitive coupling, in Proceedings of IEEE International Conference on Multimedia, Signal Processing and Communication Technologies (2013), pp. 185–188. © 2016 IEEE, Reprinted with permission
14. S.M. Kang, Y. Leblebici, *CMOS Digital Integrated Circuits: Analysis and Design*, 3rd edn. (Tata McGraw Hills, 2006)

Chapter 6
PFSCL Circuits with Reduced Gate Count

6.1 Introduction

A PFSCL gate is a single-level topology of source-coupled transistor pairs where in a parallel combination of N-input transistors is coupled to a single transistor which is driven by feedback connection thorugh gate output. This type of architecture allows implementation of only NOR/OR functions in a single gate and enables low voltage operation as stacking of transistors is not performed. Since a function must be expressed in NOR/OR form so there exist cases wherein the gate count increases by using NOR/OR approach which mitigates the advantages offered by PFSCL style. Such cases need to be identified and addressed. Therefore in this chapter, this concern is examined and methods for the efficient PFSCL circuit realization are investigated.

6.2 Realization of PFSCL Circuits (Method-1)

In this method, any arbitrary logic function in PFSCL style is realized as a cascade of NOR/OR gates [1, 2]. The concept can be illustrated through the realization of a 2:1 multiplexer (MUX). The functionality with data lines ($I0$, $I1$) and select line (SEL) can be expressed in the form of sum of product (SOP) as:

$$Y = I_0 \overline{\text{SEL}} + I_1 \text{SEL} \tag{6.1}$$

Equivalently, the functionality in NOR/OR forms can be written as:

$$Y = \left(\overline{\overline{I_0} + \text{SEL}} \right) + \left(\overline{\overline{I_1} + \overline{\text{SEL}}} \right) \tag{6.2}$$

K. Gupta et al., *Model and Design of Improved Current Mode Logic Gates*, https://doi.org/10.1007/978-981-15-0982-7_6

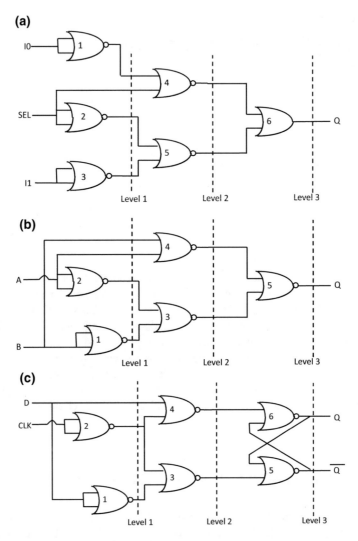

Fig. 6.1 Gate-level schematic to implement PFSCL circuits using method-1 [3, 4] **a** MUX **b** XOR gate **c** D latch

The above expression clearly shows that six PFSCL NOR/OR gates are required and should be arranged in three levels (Level 1, Level 2, and Level 3). The gate-level schematic illustrating the concept is drawn in Fig. 6.1a [3, 4]. The first level (Level 1) generates the complement of the data inputs $I0$, $I1$ and select line (SEL) while the MUX functionality is implemented in the next two levels (Level 2 and Level 3). The usage of six PFSCL NOR/OR gates results in six times more power than a single PFSCL NOR gate. Also, the arrangement of the NOR gates in three levels adds to the propagation delay. Similar observations are made from the gate-level schematic of PFSCL XOR gate and PFSCL D latch as shown in Fig. 6.1b,c [3, 4], respectively. Thus, it is clear that NOR/OR form realization of SOP logic functions has high gate count leading to performance degradation in terms of power and delay. This issue is addressed by adopting an alternate method that reduces the gate count in PFSCL circuit realization. A detailed description is presented further.

6.3 Realization of PFSCL Circuits (Method-2)

In this method, the circuits are realized by using a circuit element, named as fundamental cell [3, 4]. This cell is developed by introducing the triple-tail cell concept in PFSCL style. It comprises of two triple-tail cells ($M3$, $M4$, and $M7$) and ($M5$, $M6$, and $M8$) with X, Y, and M, and complement of M ($\overline{M}$) connected as inputs. The complete schematic is drawn in Fig. 6.2. The two triple-tail cells are biased by separate current sources of $I_{CS}/2$ value such that the cell draws the same current as a basic PFSCL gate. The transistors $M7$ and $M8$ are connected between the power supply and the common source terminal of transistor pairs ($M3$–$M4$) and ($M5$–$M6$), respectively. The output Q of the fundamental cell is formed by combining any one of the two output nodes from each of the two triple-tail cells ($O1/$ $O2$, $O3/O4$). As an example, the fundamental cell can be configured as a 2:1 multiplexer (MUX) by connecting data lines $I0$, $I1$ to Y, X terminals and connecting select lines SEL, $\overline{\text{SEL}}$ to M and $\overline{M}$, respectively. The output Q is taken by connecting nodes $O2$ and $O4$ to a load capacitance C_L. The schematic of 2:1 MUX is shown in Fig. 6.2b and is further examined and modeled.

In the MUX circuit, whenever SEL switches from low logic level to high logic level, the transistor $M7$ turns ON such that the transistor pair ($M3$–$M4$) gets deactivated. At the same time, the transistor $M8$ is turned OFF and data at the input

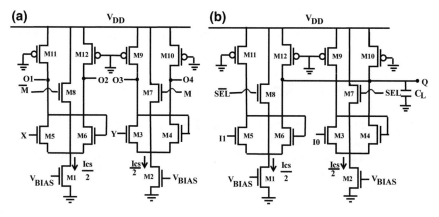

Fig. 6.2 **a** Schematic of PFSCL fundamental cell **b** fundamental cell configured as a 2:1 MUX

line $I1$ is reflected at the output through the transistor pair ($M5$–$M6$). Similarly, switching of SEL to low logic level activates the transistor pair ($M3$–$M4$) and the data from $I0$ data line is made available at the output.

6.3.1 Analysis of Fundamental Cell

With this basic understanding, it is necessary to model its functionality in terms of static parameter namely voltage swing, small-signal gain, noise margin and delay. It is assumed that the aspect ratio of transistors $M7$ and $M8$ is greater than other transistors' aspect ratio by a factor N for proper activation/deactivation of triple-tail cells [3]. To start the analysis, the load transistors $M9$–$M12$ are first modeled by equivalent linear resistance, R_{LP}. The voltage swing is evaluated by first determining the output voltage for each input combination. The expression for output voltage is written as:

$$V_Q = V_{DD} - R_{LP}[(i_{D\_M4} + i_{D\_M6})] \qquad (6.3)$$

The procedure is illustrated for one of the input combinations. It is assumed that $I0$ is high, $I1$ is low, and SEL makes a high-to-low transition. In this condition, transistors $M3$, $M6$ and $M8$ are ON while $M4$, $M5$ and $M7$ are OFF. The currents flowing through the transistors $M6$ and $M8$ can be written as

$$i_{D\_M3} = \frac{I_{CS}}{2} \qquad (6.4)$$

$$i_{D\_M6} = \frac{I_{CS}}{2} \frac{1}{1+N} \qquad (6.5)$$

$$i_{D\_M8} = \frac{I_{CS}}{2} \frac{N}{1+N} \qquad (6.6)$$

For this input condition, the output will attain high logic level and is computed using Eq. (6.3) as:

$$V_{OH1} = V_{DD} - R_{LP}[(i_{D\_M4} + i_{D\_M6})] = V_{DD} - \frac{R_{LP}I_{CS}}{2} \frac{1}{1+N} \qquad (6.7)$$

The output voltages for various input combinations are enlisted in Table 6.1. It can be observed from Table 6.1 that there are two values of both maximum output voltage V_{OH} and minimum output voltage V_{OL} for different input combinations. It can be found out that for the case when $I0$ and $I1$ are same, the voltage swing, V_{SWING1} [3] is expressed as:

Table 6.1 Output voltages for different input combinations

Inputs levels			Currents through the transistors						Output (V_Q)	
SEL	$I0$	$I1$	$M3$	$M4$	$M5$	$M6$	$M7$	$M8$	Level	$V_{DD} - R_{LP}(i_{D,4} + i_{D,6})$
L	L	L	0	$I1$	0	$I3$	0	$I2$	V_{OL1}	$V_{DD} - R_{LP}\frac{I_{CS}}{2}\left(1 + \frac{1}{1+N}\right)$
	L	H	0	$I1$	$I3$	0	0	$I2$	V_{OL2}	$V_{DD} - R_{LP}\frac{I_{CS}}{2}$
	H	L	$I1$	0	0	$I3$	0	$I2$	V_{OH2}	$V_{DD} - R_{LP}\frac{I_{CS}}{2}\left(\frac{1}{1+N}\right)$
	H	H	$I1$	0	$I3$	0	0	$I2$	V_{OH1}	V_{DD}
H	L	L	0	$I3$	0	$I1$	$I2$	0	V_{OL1}	$V_{DD} - R_{LP}\frac{I_{CS}}{2}\left(1 + \frac{1}{1+N}\right)$
	L	H	0	$I3$	$I1$	0	$I2$	0	V_{OL2}	$V_{DD} - R_{LP}\frac{I_{CS}}{2}\left(\frac{1}{1+N}\right)$
	H	L	$I3$	0	0	$I1$	$I2$	0	V_{OH2}	$V_{DD} - R_{LP}\frac{I_{CS}}{2}$
	H	H	$I3$	0	$I1$	0	$I2$	0	V_{OH1}	V_{DD}

where L/H = low/high input voltage, $I1 = \frac{I_{CS}}{2}$, $I2 = \frac{I_{CS}}{2}\left(\frac{N}{1+N}\right)$, and $I3 = \frac{I_{CS}}{2}\left(\frac{1}{1+N}\right)$

$$V_{SWING1} = V_{OH1} - V_{OL1} = \frac{R_{LP}I_{CS}}{2}\left(1 + \frac{1}{1+N}\right) \tag{6.8}$$

where V_{OH1}, V_{OL1} are maximum output voltage and minimum output voltage, respectively, for same inputs $I0$ and $I1$.

Alternatively, the voltage swing, V_{SWING2} [3] with different inputs ($I0$ and $I1$) can be expressed as:

$$V_{SWING2} = V_{OH2} - V_{OL2} = \frac{R_{LP}I_{CS}}{2}\left(\frac{N}{1+N}\right) \tag{6.9}$$

where V_{OH2}, V_{OL2} are maximum output voltage and minimum output voltage, respectively, for different inputs. As $V_{SWING2} < V_{SWING1}$, V_{SWING2} is considered as the worst case voltage swing, V_{SWING} and is further approximated as

$$V_{SWING} = V_{OH} - V_{OL} = \frac{R_{LP}I_{CS}}{2}\left(\frac{N}{1+N}\right) \tag{6.10}$$

The small-signal voltage gain (A_{v_fc}) and noise margin (NM) for the fundamental cell [3] are computed as:

$$A_{v\_fc} = \frac{g_{m,n}R_{LP}/2}{1 - g_{m,n}R_{LP}/2} \tag{6.11}$$

$$NM = \frac{V_{SWING}}{2}\left[1 - \frac{1}{A_{v\_fc}}\right] \tag{6.12}$$

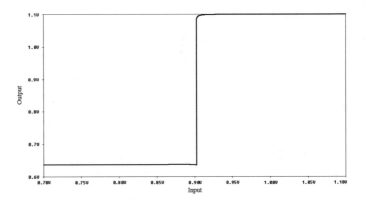

Fig. 6.3 VTC of the fundamental cell with $g_{m,n}R_{LP}/2 = 0.98$ [3]

where $g_{m,n} = \sqrt{\mu_{\text{eff},n}C_{OX}\frac{W_N}{L_N}\frac{I_{CS}}{2}}$ is the transconductance of the transistors (*M3–M6*) and W_N, L_N are the effective channel width and length of the said transistors, respectively.

The expressions of A_{v_fc} and *NM* represented in Eqs. (6.11) and (6.12), respectively, are valid for $g_{m,n}R_{LP}/2 < 1$, the circuit exhibits hysteresis otherwise [3]. To avoid large sizes of the transistors, the value of $g_{m,n}R_{LP}/2$ values close to unity is recommended for designing of PFSCL circuits [3]. The DC behavior of the fundamental cell is validated through SPICE simulations with a power supply of 1.1 V. The fundamental cell is implemented and simulated for a voltage swing of 400 mV, $N = 10$, and the bias current of 100 µA. The voltage transfer characteristic (VTC) of the fundamental cell for $g_{m,n}R_{LP}/2 = 0.98$ and $g_{m,n}R_{LP}/2 = 3$ by varying the two inputs simultaneously is shown in Figs. 6.3 and 6.4, respectively [3]. The simulation results conform to the theoretical propositions.

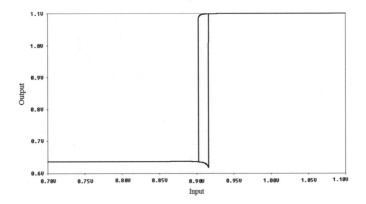

Fig. 6.4 VTC of the fundamental cell configured with $g_{m,n}R_{LP}/2 = 3$ [3]

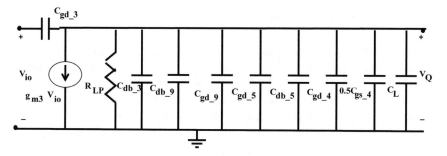

Fig. 6.5 Linear half circuit with low value of SEL input

The delay expression for the MUX is formulated by considering a high-to-low transition on SEL input, the output switch by activating (deactivating) the transistor pair $M3$–$M4$ ($M5$–$M6$) abruptly, and the circuit thus reduces to a simple PFSCL inverter. The transistors $M5$–$M6$ affect the transient response through their parasitic capacitances. The equivalent linear half circuit is shown in Fig. 6.5 where $C_{gd\_i}, C_{db\_i}, C_{db\_i}$ represent the gate-to-drain capacitance, the drain–bulk capacitance, the gate-to-source capacitance of the ith transistors.

The delay of MUX is evaluated as:

$$t_{PD} = R_{LP}\left(C_{db\_3} + C_{gd\_3} + C_{gd\_9} + C_{db\_9} + C_{db\_5} + C_{gd\_4} + \frac{1}{2}C_{gs\_4} + C_{gd\_5} + C_L\right)$$

(6.13)

with $C_{db\_3} = C_{db\_5}$, $C_{gd\_3} = C_{gd\_5} = C_{gd\_4}$ and, $R_{LP} = \frac{2\,V_{SWING}}{I_{CS}}\frac{1+N}{N}$, Eq. (6.13) can be rewritten as:

$$t_{PD} = \frac{2\,V_{SWING}}{I_{CS}}\frac{1+N}{N}\left(2C_{db\_3} + 3C_{gd\_3} + \frac{1}{2}C_{gs\_4} + C_{gd\_9} + C_{db\_9} + C_L\right)$$

(6.14)

It can be observed that the delay given in Eq. (3.12) is expressed in terms of the transistors' capacitances, which in turn depend on their aspect ratio. In practical situations, the transistor aspect ratio must be set to meet the design specifications on noise margin, power, and delay. Therefore, the dependence of the delay on the aspect ratio should also be determined. To this end, a design procedure to size the transistors is worked out and the delay model is revisited again for the purpose.

6.3.2 Design of Fundamental Cell

On the basis of the above analysis, a procedure to size the transistors is developed. The procedure assumes the value of $g_{m,n}R_{LP}/2$ as unity to maximize the available noise margin. But in practice, its value is set less than 1 and close to unity as explained in previous subsection. So, given a specified value of NM, factor N, and bias current I_{CS}, the voltage swing is calculated using Eq. (6.12) as:

$$V_{SWING} = \frac{2NM}{1 - \frac{1}{A_{v\_fc}}} \tag{6.15}$$

The above equation provides the lower limit of voltage swing. It should further be noted that the maximum value of V_{SWING} should be lower than V_T to ensure that transistors $M3$–$M6$ operates in saturation region. Once the appropriate value of voltage swing is decided, the equivalent load resistance can be found as:

$$R_{LP} = \frac{2\,V_{SWING}}{I_{CS}} \frac{1+N}{N} \tag{6.16}$$

To find the aspect ratio of the load transistors ($M9$–$M10$), the bias current I_{HIGH} corresponding to the minimum-sized PMOS transistor with equivalent resistance, R_{LP_MIN}, is determined as:

$$I_{HIGH} = \frac{2\,V_{SWING}}{R_{LP\_MIN}} \frac{1+N}{N} \tag{6.17}$$

As an example, for the adopted 0.18 μm CMOS technology, for a $V_{SWING} = 400$ mV, $N = 10$, $V_{DD} = 1.1$ V, I_{HIGH} evaluates to 49.27 μA. For $I_{CS} > I_{HIGH}$, R_{LP} is made less than R_{LP_MIN} by setting L_P to its minimum value, i.e., L_{MIN} and W_P are calculated as:

$$W_P = 0.5 \frac{N}{1+N} \frac{I_{CS}}{V_{SWING}} \frac{L_{MIN}}{\mu_{eff,p} C_{ox} (V_{DD} - |V_{T,P}|) \left\{ 1 - \frac{R_{DSW} 10^{-6}}{L_{MIN}} \left[\mu_{eff,p} C_{ox} (V_{DD} - |V_{T,P}|) \right] \right\}} \tag{6.18}$$

For $I_{CS} < I_{HIGH}$, R_{LP} is made greater than R_{LP_MIN} by setting W_P to its minimum value, i.e., W_{MIN} and L_P are calculated as:

$$L_P = W_{MIN}\, \mu_{eff,p} C_{ox} (V_{DD} - |V_{T,P}|) \left(\frac{2\,V_{SWING}}{I_{CS}} \frac{1+N}{N} - \frac{R_{DSW} 10^{-6}}{W_{MIN}} \right) \tag{6.19}$$

The width of transistors in the PDN ($M3$–$M6$) is determined by setting $g_{m,n}R_{LP}/2 = 1$. Assuming minimum channel length for these transistors, the width is computed as:

$$W_N = \frac{2}{\mu_{\text{eff},n} C_{ox}} \left(\frac{N}{1+N}\right)^2 \left(\frac{1}{V_{\text{SWING}}}\right)^2 I_{CS} L_{\text{MIN}} \tag{6.20}$$

Sometimes, in certain cases the calculated value of W_N is smaller than the minimum channel width. This happens when the bias current is lower than the current of minimum-sized NMOS transistor, I_{LOW}. Using Eq. (6.20), I_{LOW} can be computed as:

$$I_{\text{LOW}} = \frac{1}{2} \left(\frac{1+N}{N}\right)^2 \frac{W_{\text{MIN}}}{L_{\text{MIN}}} \mu_{\text{eff},n} C_{ox} V_{\text{SWING}}^2 \tag{6.21}$$

So, in such cases W_N is also set to W_{MIN}. After calculation, the width of transistors M7, M8 is made N times the width of the transistors M3–M6 for proper activation/deactivation.

According to the above design procedure, the dimensions of the transistors are being expressed in terms of bias current and the voltage swing. The parasitic capacitances associated with the delay expressions can now also be expressed in terms of these parameters. As already discussed in previous chapters, capacitance C_{xy} connected between terminals x and y can be expressed in general terms as:

$$C_{xy} = \frac{a_{xy}}{(V_{\text{SWING}})^2} I_{CS} + b_{xy} \frac{V_{\text{SWING}}}{I_{CS}} + c_{xy} \tag{6.22}$$

Using design Eqs. (6.19) and (6.20), various capacitances in Eq. (6.14) for I_{CS} ranging from I_{LOW} to I_{HIGH} may be expressed as:

$$C_{\text{gd}\_3} = C_{\text{gdo}} W_3 = 2 C_{\text{gdo}} \left(\frac{N}{1+N}\right)^2 \frac{L_{\text{MIN}}}{\mu_{\text{eff},n} C_{ox}} \frac{I_{CS}}{(V_{\text{SWING}})^2} \tag{6.23}$$

$$C_{\text{db}\_3} = W_3 \left(K_{jn} C_{jn} L_{dn} + 2 K_{jswn} C_{jswn}\right) + 2 K_{jswn} C_{jswn} L_{dn} \tag{6.24}$$

$$= 2 \frac{L_{\text{MIN}}}{\mu_{\text{eff},n} C_{ox}} \left(\frac{N}{1+N}\right)^2 \left(K_{jn} C_{jn} L_{dn} + 2 K_{jswn} C_{jswn}\right) \frac{I_{CS}}{(V_{\text{SWING}})^2} + 2 K_{jswn} C_{jswn} L_{dn}$$
$$\tag{6.25}$$

$$C_{\text{gs}\_4} = \frac{2}{3} W_5 C_{ox} L_{\text{MIN}} \tag{6.26}$$

$$= \frac{4}{3} \left(\frac{N}{1+N}\right)^2 \frac{L_{\text{MIN}}^2}{\mu_{\text{eff},n}} \frac{I_{CS}}{(V_{\text{SWING}})^2} \tag{6.27}$$

$$C_{\text{gd}.9} = C_{\text{gdo}} W_{\text{MIN}} + \frac{3}{4} A_{\text{bulk,max}} W_{\text{MIN}} L_P C_{ox}, \tag{6.28}$$

$$C_{gdo}W_{MIN} + \frac{3}{4}A_{bulk,max}W_{MIN}C_{ox}\left\{\mu_{eff,p}C_{ox}W_{MIN}\left(V_{DD} - \left|V_{T,P}\right|\right)\left[\frac{2\,V_{SWING}}{I_{CS}}\frac{1+N}{N} - \frac{R_{DSW}10^{-6}}{W_{MIN}}\right]\right\}$$

$$\text{(6.29)}$$

$$C_{db\_9} = W_{MIN}\left(K_{jp}C_{jp}L_{dp} + 2K_{jswp}C_{jswp}\right) + 2K_{jswp}C_{jswp}L_{dp}, \qquad \text{(6.30)}$$

where the symbols have their usual meaning.

The coefficients a_{xy}, b_{xy} and c_{xy} of all the capacitances in Eq. (6.14) are summarized in Table 6.2.

The various capacitance in the delay expression can now be substituted by their respective coefficients. The delay expression using Eqs. (6.22–6.30) can be written as

$$t_{PD\_TT1} = 2\,V_{SWING}\frac{1+N}{N}\left(\frac{a}{V_{SWING}^2} + b\frac{V_{SWING}}{I_{CS}^2} + \frac{c+C_L}{I_{CS}}\right) \qquad \text{(6.31)}$$

where

$$a = 2a_{db3} + 3a_{gd3} + \frac{1}{2}a_{gs4} \qquad \text{(6.32a)}$$

$$b = b_{gd9} \qquad \text{(6.32b)}$$

$$c = 2c_{db3} + c_{gd9} + c_{db9} \qquad \text{(6.32c)}$$

Table 6.2 Coefficients of the capacitances for fundamental cell-based MUX

NMOS coefficients	
a_{db3}	$\frac{2L_{MIN}}{\mu_{eff,n}C_{ox}}\left(\frac{N}{1+N}\right)^2\left(K_{jn}C_{jn}L_{dn} + 2K_{jswn}C_{jswn}\right)$
a_{gd3}	$2C_{gdo}\left(\frac{N}{1+N}\right)^2\frac{L_{MIN}}{\mu_{eff,n}C_{ox}}$
c_{db3}	$2K_{jswn}C_{jswn}L_{dn}$
a_{gs4}	$\frac{4}{3}\left(\frac{N}{1+N}\right)^2\frac{L_{MIN}^2}{\mu_{eff,n}}$
$b_{db3}, b_{gd3}, c_{gd3}$	0
PMOS coefficients	
b_{gd9}	$\frac{3}{2}\left(\frac{1+N}{N}\right)A_{bulk,max}\mu_{eff,p}C_{ox}^2W_{MIN}^2\left(V_{DD} - \left|V_{T,P}\right|\right)$
c_{gd9}	$C_{gdo}W_{MIN} - \frac{3}{4}A_{bulk,max}\mu_{eff,p}C_{ox}^2W_{MIN}\left(V_{DD} - \left|V_{T,P}\right|\right)R_{DSW}10^{-6}$
c_{db9}	$K_{jp}C_{jp}L_{dp}W_{MIN} + 2K_{jswp}C_{jswp}\left(L_{dp} + W_{MIN}\right)$
$a_{gd9}, a_{db9}, b_{db9}$	0

where the symbols have their usual meaning

The above procedure is illustrated by designing a fundamental cell-based MUX with V_{DD} = 1.8 V, V_{SWING} = 350 mV, N = 10, and I_{CS} = 30 μA for the taken 0.18 μm CMOS technology parameters. Using the corresponding equations, I_{HIGH}, I_{LOW}, L_P, and W_N are calculated as 102 μA, 30 μA, 3.5 μm, and 0.27 μm, respectively. As per the procedure, W_P and L_N are set to their minimum values. Using the values of the coefficients in Eq. (6.31), the propagation delay with the capacitance 10 fF is evaluated as 1.1 ns while a delay of 1.21 ns is obtained through simulations.

The same procedure is followed to design MUX for the bias current ranging from 10 μA to 100 μA. The same simulation condition as above is maintained. The accuracy of the delay model is validated through SPICE simulations with the load capacitance of 0 fF, 10 fF, 100 fF, 1 pF. The simulated and the predicted delay with different load capacitances are plotted in Fig. 6.6. It is found that there is a close agreement between the simulated and the predicted delay for all the operating conditions.

6.3.3 Basic Gate Realization

The study of fundamental cell in the previous section suggests that a PFSCL inverter is required to invert one of the inputs used for activation/deactivation of the triple-tail cells. Hence, the complete realization of a logic function by using method-2 requires a cascade of PFSCL inverter and fundamental cell. The complete MOS schematic to be used for method-2-based circuit realization along with its block diagram representation is shown in Fig. 6.7.

As a design example, the realization of a D latch is shown in Fig. 6.8 [3]. The PFSCL inverter (M13–M16) generates the complement of CLK which is fed as the input to the fundamental cell (M1–M12). The CLK and its complement $\overline{CLK}$ drives the transistors M7 and M8 connected between the supply terminal and the common source terminal of transistor pairs (M3–M4) and (M5–M6), respectively. A high voltage on CLK turns ON the transistor M7 and deactivates the transistor pair (M3–M4). At the same time, the transistor M8 turns OFF so that the transistor pair (M5–M6) generates the output according to the input D. Similarly, the transistor pair (M3–M4) gets activated for low voltage on CLK and preserves the previous output. Thus, the D latch models a positive level-sensitive D latch.

The functionality of D latch is verified through simulations with a power supply of 1.1 V. A voltage swing of 400 mV and a bias current of 100 μA is considered. The simulation waveforms for inputs (D and CLK) and the output Q are shown in Fig. 6.9. It can be observed that for high values of the CLK signal, the D latch is in the transparent state whereas it is in the hold state for low values of the CLK signal.

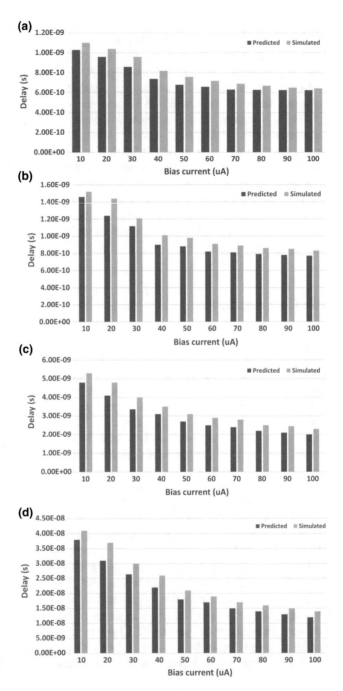

Fig. 6.6 Simulated and predicted delays of PFSCL fundamental cell-based MUX versus I_{CS} for different C_L values **a** 0 fF **b** 10 fF **c** 100 fF **d** 1 pF

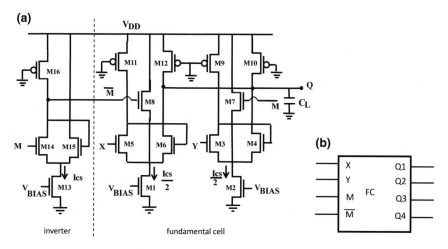

Fig. 6.7 Method-2 circuit realization, **a** complete MOS schematic [4], **b** block diagram

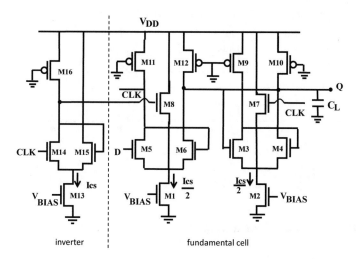

Fig. 6.8 Method-2-based realization of PFSCL D latch [3]

Similarly, realization of functions using method-2 can be worked out [4]. The mapping of the actual circuit inputs to the inputs of the inverter and fundamental cell is listed in Table 6.3.

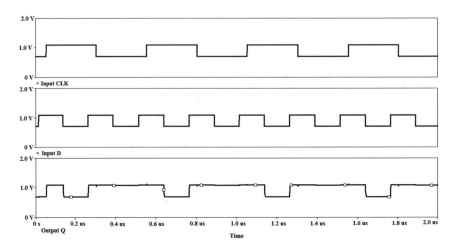

Fig. 6.9 Simulation waveform of a PFSCL D latch [3]

Table 6.3 Realization of PFSCL circuits using method-2

PFSCL circuit	Actual inputs	PFSCL inverter input	Fundamental cell inputs			Output nodes
		Z	M	X	Y	Q
OR	A, B	B	B	A	A	Q4, Q2
NOR	A, B	B	B	A	A	Q1, Q3
NAND	A, B	B	B	A	B	Q3, Q1
AND	A, B	B	B	A	B	Q4, Q2
XOR	A, B	B	B	A	A	Q1, Q4
XNOR	A, B	B	B	A	A	Q2, Q3
D Latch	CLK, D	CLK	CLK	Q	D	O2, Q4

6.4 Performance Comparison

Different PFSCL circuits are realized using both the methods and are compared on the basis of gate count and other performance parameters. The gate count for the circuits is summarized in Table 6.4. It may be noted that the NOR and OR circuits realized using method-2 require more PFSCL gates in comparison with method-1 due to the intrinsic nature of the later one. However, the realizations of NAND, AND, XOR, XNOR gates and D latch using method-1 require three to six PFCSL gates in contrast to one inverter and a fundamental cell in the second method. Thus, a reduction in the gate count is possible by following method-2-based circuit realization.

The performance of PFSCL circuits realized by using both the methods is compared through simulations for the same conditions as taken for D latch. The

Table 6.4 Comparison in the gate count

PFSCL circuit	Method-1	Method-2	Percentage reduction
OR	1	2	−50
NOR	1	2	−50
NAND	3	2	33
AND	3	2	33
XOR	5	2	60
XNOR	6	2	66
2:1 MUX	6	2	66
D Latch	6	2	66

Table 6.5 Performance comparison of PFSCL circuits

Method	PFSCL circuit							
	OR	NOR	AND	NAND	XOR	XNOR	2:1 MUX	D latch
Power consumption (μW)								
Method-1	106	108	319	319	539	424	640	640
Method-2	228	228	228	228	228	228	228	228
Propagation delay (ps)								
Method-1	563	648	710	720	1135	1119	1139	1270
Method-2	682	688	615	633	661	653	655	658
Power saving (%)								
Method-2	−53.5	−52.6	29	29	58	46	64	63
Speed Improvement (%)								
Method-2	−21	−6	13	12	41	41	42	48

simulation results are summarized in Table 6.5. It is found that the NOR and OR circuits realized using the method-1 exhibit better performance than ones realized using the fundamental method. This is can be attributed to the intrinsic nature of the former. However, the realizations of NAND, AND, XOR, XNOR gates, MUX and D latch using the fundamental cell method lower the power consumption by 64% and delay by 48% in comparison with the other method.

6.5 Design Examples

In this section, two design examples for circuit realization in PFSCL style are considered. Various circuit implementations are explored to develop a clear understanding of optimum circuit realization in this style. The first example deals with the design of PFSCL linear feedback shift register (LFSR) while the other presents PFSCL adder design.

6.5.1   LFSR Design

LFSR is a widely used circuit element in communication systems such as direct sequence spread spectrum radio, GPS satellite systems, scramblers, jamming systems, and programmable sound generators [5–8]. A LFSR comprises a shift register and a feedback network consisting of XOR/XNOR gates. The XOR function is a modulo-2 addition which represents a linear operation and hence explains the term linear in LFSR. The outputs of flip-flops in a shift register (also called taps) are fed as inputs to the XOR/XNOR gate, whose output is connected to the first flip-flop. The shift register is loaded with an initial seed value and then clocked to produce a pseudorandom sequence of 1s and 0s. A LFSR with n-flip-flops and generating $2^n - 1$ pseudorandom patterns is known as a maximal length LFSR. The selection of tap combinations in an LFSR determines if it is maximal length or not. There is no mathematical way to decide upon the tap combinations to make a maximal length LFSR; hence, designers refer to a table given by Peterson and Weldon [5].

Here, the design of 4-bit maximal length PFSCL LFSR is worked upon. The feedback polynomial is written as:

$$x^4 + x + 1 \tag{6.33}$$

The same is elaborated through a bock diagram shown in Fig. 6.10 [9]. The above polynomial indicates that tap 1 and tap 4 will be used as input to the XOR gate. The D-flip-flop shown in the block diagram is realized by configuring the D Latches in master–slave configuration, with their clocks 180° out of phase. Depending on the method used (either method-1 or method-2) for realizing the XOR gate and D Latch, four different architectures [9] for 4-bit maximal length PFSCL LFSR are designed and drawn in Fig. 6.11.

The first architecture (Architecture-1) is based on using method-1. The NOR-based realization of both XOR gate and D Latch is used. The gate-level schematic shown in Fig. 6.1 is used wherein basic PFSCL NOR/OR gates are substituted. In the second architecture (Architecture-2), both XOR gate and D latch

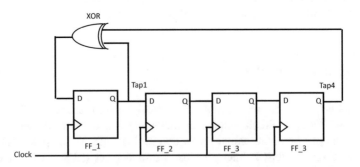

Fig. 6.10 Block diagram of a 4-bit maximal length LFSR [9]

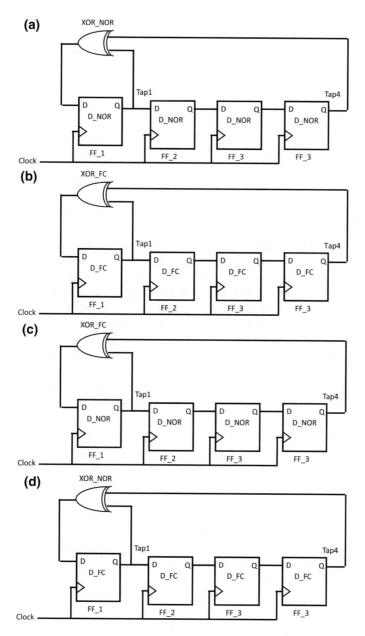

Fig. 6.11 PFSCL LFSR realization **a** Architecture-1 **b** Architecture-2 **c** Architecture-3 [9] **d** Architecture-4 [9]

are realized using method-2. The mapping table (Table 6.3) is used for configuring fundamental cell for the required functionality. The other two architectures presented here are hybrids of the above mentioned architectures. The third architecture

Table 6.6 LFSR performance comparison [9]

Architecture	Delay (ns)	Power dissipation (μW)	Power-delay product (μJ)
1	0.813	9360	7.609
2	0.485	960	0.465
3	0.707	6713	4.746
4	0.573	2015	1.154

(Architecture-3) is designed using method-2-based XOR gate and method-1-based D latch as shown in Fig. 6.11c. Similarly, by using method-2-based D latch and method-1-based XOR gate, the fourth architecture (Architecture-4) for the LFSR is realized.

The performance of these four different architectures is compared by simulating them with 0.18 μm CMOS technology parameters for a voltage swing, load capacitance of 400 mV and 50 fF, respectively. The simulation results are listed in Table 6.6 [9]. The results signify that the Architecture-2 outperforms Architecture-1. A reduction of 89.7 and 40.3% in power and delay is noted due to the reduction in the gate count as well as total stages before producing an output. Improvement in delay of LFSR will prove to be symbolic when it comes to encryption–decryption techniques which takes a significant amount of time to reach on a decision based on the random sequence pattern generated.

With hybrid Architectures-3 and -4 [9], it can be seen that simulation results are closer to one of the primary architectures depending on the type of topology used for the realization of LFSRs primary components (XOR and D Latch). In Architecture-3, we have made use of NOR-based D-flip-flops, so now the cascaded network of these flip-flops is responsible for producing majority of delay in the generation of outputs, which are eventually applied as inputs to feedback XOR gate. Therefore, using NOR-based flip-flops has made the output generation process slower and hence produces performance characteristics nearer to Architecture-1. On the same grounds, we can verify our results for Architecture-4 which uses fundamental cell-based flip-flops, and hence its performance characteristics are much closer to Architecture-2. Hence, it can be concluded that Architecture-1 (NOR/OR-based) shows the worst performance out of the four architectures, whereas Architecture-2 results in best performance PFSCL LFSR. The performance of Architecture-3 and -4 lies between the worst case and best case and is majorly affected by the choice of topology for realizing D-flip-flops.

6.5.2   Adder Design

A full adder is a combinational circuit used for performing addition of two input bits (A, B) and a input carry (C) and provides a sum bit (SUM) and a carry bit (CARRY) as outputs. The functionality of full adder can be expressed as:

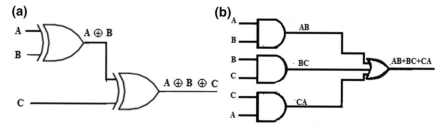

Fig. 6.12 Gate-level schematic for full adder, **a** sum circuit, **b** carry circuit

$$SUM = A \oplus B \oplus C \tag{6.34}$$

$$CARRY = AB + BC + CA \tag{6.35}$$

The gate-level schematic of the full adder is shown in Fig. 6.12. The SUM function uses two 2-input XOR gates while CARRY function is in the form of AND–OR which requires three 2-input AND gates and a single 3-input OR gate. Here, three different architectures to realize the functionality are put forward [10]. The Architecture-1 uses method-1 for PFSCL circuits that use only PFSCL NOR/ OR gates. It is drawn in Fig. 6.13. The sum expression requires two XOR gates, which is realized by employing ten PFSCL NOR gate (Fig. 6.13a). The gate-level schematic as shown in Fig. 6.1 is used and is further substituted by PFSCL NOR/ OR gate. For CARRY function realization, De Morgan's law is used to realize the

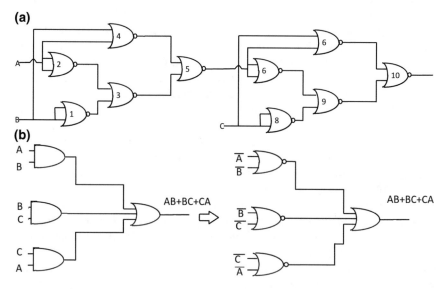

Fig. 6.13 Architecture-1 of PFSCL full adder, **a** sum, **b** carry

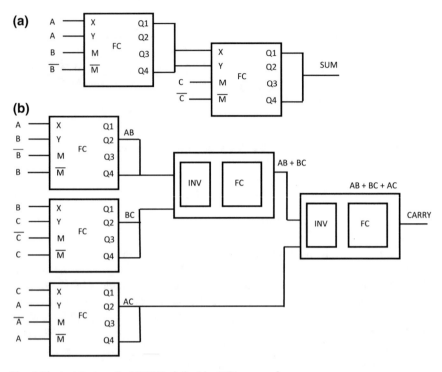

Fig. 6.14 Architecture-2 of PFSCL full adder [10], **a** sum, **b** carry

AND terms as discussed in Chap. 2. The NOR/OR gate equivalent of CARRY is shown in Fig. 6.13b. The gates are further substituted by PFSCL NOR/OR gates.

The second architecture (Architecture-2) deals with method-2-based PFSCL circuit realization [10]. The realization of SUM function is carried out by configuring the two fundamental cells as shown in Fig. 6.14a. Similarly, the CARRY circuit has fundamental cells which are configured as AND gate in the first level while the other levels implement the OR functionality as shown in Fig. 6.14b.

The third architecture (Architecture-3) is a hybrid architecture and is drawn by carefully examining the CARRY circuit in Architecture-2. It can be observed that the last two stages are basically realizing a three-input NOR function and requires two fundamental cells. Therefore, in third architecture, the last two fundamental cells of Architecture-2 are being replaced by a three-input PFSCL NOR gate. The complete block diagram is shown in Fig. 6.15.

The performance of the three architectures is compared with simulations by using the adopted 0.18 μm CMOS technology parameters and a power supply of 1.8 V. A bias current of 100 μA and voltage swing of 400 mV are maintained in the PFSCL gate. A load capacitance of 150 fF is used at the output of SUM and CARRY. The simulation results are summarized in Table 6.7 [10]. It is found that Architecture-1 is not efficient as it shows increased value of every performance

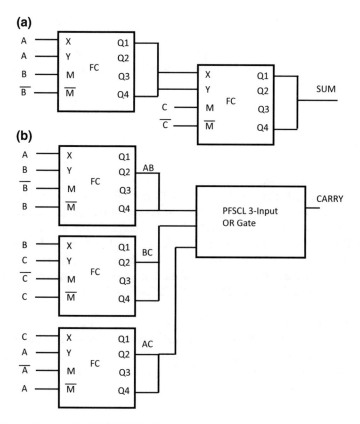

Fig. 6.15 Architecture-3 of PFSCL full adder, **a** sum, **b** carry

Table 6.7 Performance comparison of PFSCL full adder [10]

Parameter	Architecture					
	Architecture-1		Architecture-2		Architecture-3	
	Carry	Sum	Carry	Sum	Carry	Sum
Transistor count	26	50	68	24	46	24
Gate count	5	10	7	2	5	2
Delay (ns)	4.05	2.73	2.8	0.5	2.2	0.5
Power (mW)	0.9	1.8	1.26	0.36	0.9	0.36
Power-delay product (pJ)	3.6	4.9	3.5	0.18	1.98	0.18

parameter in comparison with others. This is due to the fact that the use of NOR gates leads to more number of gates and stages. Alternatively, the Architectures-2 and -3 show better results. On closer examination, it is found that the proposed Architecture-3 lowers the transistor count, gate count, power, delay, PDP by 24%, 33.3%, 21.4%, 28.5%, 43.4%, respectively, in comparison with Architecture-2.

Thus, Architecture-3 outperforms the rest and can be used in mixed-signal application design.

Thus, the above two design examples provide an insight into the efficient PFSCL circuit design. It can be concluded that the combination of both the methods can be used to realize logic functions.

6.6 Summary

In this chapter, two methods for PFSCL-based circuit realizations are elucidated. The first method inherits the feature of NOR operation and is suitable for NOR/OR-based function realization. This method results in a high gate count for logic function expressed in sum of product form. An alternate method involving the use of a PFSCL fundamental cell and an inverter is   analyzed. A fundamental cell is described next and mathematical formulation for static parameters is given which is followed by proposed delay model and design procedure. The configuration of fundamental cell as NAND, AND, XOR, XNOR gates, and D latch is presented next.

Two design examples namely LFSR and adder are included to demonstrate efficient PFSCL circuit realization. Four LFSR architectures are proposed wherein various combinations of NOR gates and fundamental cell implementations are used for its constituent components. On similar pattern, three architectures of adder architectures are also presented.

References

1. M. Alioto, L. Pancioni, S. Rocchi, V. Vignoli, Modeling and evaluation of positive-feedback source-coupled logic. IEEE Trans. Circuits Syst. I Regul. Pap. **51**(4), 2345–2355 (2004)
2. M. Alioto, L. Pancioni, S. Rocchi, V. Vignoli, Power-delay-area-noise margin trade-offs in positive-feedback source-coupled logic gates. IEEE Trans. Circuits Syst. I Regul. Pap. **54**(9), 1916–1928 (2007)
3. N. Pandey, K. Gupta, M. Gupta, An efficient triple-tail cell based PFSCL D-latch, Microelectron. J., **45**(8), 1001–1007 (2014) (Copyright (2014), with permission from Elsevier)
4. N. Pandey, M. Gupta, K. Gupta, A PFSCL based configurable logic block, *in Proceeding of Annual IEEE India International Conference INDICON* (2015), pp. 1–4 [Reprinted with permission, from © 2016 IEEE]
5. W.W. Peterson, E.J. Weldon Jr., *Error Correcting Codes* (MIT Press, Cambridge, MA, 1972)
6. K.K. Saluja, *Linear feedback shift registers theory and applications* (University of Wisconsin-Madison, Madison, updated in, 1991)
7. D. Muthiah, A. Raj, Implementation of high-speed LFSR design with parallel architectures, *in Proceedings 2012 International Conf. on Computing Communication and Applications* (2012), pp 1–6
8. P. Girard, L. Guiller, C. landrault, S. Pravossoudovitch, J. Figueras, S. Manich, P. Teixeira, M. Santos, Low-energy BIST design: impact of the LFSR TPG parameters on the weighted

switching activity, *in Proceedings of IEEE International Symposium on Circuits and Systems* (Orlando, USA, 1999)

9. N. Pandey, Abhishek, K. Gupta, PFSCL based linear feedback shift register, *in Proceedings of IEEE International Conference on Computational Techniques in Information and Communication Technologies, ICCTICT* (2016), pp. 580–585 [Reprinted with permission, from © 2016 IEEE]

10. K. Gupta, P. Shukla, N. Pandey, On the implementation of PFSCL adders, *in Proceeding of Second International Innovative Applications of Computational Intelligence on Power, Energy and Controls with their Impact on Humanity* (2016), pp. 287–291[Reprinted with permission, from © 2016 IEEE]

Chapter 7
Tri-state CML Circuits

7.1 Introduction

Tri-state circuits are the essential elements in bus organized systems such as high-performance processors, asynchronous transfer mode (ATM) crossbar switches, and programmable logic devices [1–4]. A tri-state gate assumes a high-impedance state in addition to high and low logic levels attained by a regular gate. An additional Enable signal is employed to achieve the desired functionality. These circuits can be easily designed using CMOS logic style [5] but are not favoured in mixed-signal environments due to the large switching noise generation and substantial power consumption. Therefore, a consideration on tri-state CML circuits is required which can be used in such applications. A variety of tri-state CML circuits are available and they are being classified in the category of differential tri-state CML circuits and PFSCL tri-state circuits in this chapter. The differential tri-state CML circuits are first presented and are subsequently followed by the PFSCL tri-state circuits.

7.2 Differential Tri-state CML Circuits

A differential tri-state CML gate is capable of exhibiting a high-impedance state in addition to differential operation of a regular CML gate. There exists three different ways to realize differential tri-state CML circuits. These techniques differ in the manner by which the high-impedance state is attained. The first one adds extra MOS switches to the output of the CML gate and thus is referred to as switch-based differential tri-state CML circuits. The second realization uses voltage followers and hence is called as voltage follower-based differential tri-state CML circuit. The third realization scheme modifies the load and current source sections of a CML gate to attain the tri-state operation. A discussion on all three types of differential tri-state CML circuits is presented further.

© Springer Nature Singapore Pte Ltd. 2020
K. Gupta et al., *Model and Design of Improved Current Mode Logic Gates*, https://doi.org/10.1007/978-981-15-0982-7_7

7.2.1   Switch-Based Differential Tri-state CML Circuit

The switch-based differential tri-state CML circuit adds extra MOS switches at the output of a CML gate. The complete schematic of a switch-based tri-state CML inverter/buffer [6] is shown in Fig. 7.1. It consists of a basic differential CML inverter/buffer (*M1–M5*), two PMOS transistors (*M6–M7*), and a differential to single-ended converter (*M8–M12*). The converter circuit is required to convert the reduced swing differential Enable signal to a full swing VE signal. The circuit operation is fully differential. For a high value of differential Enable signal, VE signal attains a low logic level such that the transistors *M6* and *M7* are turned ON. The logic levels of the intermediate nodes are available as the output of the CML inverter/buffer. This assures that for high value of Enable signal, CML inverter/ buffer behaves as a regular gate. Conversely, a low logic level on Enable signal makes VE signal high which makes the PMOS transistors *M6* and *M7* OFF. The output nodes are not connected to the intermediate nodes and are kept floating. Thus, the circuit enters the high-impedance state. It may be noted that a constant current is maintained in the circuit irrespective of the state as both the current sources (*M1* and *M8*) are always ON.

7.2.2   Voltage Follower-Based Differential Tri-state CML Circuit

The complete schematic of the voltage follower-based tri-state CML inverter/buffer [6] is shown in Fig. 7.2. It is pseudo-differential in nature and consists of cascade of source follower (*M1–M2* and *M10–M11*) and flipped voltage follower (*M6–M7* and

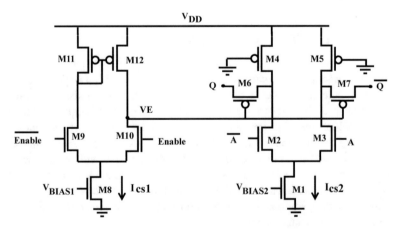

Fig. 7.1   Switch-based differential tri-state CML inverter/buffer [6]

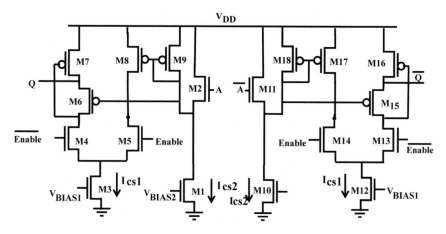

Fig. 7.2 Voltage follower-based differential tri-state CML inverter/buffer [6]

$M15$–$M16$). The circuit behaves as a regular inverter for low value of differential Enable signal. For high value of Enable, the inverter/buffer is in the high-impedance state as the transistors $M4$, $M7$, $M13$, and $M16$ are OFF. The power is consumed in both the states due to the fact that the current sources $M1$, $M3$, $M10$, and $M12$ remain always ON.

It is clear that all the current sources in both of these differential tri-state CML circuits remain ON irrespective of being in high-impedance or enabled state. This results for power consumption in both the states. Thus, in applications such as bus-based systems wherein only one inverter/buffer out of many is active at a given instant, these type of circuit realization will result in significant power consumption. So, a low-power differential tri-state CML circuit is preferable and is discussed further.

7.2.3 Low-Power Differential Tri-state CML Circuit

This realization is designed with an aim to reduce power consumption by not allowing the current source to operate in high-impedance state. The load and current source section of a regular CML gate is modified in this respect. The complete schematic of the low-power differential tri-state CML inverter/buffer [7] is shown in Fig. 7.3. It uses a differential CML inverter/buffer ($M1$–$M7$) with Enable controlled load, the current source sections and a differential to single-ended converter ($M8$–$M12$). The differential Enable signal is applied to the converter which generates a full swing VE signal that enables/disables the load transistors $M4$, $M5$ and also controls the operation of current source $M1$ via transistors $M6$ and $M7$.

When VE is low, the transistors $M4$ and $M5$ are turned ON and act as load to the CML inverter/buffer. At the same time, the transistor $M6$ charges node X to the

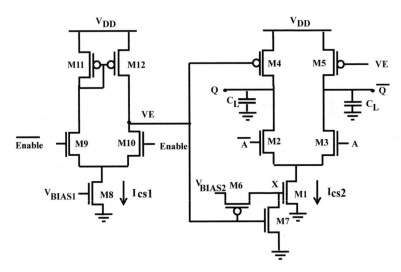

Fig. 7.3 Low-power differential tri-state CML inverter/buffer [7]

potential V_{BIAS2} since the transistor $M7$ is OFF. The transistor $M1$ begins to work as current source and provides the bias current I_{CS2} to the CML gate. Therefore, for low value of VE signal, the circuit behaves as a regular differential CML inverter/ buffer. For high value of VE signal, the transistors $M4$, $M5$, and $M6$ are turned OFF, whereas the transistor $M7$ conducts which pulls down the node X to the ground potential. Both the load and current source sections are OFF which disconnects the output nodes from the power supply as well as ground and a high impedance state is obtained at the output of the inverter/buffer.

From the above explanation, it may be noted that the current source $M1$ is OFF during the high-impedance state, in contrast to the tri-state CML inverters/buffers (Figs. 7.1 and 7.2) where all the current sources remain in ON state. Thus, the low-power feature of the CML inverter/buffer is evident and hence is named as low-power tri-state CML circuits.

7.2.4   Performance Comparison

A performance comparison of the three discussed differential tri-state CML buffers is carried out through SPICE simulations with a power supply of 1.8 V. The buffers maintain a bias current of 100 μA, voltage swing of 400 mV, and a load capacitance of 100 fF at the output. A summary of the simulation results related to different timing parameters, power consumption, and PDP is listed in Table 7.1 [7]. It may be observed that both the switch-based and the voltage follower-based differential tri-state CML buffers consume more power than the low-power tri-state buffer. This is due to the fact that in both the switch-based and the voltage

Table 7.1 Summary of the simulation results for differential tri-state CML buffers [7]

Parameter	Switch based	Voltage follower-based	Low power
Power (μW)	435	435	308
Propagation delay (ps)	481	348	340
Output enable time (ps)	1075	1052	1062
Power-delay product (fJ)	209	151	104

follower-based differential tri-state CML buffers, all the current sources remain ON in the enabled as well as in the high-impedance state whereas some of the current sources are OFF in the high-impedance state in the third one. Also, the low-power tri-state CML buffer has lowest the PDP value, thus making it power-efficient than the existing ones.

7.2.5 Application Examples

In this section, few applications are developed using the discussed tri-state CML inverter/buffer circuits.

7.2.5.1 Bus System Implementation

The CML gates are extensively used in the design of complex circuits in micro-processors. Their use can further be extended for bus architectures design wherein all the modules receive data at the same time, but only one of them transmits the data over the bus at a particular instant of time and the others remain disconnected from the bus. In general, this can be achieved by either multiplexing of the transmitters or by using open-drain or tri-state circuits [6]. The multiplexer-based method connects all the transmitters to a multiplexer and thus requires all trans-mitters to physically reside on the same location in a chip. The second method of employing open-drain circuits require a pull-up network is therefore convenient for point-to-point communication, wherein the receiver implements the pull-up net-work. The last method using tri-state circuits does not need any particular con-sideration, except that only one should be enabled at any given time. Therefore, implementation of bus system using tri-state buffers is preferred and is being chosen as one of the application examples.

A simulation test bench to model a typical bus system is shown in Fig. 7.4 [7]. It comprises of two tri-state CML buffers connected to an output node with load capacitance of 100 fF. The system is simulated by using all the three differential tri-state CML buffers. The waveforms of the applied inputs A, B, and Enable and the outputs from the three tri-state buffers are shown in Fig. 7.5 [7]. It can be observed that all the tri-state buffers conform to the functionality of a bus system.

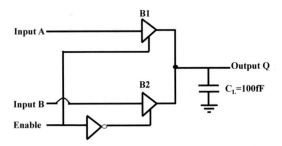

Fig. 7.4 Simulation test bench [7]

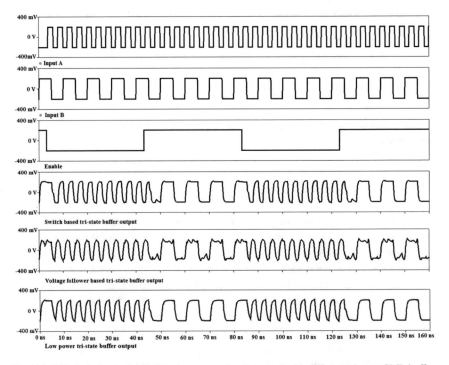

Fig. 7.5 Simulation waveform of the bus system implemented with different tri-state CML buffers [7]

7.2.5.2   D Latch Implementation

A D latch can be implemented by using tri-state inverters as shown in Fig. 7.6 [8]. It uses two tri-state inverters (I1 and I3) and a regular inverter (I2). The clock signal (CLK) controls the operation of I1 and I3. When CLK is high, I3 is in the high-impedance state and I1 is enabled such that the input data (*D*) gets transferred to the output node (*Q*) through I1 and I2. Thus, demonstrating D latch operation in

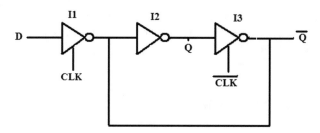

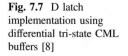

Fig. 7.6 D latch implementation using tri-state inverter [8]

Fig. 7.7 D latch
implementation using
differential tri-state CML
buffers [8]

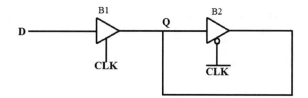

transparent mode. Alternatively, for low value of CLK signal, I1 is in
high-impedance state and no changes in the input are reflected at the output node
Q. At this point, I3 is enabled that makes the feedback loop around I2 and I3 closed
such that the last output value is preserved.

The same functionality can also be achieved by using only two tri-state buffers
instead of three inverters. This is done because in CML style, it is possible to
achieve buffer operation from the same inverter circuit by interchanging the output
nodes. The D latch design uses a cascade of two tri-state buffers B1 and B2
controlled by clock signal (CLK) and its complement as shown in Fig. 7.7 [8].
When CLK is high, B1 acts as a regular buffer while B2 enters high-impedance
state. The D latch is in transparent state by making data available on input line
(D) to the output (Q). Similarly, when CLK is low, the enabled tri-state buffer B2
preserves the last output value and none of the changes in the input are reflected at
the output node as B1 is in the high-impedance state.

The D latch shown in Fig. 7.7 is implemented and simulated by using all the
three tri-state CML buffers with a clock frequency of 500 MHz. All the buffers
maintain a bias current of 50 μA, voltage swing of 400 mV, and a load capacitance
of 20 fF. The values of power consumption and different timing parameters are

Table 7.2 Summary of the D latch simulation results

Circuit	Power (μW)	CLK → Q (ps)		D → Q (ps)	
		L → H	H → L	L → H	H → L
Switch based	180	295.8	291.6	322.9	306.8
Voltage follower based	180	340.3	345.1	299.1	288.4
Low power	90	330.1	325.1	236.7	231.6

summarized in Table 7.2. It is observed that the D latch implemented using low-power tri-state buffer shows the best performance values in comparison with the other counterparts.

7.3   Tri-state PFSCL Circuits

Tri-state circuits in PFSCL style is classified into two categories. The first category of tri-state PFSCL circuit employs a switch at the output of a regular PFSCL gate and is therefore named as switch-based tri-state PFSCL circuit. On the other hand, the concept of sleep transistor is used to achieve high-impedance state and hence the circuit is named as sleep transistor-based PFSCL tri-state circuit. A discussion on each of them and their variants is presented further. In all the circuits, it is assumed that the Enable signal is full swing signal.

7.3.1   Switch-Based Tri-state PFSCL Circuits

A switch-based PFSCL tri-state buffer [9] is shown in Fig. 7.8. A transistor $M6$ is added to the output of a regular PFSCL gate to achieve tri-state operation. For low value of Enable signal, transistor $M6$ is ON and the circuit acts as a regular buffer. Conversely, a high value of Enable signal turns transistor $M6$ OFF and provides a high-impedance state at the output by disconnecting the regular buffer output to the actual output node Q. Therefore, it can be noted that this tri-state buffer maintains current in the circuit irrespective of the state of gate. Thus, the basic structure of a switch-based tri-state PFSCL circuit can be modified to achieve low-power operation. There exist various low-power switch-based tri-state PFSCL circuit topologies. All of them use an output switch and save power by not allowing the current to flow in the high-impedance state. The current flow is restricted by modifying either the load or the current source section. The resulting topologies are accordingly classified into two categories [10]. The topology with the modified load section is

Fig. 7.8 Switch-based
PFSCL tri-state buffer [9]

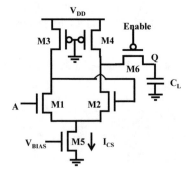

Fig. 7.9 PFSCL tri-state
buffer topology 1 [10]

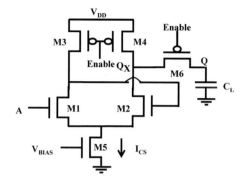

presented first and is followed by the topologies with modified current source section.

7.3.1.1 Tri-state PFSCL Circuit with Modified Load Section (Topology 1)

In this topology, the load transistors are driven by an Enable signal instead of a fixed ground potential. The modified topology is depicted in Fig. 7.9 [10]. For a low value of Enable signal, the circuit behaves as a regular PFSCL buffer. On the contrary, for high value of Enable signal, transistors $M3$, $M4$, and $M6$ are OFF, so the buffer enters in the high-impedance state. Also, the current flow in the circuit is restricted which results in a reduction of overall power consumption.

7.3.1.2 Tri-state PFSCL Circuits with Modified Current Source Section

Here, the tri-state PFSCL circuit topologies where the current source section is modified to restrict the current flow in high-impedance state are presented.

Topology 2

The topology 2 modifies the current source section by adding a PMOS transistor below the current source transistor. The circuit topology 2 for a buffer is shown in Fig. 7.10 [10]. When Enable signal is at low logic level, the circuit behaves as a regular PFSCL buffer. Conversely, for high logic level of Enable signal, the transistors $M6$ and $M7$ are OFF. This allows the circuit to enter high impedance and avoids any current flow in this duration.

Topology 3

The addition of the PMOS transistor below the current source in the topology 2 requires a higher value of bias voltage (V_{BIAS}) in comparison with the one required in conventional PFSCL buffer for maintaining the same current value (I_{CS}). This

Fig. 7.10 PFSCL tri-state
buffer topology 2 [10]

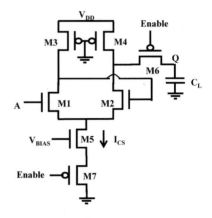

situation can be addressed by altering the placement of the two transistors. The topology 3 for the PFSCL tri-state buffer with the position of transistor $M5$ and $M7$ interchanged is shown in Fig. 7.11 [10]. A low value of Enable signal allows normal operation by providing a path to ground via transistor $M7$. Analogously, for a high value of Enable signal, the path to ground is disconnected by turning OFF the said transistor. At this point, the transistor $M6$ is OFF; therefore, the circuit enters the high-impedance state and does not consume power.

Topology 4
The topologies 2 and 3 use stacked transistors in the current source section to reduce power consumption. In topology 4, an alternate approach is followed. The availability of bias voltage to the current source is made dependent on Enable signal by using a PMOS transistor $M7$ and an NMOS transistor $M8$ as shown for the buffer topology 4 in Fig. 7.12 [10]. For a low value of Enable signal, the transistor $M5$ receives the necessary biasing through transistor $M7$. At this point, the transistor $M6$ is ON and the topology behaves as a regular buffer. Conversely, when Enable signal

Fig. 7.11 PFSCL tri-state
buffer topology 3 [10]

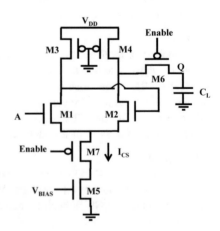

Fig. 7.12 PFSCL tri-state buffer topology 4 [10]

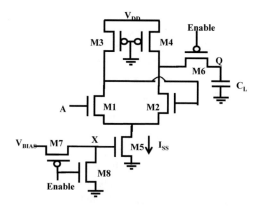

is high, the transistor $M7$ is OFF and the transistor $M8$ is ON. This discharges the potential of node X to the ground potential and consequently disables the current source. Therefore, the buffer does not consume power and high-impedance state is achieved as transistor $M6$ is turned OFF.

7.3.1.3 Performance Comparison

The PFSCL tri-state buffer topologies 1–4 (Figs. 7.9, 7.10, 7.11 and Fig. 7.12) and the conventional switch-based PFSCL tri-state buffer (Fig. 7.8) are simulated with a load capacitance of 50 fF. The performance is compared in terms of propagation delay, output enable time, power consumption, and power-delay product. The simulation results are summarized in Table 7.3 [10]. It is found that all the topologies (1–4) show 50% power reduction in comparison with the switch-based PFSCL tri-state buffer due to the fact that they all possess the provision of disabling the current flow in the high-impedance state.

In terms of propagation delay, it can be observed that all the topologies have almost equal delays since all of these possess similar loads and maintain same bias

Table 7.3 Performance comparison of switch-based PFSCL tri-state buffers [10]

Tri-state buffer	Parameter			
	Propagation delay (ps)	Output enable time (ps)	Power (µW)	Power-delay product (fJ)
Topology 1	425	553	45	19.125
Topology 2	419	348	45	18.855
Topology 3	408	132	45	18.360
Topology 4	428	438	45	19.260
Switch-based buffer	430	182	90	38.700

current in the enabled state. These two factors account for the low power-delay product values for the topologies (1–4). A maximum reduction of 47% in the power-delay product is obtained in all topologies in comparison with the switch based (Fig. 7.8). There is a variation in the output enable time of the tri-state buffers which, therefore, needs little more investigation on the behavior during high-impedance state.

- For topology 1 (Fig. 7.9), wherein the load is modified, it is to be noted that transistors in the pull-down network ($M1$–$M2$) and current source ($M5$) sections are ON. This condition leads to discharging of node QX to the ground potential. Subsequently, when the gate is enabled, the node QX will attain the valid low or high voltage levels depending upon the applied input. This explains longer output enable time in topology 1.
- For the topologies 2–4 (Figs. 7.10, 7.11 and 7.12), current source section is modified. Out of these three, the topology 4 (Fig. 7.12) shows the longest output enable time. It can be attributed to the fact that a proper V_{BIAS}, at node X, will be established through $M7$, whereas in the remaining two topologies, the path from common source coupled point to the ground is instantly established the moment the buffer is enabled. The topology 2 uses larger bias voltage than topology 3 explains its longer output enable time.
- The topology 3 shows the best output enable time among the available topologies which are due to interaction of internal node capacitances.

7.3.1.4   Bus Implementation

After performance comparison of PFSCL tri-state buffers, their suitability in bus system implementation is now explored. The test bench shown in Fig. 7.4 is considered and is simulated with all the switch-based PFSCL tri-state buffer topologies. The functioning of the setup can be understood by assuming a low value of Enable signal in conventional switch-based tri-state buffer. This condition makes transistor $M6$ in buffer B1 ON and that in buffer B2 OFF. The ON and OFF transistors for high values of input A and B are shown by bold and dotted lines in Fig. 7.13a. The tick mark in the diagram represents a current flow in the current source section. It is, therefore, clear that the output follows input A and remains unaffected by input B while both the conventional switch-based tri-state buffers consume power. The same analysis can be performed for all other variants of switch-based tri-state buffers. The simulation waveforms are shown in Fig. 7.13b. It is found that all tri-state buffers maintain the same voltage levels and conform to the functionality.

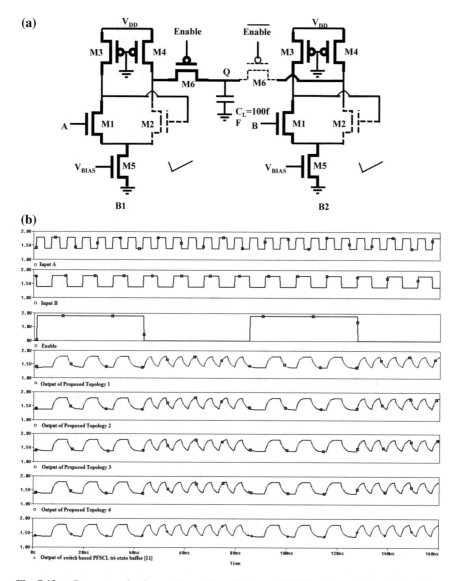

Fig. 7.13 **a** Bus system implementation with switch-based PFSCL tri-state buffers, **b** simulation waveforms [10]

7.3.2 Sleep Transistor-Based PFSCL Tri-state Circuits

This category of PFSCL tri-state circuit uses a sleep transistor in series with the power supply terminal of the basic PFSCL buffer. The schematic for a sleep transistor-based PFSCL tri-state buffer is shown in Fig. 7.14 [9]. It acts as regular

Fig. 7.14 Sleep
transistor-based PFSCL
tri-state buffer [9]

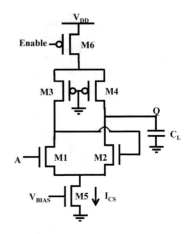

buffer for low value of Enable signal by turning ON transistor $M6$ while providing a
high-impedance state at the output, otherwise. The sleep-based tri-state buffer is
claimed to be more power-efficient over conventional switch-based counterpart
(Fig. 7.8) as no current flows in the circuit (Fig. 7.1b) during high-impedance state.

7.3.2.1   Issue in Bus Implementation

The bus implementation using sleep transistor-based PFSCL tri-state buffers
however suffers a major drawback due to the incomplete isolation of the common
output node from the tri-state disabled buffers. To illustrate this, a typical bus
environment consisting of two tri-state buffers driving a common output node as
shown in Fig. 7.4 is considered. The test bench is simulated by using the sleep
tri-state PFSCL buffers (Fig. 7.14).

A low value of Enable signal enables B1, whereas B2 moves in high-impedance
state by disconnecting the output node from its power supply. In this condition, a
careful examination reveals that the pull-down network (PDN) of B2 is still connected to the output node, and a path for the current to flow from the power supply
of B1 to ground via the output node Q and B2 still exists. To make this point clear,
let us consider both inputs A and B as high. In this condition, transistor $M1$ of buffer
B1 and both the transistors in PDN of buffer B2 would be ON leading to drawing
more bias current from power supply than that of an individual enabled buffer. It is
pictorially represented in Fig. 7.15 by marking ON transistors by bold lines and
OFF transistors by dotted lines [10]. The tick mark in the figure signifies a current
flow in the current source section. Hence, the isolation of the output node Q from
the buffer B2 is not established. This causes malfunctioning of the whole bus
system by altering the magnitude of the high and low logic levels. The degradation
in the output levels will increase with the increase in number of gates connected to
the common node Q. Also, the functionality of the device which will be driven by
the output of sleep-based tri-state buffer may completely be disrupted.

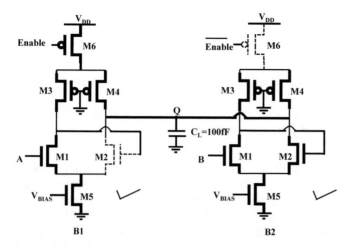

Fig. 7.15 Bus system implementation with sleep-based PFSCL tri-state buffers [10]

In the next section, sleep-based tri-state PFSCL topologies [11] to overcome this shortcoming are presented. The scheme is extended to develop generalized sleep transistor-based PFSCL tri-state circuit as shown in Fig. 7.16. The generalized circuit has a load implemented using PMOS transistors, the PDN corresponding to the functionality to be realized, and a NMOS operating in saturation region as

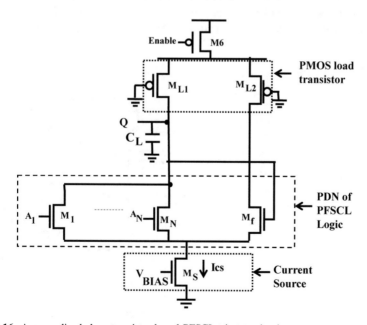

Fig. 7.16 A generalized sleep transistor-based PFSCL tri-state circuit

current source. The PMOS transistor *M6* driven by Enable signal is responsible for driving the PFSCL gate into the high-impedance state.

7.3.2.2 Improved Sleep Transistor-Based PFSCL Tri-state Topologies

In this section, the topologies that eliminate the drawback of conventional sleep-based PFSCL tri-state circuits are explored [11].

Topology 5
In this topology, a PMOS transistor (MCS) is added in the current source section of the sleep transistor-based PFSCL tri-state circuit. This modification disconnects the output node from the ground, thereby ensuring proper functionality in bus systems. The schematic of the generalized PFSCL tri-state circuit (topology 5) is shown in Fig. 7.17. The circuit behaves as a regular buffer for a low value of Enable signal. Conversely, when Enable signal is at high voltage value, the transistor *M6* and *M7* are OFF and no current flows in the circuit. Thus, the circuit achieves high-impedance state and does not consume power during this state.

Topology 6
With the transistor arrangement as shown in Fig. 7.17, it is clear that a higher bias voltage (V_{BIAS}) is required to produce desired bias current I_{CS} due to voltage headroom. This can be avoided by placing the transistor MCS above the current source as shown in Fig. 7.18. The circuit behaves in a similar manner as the previous topology. It works as a regular PFSCL gate for low value of Enable signal since both the power supplies get connected to the circuits. Alternatively, no current flows in the circuit as transistor *M6* and MCS becomes OFF due to high value of the

Fig. 7.17 PFSCL tri-state circuit topology 5

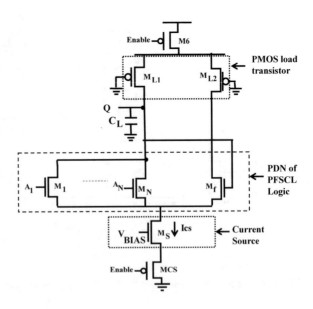

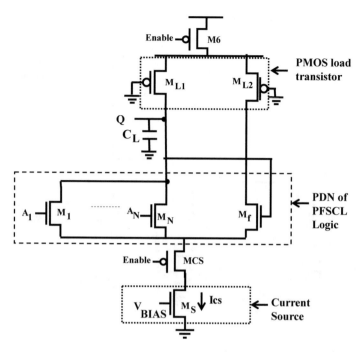

Fig. 7.18 PFSCL tri-state circuit topology 6

Enable signal. The circuit exhibits high-impedance state and no power is consumed during this state.

Topology 7

The stacking of transistors is followed in topologies 5 and 6 to obtain the tri-state behavior in sleep transistor-based PFSCL circuits. Alternatively, the stacking of transistors can be avoided by scheme depicted in Fig. 7.19. Two transistors, a PMOS transistor $M7$ and an NMOS transistor $M8$ are used for controlling the operation of the current source. The Enable signal controls the two transistors. The PMOS transistor $M7$ passes the bias voltage (V_{BIAS}) to the current source for low value of Enable signal. Since $M8$ is OFF during this interval, proper bias current flows through the gate and it works as a regular PFSCL gate. Conversely, for high Enable signal value, the transistor $M7$ gets OFF and the potential of node X discharges to ground potential since transistor $M8$ is ON. Consequently, the current source is disabled and a high-impedance state is achieved with no power consumption in this state.

The sleep transistor-based PFSCL tri-state topologies can further be optimized by modifying the PMOS load transistors. It is clear from the above explanations that the role of transistor $M6$ is to disconnect the power supply for high values of Enable signal. This functionality can also be achieved if the PMOS load transistors are driven by Enable signal instead of connecting them to the ground potential.

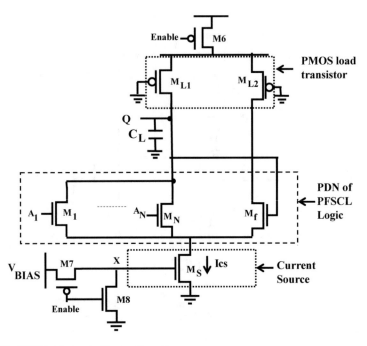

Fig. 7.19 PFSCL tri-state buffer topology 7

Applying the concept in the above three topologies (topologies 5–7), the optimized topologies (topologies 8–10) are drawn in Fig. 7.20.

7.3.2.3   Performance Comparison

The performance of the sleep transistor-based PFSCL tri-state topologies 5–10 (Figs. 7.16, 7.17, 7.18 and 7.19) is compared. A tri-state buffer is configured and simulated. All the SPICE simulations are carried out using of 0.18 μm TSMC CMOS technology parameters with a power supply of 1.1 V. All the buffers maintain a bias current of 100 μA, voltage swing of 350 mV, and a load capacitance of 100 fF, respectively. A switch-based PFSCL tri-state buffer (Fig. 7.8) is also included for the sake of completeness and is considered as reference to evaluate the performance. The performance is compared in terms of the power consumption, the propagation delay, the output Enable time, and power-delay product (PDP). The simulation results are listed in Table 7.4. All the PFSCL tri-state buffer topologies consume same power thus satisfying the low-power aim due to the fact that they all possess the provision of disabling the current flow in the

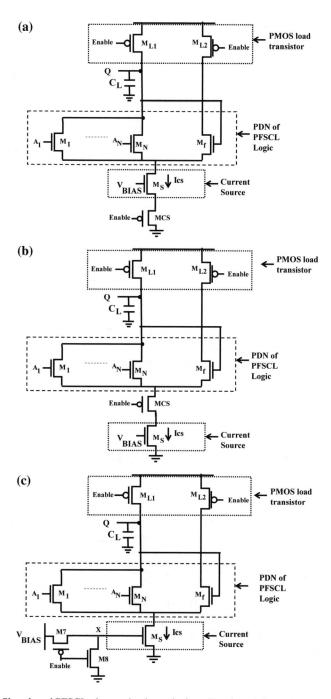

Fig. 7.20 Sleep-based PFSCL tri-state circuit topologies **a** Topology 8, **b** topology 9, **c** topology 10

Table 7.4 Performance comparison of sleep transistor-based PFSCL tri-state buffer with load capacitance (C_L = 100 fF)

Tri-state buffer	Parameter				
	Switching current (μA)	Propagation delay (ps)	Output enable time (ps)	Power (μW)	Power-delay product (fJ)
Topology 5	1.99	0.87	2.74	1	0.87
Topology 6	1.99	0.78	1.36	1	0.78
Topology 7	2.0	0.87	3.06	1	0.87
Topology 8	0.93	0.79	2.8	1	0.79
Topology 9	0.92	0.75	0.83	1	0.75
Topology 10	0.944	0.81	3.27	1	0.81
Conventional sleep-based topology	1.56	0.84	2.81	1	0.84
Conventional switch-based topology	1	1	1	1	1

high-impedance state. All the improved sleep-based tri-state buffer topologies show reduction in the propagation delay but have value of output enable time in comparison with the conventional switch and sleep-based PFSCL tri-state buffers.

7.4   Summary

In this chapter, three types of differential ended tri-state CML circuits are presented. All the current sources used in switch and voltage follower-based differential tri-state CML circuits remain ON during the enabled and high-impedance states. The low-power differential tri-state CML gate uses a mechanism to put some of the current sources OFF and reaps the advantage of reduced power consumption. The usefulness of these buffers is illustrated through bus implementation and D latch.

Ten PFSCL-based tri-state CML circuits are discussed which is based on four different methodologies. Firstly, the switch-based tri-state buffer is presented and modifications are subsequently described that help in reducing power consumption. Load section is modified in one whereas remaining three work on modifying current source. Thereafter, current source modifications are applied in sleep-based tri-state buffer. Remaining three topologies are based on simultaneous modification of load and current source sections.

References

1. H.C. Jonathan, C.A. Johnston, L.S. Smoot, A packet video/audio system using the asynchronous transfer mode technique. IEEE Trans. Consum. Electron. **35**(2), 97–105 (1989)
2. R. Golshan, B. Haroun, A novel reduced swing CMOS bus interface circuit for high-speed low-power VLSI systems, in Proccedings of the International Symposium on Circuits and System (1994), pp. 351–354
3. M. Akata, S. Karube, T. Sakamoto, T. Saito, S. Yoshida, T. Maeda, A 250 Mb/s 32 × 32 CMOS cross point LSI for ATM switching systems, in Proceedings of IEEE International Solid-State Circuits Conference (1990), pp. 30–31
4. L. Louis, J. Chroma, J. Draper, A self-sensing tri-state pad driver for control signals of multiple bus controller, in Proceedings of the IEEE International Symposium on Circuits and Systems (1999), pp. 447–450
5. S.M. Kang, Y. Leblebici, *CMOS Digital Integrated Circuits: Analysis and Design*, 3rd edn. (Tata McGraw Hills, 2006)
6. S. Badel, Y. Leblebici, Tri-state buffer/bus driver circuits in MOS current-mode logic, in Proceedings of Research in Microelectronics and Electronics Conference, Bordeaux, (2007), pp. 237–240. © 2007 IEEE, Reprinted with permission
7. K. Gupta, N. Pandey, M. Gupta, Low-power tri-state buffer in MOS current mode logic. Analog Integr. Circuits Signal Process. **75**(1), 157–160 (2013). [COPYRIGHT]. Reprinted by permission from Springer Nature Customer Service Centre GmbH: Springer, Analog Integrated Circuits and Signal Processing
8. Radhika, N. Pandey, K. Gupta, M. Gupta, Low power D-latch design using MCML tri-state buffers, in Proceedings of IEEE International Conference on Signal Processing and Integrated Networks (SPIN) (2014), pp. 531–534. © 2016 IEEE, Reprinted with permission
9. K. Gupta, R. Sridhar, J. Chaudhary, N. Pandey, M. Gupta, New low power tri-state circuits in positive feedback source coupled logic. J. Electr. Comput. Eng. **2011**, 6 (2011). Article ID 670508
10. N. Pandey, B. Choudhary, K. Gupta, A. Mittal, Bus implementation using new low power PFSCL tristate buffers, Act. Passiv. Electron. Compon., **2016**, 8 (2016). Article ID 4517292
11. N. Pandey, B. Choudhary, K. Gupta, A. Mittal, New sleep-based PFSCL tri-state inverter/ buffer topologies. J. Circuits, Syst. Comput. 15 (2017). Article ID 1750186

Printed in the United States
By Bookmasters